ENDORSEMENTS FOR
A FELLOWSHIP OF DIFFERENTS

Fifty years from now, pastors, scholars, and Christians from a wide variety of denominations will look back say, "God used *Fellowship of Differents* to change the church in America!" This is the most important book you may ever read outside of the Bible. The staff of Transformation Church will be reading this phenomenal book.

— Derwin L. Gray, lead pastor of Transformation
Church; author, *Limitless Life*

I love this book! It's the theological mac to my social-psychological cheese. The pursuit of unity in the midst of difference is a trek across a minefield. With each step, we must contend with challenges that threaten to send us running back to the "safety" of similar others. That's why I'm so thankful for *A Fellowship of Differents*. McKnight draws from Paul's letters to give readers the robust foundation and action steps needed to keep pursuing unity at all costs.

— Christena Cleveland, author *Disunity in Christ*;
associate professor of reconciliation studies, Bethel
University

For over twenty-five years I've served as a church planter and pastor of churches that wrestled with being pots of stew (or "salad bowls," as Scot McKnight would put it). Pastors in my situation found ourselves — sometimes unwittingly — in conflict with the so-called "homogenous unit principle," that highly pragmatic perspective at work in megachurches whose explosive growth had many of us drooling and sitting at the feet of CEO-pastors. Yet I craved something else: a resource to encourage and challenge us from the Scriptures, affirming our work among people of various backgrounds, different races, ethnicities, genders, and economic groups. McKnight has blended his expertise in the NT and his passion as a life-long participant in the church to address just about every topic we can imagine! I enthusiastically recommend this book!

— Rev. Dennis R. Edwards, PhD, senior pastor
of The Sanctuary Covenant Church in Minneapolis;
adjunct seminary instructor in biblical studies

Pour yourself a cup of coffee and settle into this timely, provocative, and challenging book on what it means to be the church. McKnight's conversational style and his perceptive insights to American Christian culture combine with his expert analysis of Scripture to illuminate God's design for Christian fellowship. An essential read for all who long for the church to live out its calling.

Lynn H. Cohick, professor of New Testament,
Wheaton College

A Fellowship of Differents echoes God's plea for true community: for the church to become the real deal embracing all of God's different kinds of people, to unite in a "wild revolution of equality" through Him, to bring visibility to the otherwise invisible. Most importantly, this book shows us how true unity is the only way to achieve Jesus' heart for his bride, the church.

— Bruxy Cavey, author of bestseller *The End of
Religion*; teaching pastor at The Meeting House

At a moment when so many are questioning what the church is and wondering if it even matters, McKnight's claim — that the way we follow Jesus is shaped by our local church more than any other source — is a bold, prophetic, and compelling idea. Reading this book gave me a new vision for what my church is and what it could be. It was nothing short of a love affair with Jesus' bride all over again.

— John Mark Comer, Pastor of Teaching and
Vision, Bridgetown: A Jesus Church

A Fellowship of Differents is an impressive achievement: it puts the church in conversation with today's most difficult differences and differents — and the church comes out making sense. Scot McKnight's work is precisely in step with Jesus' famous words: "I will build my church." We need this book because all of us different people in the modern church are the ones Jesus has trusted with the keys to the kingdom!

> — Anglican Bishop Todd Hunter, author, *Giving Church Another Chance*

In the context of a rapidly changing world, our ecclesiology must go deeper. In a winsome manner, Scot McKnight brings the teachings of the apostle Paul to life so that we may rediscover what the church is supposed to be. *A Fellowship of Differents* provides a hopeful and an applicable ecclesiology for the twenty-first century that provides insight into the burden and joy of being the church.

> — Soong-Chan Rah, Milton B. Engebretson Professor of Church Growth and Evangelism; author of *The Next Evangelicalism*

Ever wonder what Paul would say to the Church today? This is it. Scot McKnight has captured the mind and heart of our beloved apostle, who spent his whole life pursuing one dream, preaching one gospel, sacrificing everything for one beautiful vision: that all people would believe in the Lord because the church — this strange collection of humanity united by the miraculous work of the Holy Spirit for one purpose — is the very body of Christ.

> — Rodney Reeves, professor of biblical studies, Southwest Baptist University

One of my life values is that uniqueness is better than conformity, firmly believing (though I realize this is strong) that conformity only leads to death. My work with church leaders shows me that healthy thriving churches are not only places of diversity, but they love that about themselves. *A Fellowship of Differents* will feel like a commendation to churches who already live in this tension, and like a loving and prophetic intervention for those who wrongly worship the god of sameness.

– Mark Oestreicher, partner, The Youth Cartel;
Author, *Hopecasting*

Scot McKnight applies a professor's mind with a pastor's heart to one of the greatest enemies of God's plan for his church: disunity. Instead of being a "salad bowl" fellowship of difference and differents, we've segregated ourselves into homogeneous groups so remote that we are virtually invisible to each another. The author doesn't stop by describing this inconvenient truth, but identifies six themes of the Christian life that, when implemented in the church by God's grace, will help us to love one another and flourish as one people of God. No Christ-follower who cares about the beauty of Christ's bride, the church, should miss this masterful guide to creating a fellowship of differents!"

– Dr. E. Andrew McQuitty, senior pastor of Irving
Bible Church, author of *Notes from the Valley*.

The local church certainly has its failings and therefore, its critics. Most critics are just angry and few are helpful. Scot McKnight loves the local church and because he loves the local church, his words of criticism don't wound as much as they remind us – of who we once were, of who we're called to be, and who we can yet become. Like a parent showing a child the child's baby picture, Scot McKnight, in his book, The Fellowship of Differents, calls us back to the original dreams of fellowship and transformational love Jesus first intended for us – and still intends for us now.

—Mike Glenn , Senior Pastor, Brentwood Baptist
Church, Brentwood, TN

A
FELLOWSHIP
of
DIFFERENTS

SHOWING *the* WORLD
GOD'S DESIGN *for* LIFE TOGETHER

A
FELLOWSHIP
of
DIFFERENTS

SCOT MCKNIGHT

 ZONDERVAN®

ZONDERVAN

A Fellowship of Differents
Copyright © 2014 by Scot McKnight

This title is also available as a Zondervan ebook.

Requests for information should be addressed to:
Zondervan, 3900 *Sparks Dr. SE, Grand Rapids, Michigan 49546*

Library of Congress Cataloging-in-Publication Data

McKnight, Scot.
      A fellowship of differents : showing the world God's design for life together / Scot
McKnight. — 1st [edition].
           pages   cm
      Includes index.
      ISBN 978-0-310-27767-5 (hardcover)
      1. Church. I. Title.
BV600.3.M357   2015
      262 — dc23   2014040112

Cover design: Dual Identity
Cover photography: © Kues / Shutterstock
Interior design and composition: Greg Johnson/Textbook Perfect

First printing January 2015 / Printed in the United States of America

TO

Church of the Redeemer
and
Jay and Susan Greener
Amanda and Erik Rosengren

Contents

Part 5 NEWNESS

Part 6 FLOURISHING

1

Growing Up
in Church

WHEN I WAS A TEENAGER, MY YOUTH PASTOR asked me to preach one Wednesday night to the youth, which was a *big* deal in my church. Truth be told, we all went to church on Sundays just to hear our head pastor give the sermon upstairs, which was the biggest deal of all. He would preach through books in the Bible *verse-by-verse* in what we called *expository preaching*. Other churches called their sermons "homilies," which lasted about ten minutes or less, though most of us had no idea whether this was true since we never stepped through their doors anyway. They also called their pastors "priests" or "fathers" — a sure sign you weren't saved. We weren't even sure they believed in the Bible.

For my sermon that Wednesday, I chose one line from the apostle Paul in the King James Bible that read, *"Be ye separate."* I talked about how important it was to stay away from sin and sinners like Methodists and to avoid the temptation to go to movies and to resist with all our might the evil of drink and dancing and cursing and tobacco. I went on and on, until about an hour later "Pastor Dave," our youth leader, told me to knock it off, and I sat down among my glassy-eyed peers. We sang and prayed some more, and finally all of us went home into the night.

Growing up in First Baptist Church in Freeport, Illinois, I observed that our church was about four things: getting people saved, separating from the world, singing full throttle, and listening to sermons by our pastor — though certainly not in that order. Getting people saved mostly meant getting Methodists, Presbyterians, and Lutherans to come to our church, preferably for a revival. We would ramp up our efforts and try to get them to walk down the aisle and accept Christ into their heart, going to the backroom to say the Sinner's Prayer. Our biggest prize came when a Catholic prayed to receive Christ, but that didn't happen often. When it did, we sang louder and told the story over and over.

Singing was big for us too. The Sunday morning official choir wore Old Testament-like priestly robes and sashes. I sang in the young peoples' choir, where the show-offs sang the main parts while the rest of us sang harmony, if we could. I never really got to that level, so when I could hit the notes, I pressed the gas a little harder to show the show-offs what I was capable of.

The worst part about singing in my church was that someone, no doubt with a holy motive, made us guys a vest, a kind of mustard yellow Ringo Starr vest with no buttons. We wore light-colored, long-cuffed, four-inch collar shirts; brown bell bottom burlap-bag-like pants; and hip sixties shoes. The girls wore the same outfit as the guys except with skirts, because wearing pants was worldly and secular and modernist, the words we used for everyone else in the town who didn't go to our church. Another sign of worldliness was rock music, so we had no guitars for our choir. Playing the instrument might make someone's hair grow over his ears.

If you haven't figured it out yet, going to church for us was also about being separate, or holy. Someone way back in our denominational history had drunk the wine of the Puritans, though I'd have to admit that's a serious license, since neither the Puritans nor we drank wine or beer — or anything alcoholic for that matter. We even protested grocery stores that sold alcohol, and my friend's mom inked out *alcohol* after the word *Isopropyl* to preserve her testimony.

We were definitely separate, which means we *didn't* (or weren't supposed to) do all sorts of things. We didn't drink alcohol, we didn't go to school dances or smoke cigarettes *of any kind*, we didn't "do sex" before marriage, and we didn't go to movies that popped some skin and created lust in teenagers. We kept away from the world lest we fall away and become Lutheran or Methodist or Presbyterian or, worst of all, Catholic. In our town the Catholics would team up with the Lutherans, Methodists, and Presbyterians for dances and movies, while we felt excluded or holy.

Now don't get me wrong. There was plenty of godliness and goodness in the folks at First Baptist Church, Freeport, Illinois. Nor do I want to suggest that our church didn't do a lot of good for the kingdom of God, because it certainly did. But some of the stuff we did was ... well, just weird.

Since marrying my wife, Kris, who grew up among the Presbyterians, we've been to all sorts of churches in our hometown over the decades. We've "gone to church" with the Anglicans, the Baptists, the Presbyterians, the Methodists, the Episcopalians, the Plymouth Brethren, the Evangelical Free, the Evangelical Covenant, and all sorts of evangelical nondenominational churches. We went to a Catholic church, San Giorgio Maggiore, on a little island in Venice, and though we hardly understood a word, it was cool being in such a historic church on Pentecost. Each of these churches we've attended over the years is a shade different from the others, but — when you get down to it — they're really not all *that* different.

So here's my claim after that romp through the church of my youth: *Everything I learned about the Christian life I learned from my church.* I will make this a bigger principle: *a local church determines what the Christian life looks like for the people in that church.* Now I'll make it even bigger still: *we all learn the Christian life from how our local church shapes us.* These three principles are a way of saying that local churches matter far more than we often know.

Some churches focus on holiness, some on love, some on fellowship with one another, and some on evangelizing outsiders. Some focus on sermons and Sunday School classes and Bible studies and theology and orthodoxy. Others focus on worship and have all kinds of beliefs determining who says what from where and how it is said and who can do what from where and when and why. Whether we admit it or not, *a local church really does shape what we think the Christian life is all about.*

Richard Foster, who has studied what we call "spiritual formation" his entire life, breaks down the history of how churches have understood the Christian life into six themes:[1]

1. A prayer-filled life
2. A holy and virtuous life
3. A Spirit-empowered life
4. A compassionate or just life
5. A Word-centered life
6. A sacramental life

I could easily find the church of my youth in the first, second, and fifth of these, because we were into prayer, holiness, and the Word, though our first note was about holiness. But these elements don't exist on their own; it was my church that shaped, led, guided, and drove me to those three items all the time in my Christian development. I never thought about justice and barely thought about the Spirit, and we wouldn't have been caught dead talking about sacraments, because other churches in Freeport did *that*. Churches determine the direction of our discipleship.

Which leads to one big question:

What then is the church supposed to be?

I believe for most of us the church is a *place we go on Sunday to hear a sermon, or to participate in worship, or to partake in communion.* Some will add Sunday School classes and time together in the fellowship hall. But by and large it is all contained within one or two hours on Sunday morning. After two hours, we go home and "church" is over. No one wants to admit that is what church really is in practice, but it's true!

So we ask that question again, only this time we add a second one:

What is the church supposed to be?

and

**If the church is what it is supposed to be,
what does the Christian life look like?**

To answer *that* question I want us to explore the image of the salad bowl, which reflects the ways all us "differents" — from different socioeconomic groups, genders, educational and ethnic backgrounds, and life situations — struggle to come together in fellowship as the church God intended.

2

A Salad Bowl

THERE ARE THREE WAYS TO EAT A SALAD: the American Way, the Weird Way, and the Right Way.

The American Way of eating a salad is to fill your bowl with some iceberg lettuce or some spinach leaves, some tomato slices and olives, and maybe some carrots, then smother it with salad dressing — Ranch or Thousand Island or Italian or, for special occasions, Caesar.

The Weird Way is to separate each item in your salad around on your plate, then eat them as separate items. People who do this often do not even use dressing. As I said, weird.

Now the Right Way to make and eat a salad is to gather all your ingredients — some spinach, kale, chard, arugula, iceberg lettuce (if you must) — and chop them into smaller bits. Then cut up some tomatoes, carrots, onions, red pepper, and purple cabbage. Add some nuts and dried berries, sprinkle some pecorino romano cheese, and finally drizzle over the salad some good olive oil, which somehow brings the taste of each item to its fullest. Surely this is what God intended when he created "mixed salad."

THE CHURCH IS A SALAD

In our last chapter, I highlighted just how important the church is in our spiritual formation, so if we want to get the church right, we have to learn to see it as a salad in a bowl, made the Right Way of course. For a good salad is a fellowship of different tastes, all mixed together with the olive oil accentuating the taste of each. The earliest Christian churches were made up of folks from all over the social map, but they formed a fellowship of "different tastes," a mixed salad of the best kind.

Understand that these early Christians did not meet in churches and sit apart from one another in pews, and then when the music ended get in their chariots and go home. No, their churches were small, and they met in homes or house churches. A recent study by a British scholar has concluded that if the apostle Paul's house churches were composed of about thirty people, this would have been their approximate make-up:[1]

+ a craftworker in whose home they meet, along with his wife, children, a couple of male slaves, a female domestic slave, and a dependent relative
+ some tenants, with families and slaves and dependents, also living in the same home in rented rooms
+ some family members of a householder who himself does not participate in the house church
+ a couple of slaves whose owners do not attend
+ some freed slaves who do not participate in the church
+ a couple homeless people
+ a few migrant workers renting small rooms in the home

Add to this mix some Jewish folks and a perhaps an enslaved prostitute and we see how many "different tastes" were in a typical house church in Rome: men and women, citizens and freed slaves and slaves (who had no legal rights), Jews and Gentiles, people from all moral walks of life, and perhaps, most notably, people from elite classes all the way down the social scale to homeless people.

Do you think these folks agreed on everything? (Impossible is the right answer.) Were they a fellowship of "differents"? (Yes is the right answer.) Was life together hard? (Yes, again.) That's the whole point of what it means to be a church. The Christian life is not just about how I am doing as an individual, but especially about how we are doing as a church, and how and what I am doing in that mix of others called the church.

God has designed the church — and this is the heart of Paul's mission — to be *a fellowship of difference and differents*. It is a mixture of people from all across the map and spectrum: men and women, rich and poor. It is a mix of races and ethnicities: Caucasians, African Americans, Mexican Americans, Latin Americans, Asian Americans, Indian Americans — I could go on, but you see the point. The church I grew up in, bless its heart, was a fellowship of sames and likes. There was almost no variety in our church. It was composed entirely of white folks with the same beliefs, the same tastes in music and worship and sermons and lifestyle; men wore suits and ties and women wore dresses and not a few of them wore church hats.

Getting the church right is so important. The church is *God's world-changing social experiment* of bringing unlikes and differents to the table to share life with one another as a new kind of family. When this happens, we show the world what love, justice, peace, reconciliation, and life together are designed by God to be. The church is God's show-and-tell for the world to see how God wants us to live as a family. But there's something deeper going on too.

CHURCH LIFE SHOULD MODEL THE CHRISTIAN LIFE

My claim is also that *local churches shape how its people understand the Christian life*, so let's think about this briefly. *If the church is a mixed salad, or a fellowship of differents, then...*

We should see different genders at church. Do we?
We should see different socioeconomic groups at church. Do we?
We should see different races at church. Do we?
We should see different cultures at church. Do we?
We should see different music styles at church. Do we?
We should see different artistic styles at church. Do we?

We should see different moral histories at church. Do we?

We should see different forms of communication at church. Do we?

We should see different ages involved at church. Do we?

We should see different marital statuses at church. Do we?

Even more, *if the church is a mixed salad in a bowl*...

We should understand the Christian life as a fellowship. Do we?

We should understand it as a social revolution. Do we?

We should understand it as life together. Do we?

We should understand it as transcending difference. Do we?

We should understand it as honoring difference. Do we?

We should understand it as enjoying difference. Do we?

We should understand it as love, justice, and reconciliation. Do we?

No, in fact, we don't. We've turned the church, as we have done with some of our salad making, into the American Way and the Weird Way.

What does that mean? If the American Way is smothering the salad with dressing so that it all tastes like dressing, we have smothered all differences in the church so that everything is the same: designed for one gender, one socioeconomic group, one race, one culture, and one theology. We have become ingrown, like a toenail. Anyone who doesn't fit becomes invisible, gets ignored, is shelved, or goes AWOL.

Put differently, we've made the church into the American dream for our own ethnic group with the same set of convictions about next to everything. No one else feels welcome. What Jesus and the apostles taught was that you were welcomed *because the church welcomed all to the table.*

Let's be even more honest. While we might like to think we have smothered everyone with one tasty culture, what we have actually accomplished is closer to the Weird Way of making and eating a salad. We like ourselves, our way of thinking, our music, and our ... our everything. So we separate all the difference and differents and scatter them across the towns and cities so that each group worships on its own. Churches for men and not really for women, churches for the wealthy and churches for the middle class and churches for the poor, churches for whites and

Mexican Americans and African Americans and Asian Americans and Indian Americans. Churches for liberals and churches for fundamentalists, churches for those who follow Calvin, Wesley, Luther, Aquinas, Menno — or for those who follow Hybels, Warren, Stanley, Hamilton, Chandler, or Driscoll. Sunday morning then becomes an exercise in cultural and spiritual segregation, and this has a colossally important impact on *the Christian life itself!*

The reality is that each of our churches has created a Christian culture and Christian life for likes and sames and similiarities and identicals. Instead of powering God's grand social experiment, we've cut up God's plan into segregated groups, with the incredibly aggravating and God-dishonoring result that *most of us are invisible to one another.*

Here's a heart-breaking example. Recently I was having lunch with a gifted Northern Seminary student named Phil, during which he mentioned to me the Hampton Ministers' Conference. I must have looked stone-faced because he said to me, "Have you ever been to the Hampton Conference?" I said, "Well, no, and neither have I ever heard of it." So he told me about it (you can Google it yourself). In June 2014, the Hampton University Ministers' Conference gathered for its one hundredth annual event. So I wrote to a few publishers and to some of my pastor friends to ask if they had ever been to the Hampton Conference, and I got back the same stunning response from each person I wrote: "Never heard of it." Not one person — pastor or publisher — I wrote to had ever heard of it. It is the longest running pastors' conference in the USA, attended by seven thousand, and I was embarrassed at my whiteness for not knowing that my brothers and sisters were gathering. They were invisible to me.

Groups and groups of wonderful Christian people — and not just those of different ethnicities — have become *invisible* to one another. We no longer even see one another. God designed the church to *make the previously invisible visible to God and to one another in a new kind of fellowship that the Roman Empire and the Jewish world had never seen before.* That was the fellowship of God. Let me tell a story and then ask a test question.

INVISIBLE PEOPLE

In 1953, Ralph Ellison won the National Book Award for *The Invisible Man*, a novel about the journey of an African American man from his southern roots and dreams of leadership at an African American college to sudden expulsion from that school. He struggles to find employment so he can return to college and enter into the American dream, and he discovers that the dean at his former school has lied to him and that he will never be readmitted. He then explores two options in New York City for a transplanted southern black: the path of communism or the path of violent subversion of white power and culture.

A frustrating feature of Ellison's brilliant novel is that his central character has no name. Why? Because the black person was (and still often is) invisible and anonymous in American society. Ellison's descriptions of the experience of invisibility pierce into the soul of America and, more alarmingly, into the soul of the church: "About eighty-five years ago they were told that they were free, united with others of our country in everything pertaining to the common good, and, in everything social, *separate like the fingers of a hand*."[2] In American history, this experience found its way into the social "policy" of separate but equal, a policy many of us learned on Sunday morning at 11:00 a.m. — and which really meant "separate because unequal." Later Ellison's character embraces the new mantra that "when I discover who I am, I'll be free."[3] Our soul-numbing system made the African American invisible by overwhelming African American culture with a dominant white Protestant culture.

But it is not just African Americans who are invisible in American culture and in churches today. Gentile invisibility to the Jewish community is not identical to the African American experience of invisibility in the U.S., but Paul is still incredibly relevant to us today because his ambition of breaking down ethnic barriers is the preeminent twenty-first-century church problem. The first-century Jewish synagogue and the twenty-first-century American church are so much alike in that visibility is connected to ethnicity.

Paul yearned that there be no invisible people in the fellowship because he knew the power of God's grace. He knew grace was the new creation at work in the present to make one family, Jews and Gentiles, under one Lord, King Jesus. Paul's vision contrasts violently with American churches. Fully 90 percent of American churches draw 90 percent of their people from one ethnic group, and only about 8 percent of American churches can be called multiracial, multiethnic, or interracial. But let's scrape the mud off even that 8 percent. Studies show that interracial churches are often little more than a white-culture church sprinkled with ethnic mixture in the congregation.[4] That is, interracial churches tend toward the coercive forces of a salad made the American Way or the Weird Way.

Which brings us to our test question:

WHO IS INVISIBLE IN YOUR CHURCH?

To the degree that folks are invisible in our church, we don't have the right view of the church and the right view of the Christian life. In fact, *the success of a church is first determined by how many invisible people become visible to those not like them.* So let's explore who is most invisible in our churches today. Here are some examples:

Widows. Listen to how Miriam Neff, a widow, tells her story:

I am part of the fastest growing demographic in the United States. We are targeted by new-home builders and surveyed by designers. We are a lucrative niche for health and beauty products, and financial planners invite us to dinners. It's no wonder the marketers are after us: 800,000 join our ranks every year.[5]

Who are we? We are the *invisible* among you — the widows.

Studies show that widows lose 75 percent of their friendship network when they lose a spouse. Sixty percent of us experience serious health issues in that first year. One third of us meet the criteria for clinical depression in the first month after our spouse's death, and half of us remain clinically depressed a year later. Most experience financial decline. One pastor described us by saying we move from the front row of the church to the back, and then out the door. We move from serving and singing in choir to solitude and silent sobbing, and then on to find a place where we belong.

We could go on, but you get the picture. Are widows visible or invisible in your church?

What about *children*? Are they wall flowers and decorations, isolated and segregated, or are they truly part of your church? What about *young adults*? Are they segregated or are they being brought to the table? What about *seniors*? Are they sitting up front or in the back (on their way out the door with the widows)?

What about *races*? How many races are present in your church? Are there Asian Christians in your church? Do you know Asian Americans are the fastest growing ethnic group in the U.S. and that nearly 50 percent identify themselves as Christians? Are they invisible to you? Can you name some Asian Christian leaders? What about Latin and Mexican Americans — any names of leaders come to mind? (We'll ignore my own heritage, for the moment, the Scottish.) Measure that against your community. Is your church representative of the community, or is it more mono-ethnic?

What about *women*? How involved are women in your church? How are women involved? Are they at the table where decisions are made? Or do men make the decision and women do the work? In the words of Carolyn Custis James, who called her book about women *Half the Church*: "It is no small matter that women comprise half the church. In many countries women make up a significantly higher percentage of believers — 80 percent in China and 90 percent in Japan ... maybe these high percentages of women should make us wonder what God is doing, for he often forges significant inroads for the gospel by beginning with women.... When you stop to think of it, in sheer numbers, the potential we possess for expanding the kingdom is staggering."[6] Is your church unleashing the spiritual power of women? Is their voice heard?

What about the *poor*? How many poor people, unemployed people, financially struggling people are in your church? Are they even willing to let those facts be known? If not, why not?

What about *inner city* versus *suburban*? In the U.S., it has become a sign of special devotion to stake a claim for Jesus by dwelling among the "least of these" through church planting in the inner city. The implication is that the suburban folks are just too compromised with the wealth of this world to care about those in the urban settings. Another way to look at this is that some in the suburban churches don't know about the inner city and consequently don't care. So let's think about this together: Do we need to make the inner city folks visible in our churches? Do some inner city folks need to make the suburban folks visible at their churches? As Osheta Moore says so well, "geography does not indicate fidelity."[7]

What about *those struggling with faith*? How many folks in your church are struggling with the truth of the Bible, with the relationship between science and faith, with the atonement, with hell, with what the Old Testament says about God? Do you know? Are they free to inform you? What would happen if their problems became visible?

What about the *non-university educated*? Is your local church designed by a college graduate (almost certainly) and seminary graduate (good chance)? Does it appeal to college graduates? (Probably). What about those who don't give a rip about college, but like to cut wood or do landscaping, to paint or work on cars? Does your church see them when it makes plans?

What about *gays and lesbians*? Let's ignore for the moment the debates about what the Bible teaches and ask this question: Are people in your church able to be honest about their sexuality? Or do they catch the message that the gospel is not for them? Does your church want redemption or exclusion?

What about *introverts*? Is your church designed by extroverts (almost certainly) and engaging for extroverts (almost certainly) — but not introverts (very likely)?

What about those ... well, how to put this? Some people have somehow managed to compile a history of one nonsensical episode after another, while others seem to have walked straight out of the script of the American dream. Joseph Epstein speaks of such people as "men and women who have drawn lucky numbers in life's lottery."[8] We know what he means, so what about *mixing different walks of life?* Is your church only for the "successful and scripted," those with lucky numbers?

What about those suffering from *sexual abuse, dysfunctional families, depression, anxiety, or post-traumatic syndrome?* Or is your church for the (seemingly) mentally healthy extrovert?

The apostle Paul laid down one of the most brilliant lines in the history of mankind, a set of lines that reveal God's grand social experiment called "church," a set of lines that reveals what God wants the church to be and, therefore, how the Christian life is to be understood. I will reformat the lines so you see how central the grand experiment, the church, was for Paul:

"There is neither Jew nor Gentile [ethnic],
neither slave nor free [social or socio-economic class]
nor is there male and female [gender]."

(Why is there no ordering of life on the basis of ethnicity, class, or gender?)

"For you are all *one* in Christ Jesus." (Galatians 3:28)

The church is God's grand experiment, in which differents get connected, unlikes form a fellowship, and the formerly segregated are integrated. They are to be *one* — not scattered all over the city — and they are one *in Christ Jesus*, in the salad bowl that holds the differents together.

There are different cultures, there are different socioeconomic classes, there are different genders, and there are different sexualities. And there are different educations, incomes, kinds of work done, and preferences in music and art, worship style and sermon length. And they are all together at the table, in the salad bowl, thrashing it out with one another. That thrashing it out is what the church is about — *and that is what the Christian life is all about: learning to love one another, by the power of God's grace, so we can flourish as the people of God in this world.* The purpose of the church is to be the kingdom in the present world, and the Christian life is all about learning to live into that kingdom reality in the here and now.

ONE BIG MOSH PIT

Jen Hatmaker is a mom of two adopted kids from Ethiopia, and she took her adopted kids and three "bio" kids to a camp. I pick her story up there because it beautifully illustrates what the church is supposed to be and what the Christian life looks like when the church is what it is supposed to be:

> We went to *Encompass Adoption Family Camp* last week in Montana. All five of our kids gave us the side eye before the trip, pre-assigning adjectives: *"lame," "awkward," "weird," "random."* (Our brown children participated in this advance disparagement.) Brandon and I were convinced that spending time with other families who looked like ours and needed no explanation would be healing and powerful, not just for our little survivors but the whole family.
>
> We were right. (BOOM, kids. We OWN you.)
>
> Different skin, languages, countries of origin, accents, birth stories, siblings, experiences: nothing to see here. **The kids mixed and melded like it was the easiest thing they've ever done.** We thought maybe the bio kids would find common ground and the adopted kids would circle up, or perhaps the Ethiopians would form a tribe or the Sierra Leone gang would combine, but instead *it was one big mosh pit.*
>
> The teenagers were *inseparable,* says the mom who sent her husband over to the cafeteria at midnight to check on their (endless) poker game because I AM A MOM AND WORRYING IS MY TERRITORY. The littles never stopped playing; all the whites and tans and browns and blacks. I don't even know who was adopted and who wasn't. I couldn't even find my own kids in the pack. Everyone looked the same. And different. Which in our families is the same....
>
> I got a taste of heaven, and I mean that in the most non-overspiritualized way ever. **Through our kids, we glimpsed a world where the playing field is level, everyone is welcomed, all are valued, everyone is in.** The dividing lines that mark our adult lives are absent.

Your ethnicity is honored and fully celebrated, but it doesn't separate us. Are you on Instagram? Then you are a part of the teenage tribe. Can you traverse monkey bars? Then you are a part of the elementary crew. Are you a cute, pudgy baby? Then every human at camp will try to hold you.[9]

Jen, one slight correction. You got a taste not just of heaven, but of the church as God wants it to be in the here and now.

Pick your church and its image, and it will shape your Christian life — salad bowl, mosh pit, whatever — for they reflect the design that Jesus lived and Paul strove for daily.

THE CHALLENGE

The church as a salad bowl is such a wonderful, even utopian image. I love Miriam Neff's idea of including widows, and I love the image of a mosh pit we read about in Jen Hatmaker's blog. Ideas are easy — but living out those ideas is hard. (So invite the widow on your block over for coffee or dinner.) Inclusion, or fellowship of differents, is a great idea, but it's also the church's biggest challenge. How we understand the church determines how we see the Christian life. If the church is a fellowship of differents, what does the Christian life look like? I suggest the following six themes become central to the Christian life, and in the book that follows we will find ourselves in a church in need of each of these ideas:

Grace
Love
Table
Holiness
Newness
Flourishing

PART 1

GRACE

3

Space for Yes

Ever wonder what God was doing way back before time, before creation, billions of years ago? I confess to wondering about this, and the greatest theologians of the church have an answer: since God is love, God was loving. What God was doing was dwelling in love — Father loving Son, Son loving Father; Father loving Spirit, Spirit loving Father; Son loving Spirit, and Spirit loving Son. Endless, ceaseless, expanding, entirely satisfying, and creating love from one to the other. God was loving, God is loving, and God always will be loving. Love is who God is, and love is what God does.

It is a fact too sad not to report that many think of God in less than loving terms, and somehow they come away with the view that our God is a cosmic, moral monster. Dorothy Sayers once put this in admirable prose: "The God of Christians is too often looked upon as an old gentleman of irritable nerves who beats people for whistling."[1] But in fact, anything more than a prejudiced reading of the Bible reveals a God rich in mercy, abounding in compassion, patient in forgiveness, and altogether intent on reconciliation.

God created us, and that means too that God's love expanded to us. God is love and God can do no other. God looks at all of us and says, Yes. Do you hear God's grand Yes to you? My friend Mike Glenn wrote a whole book on this and called it *The Gospel of Yes*. It's the best title of a book I've ever seen (except for *The Blue Parakeet*). It's also the best news ever, that God looks at you and says, *Yes, I want you in my company.* God's Yes echoes throughout the cosmic expanse and promises, *I will do what it takes to make that happen.* God's Yes to us, which is the foundation for our learning to say Yes to those who are different from us in the church, can be seen in two majestic "acts" of God.

JESUS, GOD'S GRAND YES

God's biggest Yes was said to Jesus. As Paul put it, "For no matter how many promises God has made, they are 'Yes' in Christ" (2 Corinthians 1:20). Jesus is God's grandest Yes of all his Yeses. If you want to know what God thinks of you, look to Jesus, for in Jesus God says to the entire world, *Yes!*

We often get this backwards. We sometimes wonder if Jesus is God. So we compare what we believe about God — eternal, unchangeable, invisible, independent, omniscient, omnipotent, omnipresent, spiritual, wise, true, good, holy, loving, just, supremely creative, timeless — to see how Jesus stacks up with God. If Jesus fits, we believe, then he's God. If not, well then, he's not. But here is a startling Christian conviction, one that stands out like a seven-footer in a crowd of normal-size teenagers: we don't know Jesus is God because we know who God is, but we know who God is because we know Jesus! Jesus, the Gospel of John tells us, is the very incarnation of God. We see God perfectly in Jesus. We need to be asking the question: Is our view of God like Jesus?

If we read Paul front to back, we cannot help but observe that the man was intoxicated with Jesus. Paul tells us in the heart of his early ministry that Christ *is* our wisdom, our righteousness, our holiness, and our redemption (1 Corinthians 1:30 – 31). Notice something here: Jesus *is* these things; he doesn't just *give* us these things. Toward the end of his ministry Paul said that compared to Jesus, everything else was garbage (he uses a term stronger than this, but editors and publishers are sensitive about such terms). All he wanted in life was "to know Christ"

(Philippians 3:10), and Paul can't say enough about him: "In Christ all the fullness of the Deity lives in bodily form, and in Christ you have been brought to fullness" (Colossians 2:9 – 10). History closes when God brings "unity to all things in heaven and on earth" — *where?* — "under Christ" (Ephesians 1:10). Paul writes that "speaking the truth in love, we will grow to become in every respect the mature body of him who is the head, that is, Christ" (4:15).

If you want to know what God thinks of you, Paul wants you to know, look at Jesus. In him you will see that great Yes that God is for us. If you wonder if you are accepted by God, ask this: Has the Father accepted the Son? If God has, God has accepted you. If you want to know if God loves you, ask this: Does the Father love Jesus? If God does, then God loves you. What God thinks of you is what God thinks of Jesus. That is the greatest Yes echoing back through the galaxies of time and forward into all eternity. That Yes is the only Yes that matters.

GOD'S YES TO ALL OF US

Look around you in all directions, then look farther — to the northern countries and to the southern countries, to the west and to the east. God's Yes in Jesus is for everyone. Because there is so much variety in this world and because we are so invisible to one another, we need to let God's Yes in Christ penetrate so deeply that we embrace all others as the objects of God's Yes. We need to know that those who are invisible to us are visible to God and, if they listen, that they too can hear God's Yes.

Paul's new vision of God's grand experiment rubbed raw the delicate skin over ethnic privilege. Jews would have to learn that God was saying Yes to Gentiles; Gentiles — the Greeks and Romans — would have to learn that God was saying Yes to Jews. Males would have to learn God's Yes spoken to women, and women would have to learn God's Yes spoken to men. The economically elite would have to learn that God's Yes included the poor, and the poor would have to learn that God's Yes involved the rich. The morally kosher would have to listen with better ears for God's Yes to the morally nonkosher — the alcoholics, the prostitutes, and the all-too-common thieves.

God's Yes is why the church is God's great mystery in this world, the place where he is doing something altogether radical and new. Sadly, God's Yes is often the first notion rejected by whites about African Americans, by African Americans about Latin Americans, by Latin Americans about women, by women about men, by rich white men about poor minorities. The revolution God creates in the church begins or ends with this first step: either we embrace that God's Yes is for all or we don't.

Christena Cleveland, in her new book with the potent title *Disunity in Christ*, opens up her own heart about divisiveness and unity with this wondrous beginning in her own journey of faith:

> When I first began walking with Christ, I felt an immediate and authentic connection with any other Christian who crossed my path. Orthodox, Catholic, charismatic, Lutheran, evangelical, black, white, Asian, Ben [she tells about her encounter with him earlier] — didn't matter. We were family.

But something sinister and divisive arose:

> But as I walked with Jesus, somehow my "growth" had been coupled with increasingly stronger opinions about the "right" way to be a follower. I started keeping people I didn't enjoy or agree with at arm's length. I managed to avoid most of the Bens in my life by locating them, categorizing them and gracefully shunning them, all while appearing to be both spiritual and community-oriented.

Then the stinger:

> I chose to build community with people with whom I could pretty much agree on everything.[2]

The only way to recover that first love for all is to listen one more time to God's Yes to all — the Yes God speaks in Jesus Christ. When we absorb the indiscriminate love of God for all as displayed in the life of Jesus, we can learn to see others as God sees them. But there's one more Yes.

SPIRIT, GOD'S GRAND YES

The Father not only sends the Son; he also sends the Spirit "into" us. The Spirit, too, is God's Yes. If you want to know what God thinks of you, look at the Spirit at work in you. One of my favorite expressions of Paul's is that the Holy Spirit is God's "deposit" in us: the Spirit "is a deposit guaranteeing our inheritance until the redemption of those who are God's possession" (Ephesians 1:14). The Spirit reveals that God is working in us to transform us.

When I was a seventeen-year-old athlete considering college scholarships as a high jumper (no kidding), my parents and youth pastor conspired to get me to go with my girlfriend (now my wife, Kris) with some other high school friends to a church camp in Muscatine, Iowa. On the first night our camp counselor asked the Bible teacher for the camp, Dr. Benson (the president of some Bible college in the Midwest), to speak to us at bedtime. The lights were all but out, and we had nowhere to go and nothing to do in that deserted Iowa campground, so we listened — or at least I did.

Dr. Benson talked about the "filling of the Holy Spirit," and I had no real idea what he was talking about — at least at the existential, real-life level. For some reason, this gray-headed, unathletic man in cuffed pants and a dress shirt had my attention. He asked us to spend some time with God before breakfast the next morning, and he urged us to ask the Spirit into our lives, to make room for the Spirit. It sounded so weird, but I went to bed thinking about what he said.

The next morning, I got to breakfast before the crew was ready to serve, so I wandered down a hill to the small outdoor chapel. I sat down under a tree and, completely unaware of what might happen, I did what Dr. Benson told us to do the night before. I simply said, "God, fill me with your Spirit." I opened that door and, mysteriously enough, Someone entered. Something mighty in my life happened at that moment. My whole life was changed — and I'm writing this book because of what happened that morning before breakfast.

I asked for the Spirit, and God gave his Spirit. I felt a mighty rushing wind in my soul, I was awakened spiritually, I became convinced of the truth of the gospel, and I began to read my Bible seriously. My girlfriend caught the same fire at the same camp, and I cared less about being an athlete and everything about being a follower of Jesus. We went off to Cornerstone University the next year and got married a year after that. Since then, I have had one passion in life: to know God, to know him through his Word, and to teach the Bible to others. I asked for the Spirit, and I got the Spirit — because God is for us in giving us the Spirit to create new life. Nothing is more convincing to me that God is for us than the gift of the Spirit — and in God's Spirit, I have heard his Yes time and time again.

IF GOD SAYS YES, WHO CAN SAY NO?

One of Paul's grandest statements is Romans 8:31: "If God is for us, who can be against us?" This is not a Big Question Mark: "*If it so happens, but it's not clear, that God is for us....*" Instead, this is an assumption: *Since it is absolutely true that God is for us....*" Another way of phrasing this is, "If God has said Yes to you...."

When did you realize someone was *for* you? Often enough we learn someone's for-ness through their performance. You learn your parents are for you when they cheer for you or when they congratulate you on some performance. I believe most of us learn someone is for us when we hear their Yes in response to our performance.

But there's a deeper, louder Yes than this when it comes to God, and it is sad that many people don't experience this deeply enough or often enough. God's Yes is not rooted in our performance, but rather in our are-ness. God loves us because we *are* made in his image. God's Yes is this: "I love because you *are* you!"

God loves everyone, including you and me, for who we are, not for what we have done or for what we might accomplish. If God has said Yes to us, Paul asked, *who can say No?* So let me say it all over again a different way:

No matter what you have done,
not because you go to church,
not because you read your Bible,
not because folks think you are spiritual,

and

no matter what sins you have committed,
no matter how vicious or mean or vile they were,
no matter how calloused your heart and soul have become,

God loves you.

Not because you are good,
not because you do good things,
not because you are famous or have served others,
but *because you are you.*

To you, God has said Yes,
God is saying Yes,
and God will eternally say Yes.

God is for the You that is You.

GOD'S YES IS UNSTOPPABLE

There is something else in Romans 8:31 – 39, namely, that God's Yes is unstoppable. Let's transport ourselves back to one of Paul's house churches and imagine yet again the make-up of that group — the morally unkosher sitting with the unpowerful standing with an arm around the financially drained, addressed by an apostle who was being chased daily by opponents of the gospel. In that context, with all those people around, hear again the grand Yes of God.

"Who can be against us?" Paul tauntingly thunders. The answer, No one! Can anyone bring secure charges against us? Never! Why? Because "it is God who justifies." Can anyone condemn us? No! Why? Jesus died for us and is now "at the right hand of God and is also interceding for us." The ultimate mode of Yes is the lawyer advocate, and here Jesus' role is to have our back, to be our defender before the gracious throne of God. Can anything separate us from God's love? Here are Paul's matchless words to that ramshackle bundle of new Roman Christians about God's unstoppable, relentless Yes:

> No, in all these things we are more than conquerors through him who loved us. For I am convinced that
> neither death nor life,
> neither angels nor demons,
> neither the present nor the future,
> nor any powers,
> neither height nor depth,
> nor anything else in all creation,
> will be able to separate us from the love of God that is in Christ Jesus our Lord.

Do you hear God's Yes? Stop whatever you are doing and tell yourself, "God's Yes is for me." If you think this is too simple, too basic, too below your level, say it twice. For this is the beginning of God's grand experiment in this world called the church. The church is God's space for Yes.

4

Space for Grace

The Man not only despised Christians, he sought to eliminate them. He began with threatening emails to some Christians he knew; then, under a bogus name, he opened a website where he pumped out vicious accusations and fierce warnings. Some in the community begged Christian family members to abandon their faith and the church.

The Man occasionally beat up a Christian or two when he knew no one was watching, but he also knew the authorities would not come to their aid if they noticed his abuse. His religiously informed and passionate pleadings with the police coaxed the powers to his side. The police began their surveillance, and some devout believers were brought in for questionings and threatened with danger to their families and life imprisonment or worse. Some Christians were tortured, and rumors began to circulate that a young Christian leader had been killed to set an example. Fear struck the Christian communities, and their fear fed The Man's fury into further abuse.

No, The Man is not a modern day Muslim.

No, The Man is not a terrorist.

No, The Man is not an Iron Curtain Lenin or Stalin.

No, The Man is not an Idi Amin, or a Robert Mugabe, or an apartheid supporter, or a secretive sleuth or drug lord.

That Man is the apostle Paul, and I simply updated him to illustrate how persecution occurs in our world today.

Paul was Enemy #1 to the first Jewish Christian community's faith. They all agreed Paul was an enemy of God, of Christ, of the Spirit, of the Christians. But God drew That Man away from persecuting zeal into the church. Paul's zeal for the Torah became a zeal for the Messiah. That transformation is grace.

Maybe you've not read Paul's story enough to know the details, but Paul once left Jerusalem under orders from Caiaphas, the high priest, to arrest Christians. He was successfully carrying out those orders when God stepped into his life and transformed him. Remarkably, Paul returned to Jerusalem three years later as a defector from his former rabbi's ways and as a convert to Jesus' ways. Ever wonder what Caiaphas or Paul's famous majordomo rabbi, Gamaliel, thought of their former comrade and student who was now a follower of Jesus? How did those in Paul's former circles describe what had happened to him? That didn't matter to Paul, who was so overwhelmed by God's grace; he no longer cared what they thought. Paul knew he was in a place called grace.

> Grace is the opening word that tumbles out of Paul's mouth.
> Grace is more than being lucky to be on God's side.
> Grace is God's goodness showered on people who have failed.
> Grace is God's love on those who think they are unlovable.
> Grace is God knowing what we are designed to be.
> Grace is God believing in us when we have given up.
> Grace is someone at the end of their rope finding new strength.

But there's more to grace. Grace is both a place and a power.

> Grace is God unleashing his transforming power.
> Grace realigns and reroutes a life and a community.
> Grace is when you turn your worst enemy into your best friend.
> Grace takes people as they are and makes them what they can be.
> Grace ennobles; grace empowers.

Grace forgives; grace frees.

Grace transcends, and grace transforms.

Grace turns a Christian-baiting, Torah-loving Pharisee such as the apostle Paul into a Christian-loving, Christ-following apostle. One of my favorite lines in the whole Bible is found at the end of the first chapter of Galatians: "The man [Paul] who formerly persecuted us is now preaching the faith he once tried to destroy" (Galatians 1:23). Grace turns persecutors into preachers. As The Man himself claimed, "I was just as zealous for God as any of you are today. I persecuted the followers of this Way to their death, arresting both men and women and throwing them into prison" (Acts 22:3 – 4). Toward the end of his life he uses three terms for his pre-Jesus days: "I was once a *blasphemer* and a *persecutor* and a *violent* man." But the next words explain the transformation: "I was shown *mercy* ... the *grace* of our Lord was poured out on me abundantly" (1 Timothy 1:13 – 14). If we were to sum up Paul's life in three words it would be these: zeal, grace, transformation.

Grace turns God-fighters into God-defenders.

Grace turns Jesus-haters into Jesus-lovers.

Grace turns Spirit-resisters into Spirit-listeners.

To do this, grace forgives; grace heals; grace transforms; grace ennobles; grace empowers. Grace makes people in the salad bowl comfortable with another. Only grace can do that. But grace can do that.

FROM GRACE TO GRACES

Paul doesn't call the place of grace or the church a "salad bowl." Instead he calls it being "in Christ." Have you ever looked up all the references to "in Christ" in the New Testament and considered what we get when we find ourselves "in Christ"? To be "in Christ" means to be connected to, joined to, and participating in who Jesus is and what Jesus has done. To be in Christ means we live in him, we die in him, and we are raised in him.

To be in Christ means to be joined to others who are in Christ. To be in Christ means to be in God.

God promises — literally — the world to those who are in Christ. To be in Christ means one kind of grace piled on top of another. Grace places us in the salad bowl, gives us an assignment in the salad bowl, and gives us the courage and power to live with others in the salad bowl. I can only give you a sampling here of all we get "in Christ," but pride of place is given to 1 Corinthians 1:4:[1]

> I [Paul] always thank my God for you because of his *grace given you in Christ Jesus.*

Grace spreads itself out in all directions and we receive the following "graces" in Christ.[2]

Freedom
Justification, or being declared right with God
Eternal life
Sanctification, or being made holy
Reconciliation, or being at peace with God
Blessed with every spiritual blessing
Raised and seated with Christ in God's presence
Created to do good works
Forgiveness
Peace
Our needs met
Faith and love

It's all grace, the kind of grace that transformed the apostle Paul from a persecutor to an apostle. The kind of grace that can face the challenge of the fellowship of differents and turn those differents into best friends. It's the kind of grace Paul saw at work in house churches when he saw an enslaved prostitute, who did not have control of her own body because her master owned her, a homeless man for whom the Roman dole was not designed, a craft worker whose own workers had formed a riot with another craft worker's slaves over the prices they were charging — this is what Paul had in mind when he knew what God's grace was doing in house churches all around the Roman Empire. Ordinary people were becoming extraordinary ordinaries!

ORDINARY PEOPLE TOO

We Christians are too often addicted to stories of dramatic and extraordinary grace. We love the big story such as Paul's — but grace isn't just found in the dramatic.

Grace is at work in the stories of ordinary girls and boys who grow up in ordinary homes and who go on to live ordinary Christian lives in ordinary churches with ordinary jobs. It's the same power of grace at work. Slow, steady transformation remains transformation. Most of God's work is with ordinary people because that's the sort of people who populate this world. God's grace makes ordinary people better. An angry friend who becomes a gentle companion is God's grace. A selfish mom who becomes a giving mom is God's grace. A distant husband who becomes an emotionally present husband is God's grace. A bitter teen who becomes a family member all over again is God's grace. A backbiting church friend who learns to bite the lip is God's grace.

Here's one for you. A student of mine at Northern Seminary, Tara Beth, grew up in a family of what she calls "ChrEasters" — the sort who goes to church on Christmas and Easter. But with little family mentoring, Tara Beth — who openly admits she's ordinary — describes what happened in her spiritual journey:

> At fifteen I experienced an inexplicable longing to know the true God. This also coupled with a time in my life when I was terribly lonely and without a friend. I was seeking companionship and meaning in my life.
>
> I sought out the local Campus Life Director. This man encouraged me to start reading my Bible for the answers I was seeking. Every night I would find myself alone in my bedroom reading through the Bible. I

began in the Old Testament and found myself enthralled by the story of creation, Abraham, Moses, and Israel.

Every single evening, as soon as my homework was finished, I would race to my bedroom with genuine delight to continue reading this awe-inspiring Story. Then I landed on the Gospel of Luke. I was captivated. I could not get away from the compassion, love, and grace exemplified in Jesus Christ, the Messiah. Every single night I had a deep hunger and the desire to seek Jesus through the Gospel of Luke. One night I came to the story of the cross. I was overwhelmed with joy as at once everything started to make sense. That night I fell to my knees, raised my hands in the air and wept with tears of joy. I found grace and hope ... or it found me.

The only words able to slip out of my mouth were, "Thank you, Jesus. Thank you, Jesus. Thank you, Jesus." I said this over and over for the next hour as I wept on my knees. It was there that I met Him and fell totally in love.

After that evening there was no turning back. I had met Jesus our King.

Grace takes lonely people and gives them friendship with God. Grace takes our longings for love and ushers us into the presence of God. Grace transforms our yearnings for significance into gifts of significance. God's grace speaks to us when we are alone and draws us into fellowship with God and with others. Tara Beth experienced the same grace, the same transforming power that Paul experienced. She's loved; she's in seminary today; she's married; she's a mother; she's serving in a church; she's gifted.

After reading an early version of this chapter, this is what Tara Beth wrote in response:

Ever since I was a child I struggled academically. Severely. I took home report cards in grade school that were littered with bad grades. I can remember being humiliated in the classroom for not understanding a concept or not knowing the answer. I was put in many smaller classrooms with Special Ed students and had to have one-on-one help. I also had a severe speech impediment and had to go through loads of therapy for that. I *barely* graduated high school.

So when I knew that God was calling me to ministry, I was terrified not only for the speaking part but also the academics. How would I *ever* make it through college? But I did. In fact, when I was sixteen I read how Jesus "increased in wisdom." I so desperately wanted to understand God's Word and teach it in a way that was God honoring. So I prayed fervently every single night, "Jesus, increase my wisdom." I can remember praying it to tears. I was so incredibly insecure about my speech and academics that I thought I could never be a vessel for God. When I got to college, things began to transform. I started to understand complex theological concepts and biblical concepts. I began to blossom. But my insecurities never went away.

When God called me to Northern Seminary, I almost vomited at the thought of revisiting academia. The old fears haunted me yet again. So I prayed and prayed and prayed, "Lord increase my wisdom." I've recently experienced a breakthrough. Major. When I think back to who I was and where I've come from, I know that it has been nothing but God's rich, pure, lavish, and extravagant GRACE.

God heard the prayer of a young sixteen-year-old girl just wanting to *understand* God's Word in a way that would spur on growth. It has been God's grace every time I write a paper, read a book, or preach a sermon. It was God's grace through the Spirit that spoke deeply into my soul to say, let go of your insecurities and trust that I am at work.

Tara Beth was invisible, and by God's grace has become visible. She's now "in Christ" with all those differents seeking to make sense of how to live when everyone around you also is different. The only way we can ever be the church God wants is to be bathed and soaked in grace.

GRACE: SHORT STORY OR FULL STORY?

Sadly, the full story of grace is often reduced to a short story. Frederick Buechner tilts in this direction when he says that "a good sleep is grace and so are good dreams." "The smell of rain is grace."[3] I like dreamy sleep and the pitter-patter of rain, but we do the word "grace" a disservice when we reduce it to pleasant life experiences.

The second misunderstanding is a sad face — that is, when grace is what God does for bad people in such a way they are reminded how bad they are. Here's the short story it tells: "God was against us, but God was gracious and now we're just flat-out lucky to be on his good side." Here are three standard definitions of short-story grace:

B. B. Warfield: "Grace is free sovereign favor to the ill-deserving."

Jerry Bridges: "[Grace] is God reaching downward to people who are in rebellion against Him."

Paul Zahl: "Grace is unconditional love toward a person who does not deserve it."[4]

In each of these three definitions, the accent falls on our unworthiness. That's the short story of grace.

The full story starts where these definers started, but it goes well beyond. As Anne Lamott once put it, "I do not understand the mystery of grace — only that it meets us where we are but does not leave us there."[5] That's the full story of grace — one that invades my space, but never leaves me in my space. No, grace creates new space.

It is also vital to know that grace does not begin with God's anger or wrath. No, God's grace begins on the Yes-note of love; grace begins with his unconquerable love for us. He gives us a place "in Christ," and then God's grace empowers us to thrive "in Christ." Grace invades our world to transform us until we are fully outfitted for eternal life. Grace is God's loving, new creation power at work in us. Kathleen Norris stands closer to the apostle Paul when she describes God's artistic grace this way: "Peter denied Jesus, and Saul persecuted the early Christians, but God could see the apostles they would become."[6] Dorothy Sayers once said that the artist does "not see life as a problem to be solved, but as a medium for creation."[7]

The church, if it is going to be the church God designed it to be, must become a space for the full story of God's artistic grace — the story about where we were, where we are now, and where we will be someday.

GRACE TRANSFORMS

Notice how often — dozens of times — The Man Paul uses "grace" for his entire life. Read these lines from Paul carefully (bold added below):

> But when God, who set me apart from my mother's womb and called me by his **grace**, was pleased to reveal his Son in me so that I might preach him among the Gentiles. (Galatians 1:15 – 16)

God revealed himself to Paul personally by grace.

> James, Cephas and John, those esteemed as pillars, gave me and Barnabas the right hand of fellowship when they recognized the **grace** given to me. They agreed that we should go to the Gentiles, and they to the circumcised. (Galatians 2:9)

Paul's mission to the Gentiles was God's grace, as evidenced here in his letter to the Romans:

> Through him we received **grace** and apostleship to call all the Gentiles to the obedience that comes from faith for his name's sake. (Romans 1:5)

Each of our "gifts" is from God's grace:

> We have different gifts, according to the **grace** given to each of us. If your gift is prophesying, then prophesy in accordance with your faith. (Romans 12:6)

Here is grace on top of grace on top of grace — the apostle says *everything he is and everything he has done is God's grace!*

> But by the **grace** of God I am what I am, and his **grace** to me was not without effect. No, I worked harder than all of them — yet not I, but the **grace** of God that was with me. (1 Corinthians 15:10)

Yes, Paul has a terrible past to tell, and grace includes that story.[8] Paul's idea of grace will not stop with a short story; it tells the whole story of that grace at work in us — and that was at work in a man named "Jack."

GRACE FOR A MAN NAMED JACK

In World War I, in France, some English military were struck by German fire. Harry Ayres was killed, while the man next to him lived. The man who survived was "Jack," or as he was named by his parents, "Clive Staples." As in C. S. Lewis[9] — the one we love. Alan Jacobs, an expert on Lewis, observed that the "pre-conversion Lewis [was ...] neither a particularly likable nor a particularly interesting person." In his famous *Mere Christianity*, Lewis insightfully describes "The Great Sin" as pride or self-conceit. Lewis says it is the "complete anti-God state of mind,"[10] and he knew by experience that anti-God state of mind well.

What Jacobs said of Lewis in his middle teens can perhaps fit most of his preconversion life: he was a "thoroughly obnoxious, arrogant, condescending intellectual prig." As a teenager, Lewis became an atheist but irreverently faked his way through a confirmation at his father's church in (now) Northern Ireland. He was later to say, "The man Yeshua or Jesus did actually exist ... but all the other tomfoolery about virgin birth, magic healings, apparitions and so forth is on exactly the same footing as any other mythology." As a young man, he had to say this about Christianity and any religious faith: they are "a kind of endemic nonsense into which humanity tended to blunder," and he said of God that he was "a bogey who is prepared to torture me for ever and ever." Reflecting on his time in World War I, when asked if he was afraid, Lewis' steely resistance to God finds its way to a timeless expression of hubris: "All the time, but I never sank so low as to pray." As an Oxford student, to a friend Lewis "cried out in an angry crescendo, 'You take too many things for granted. You can't start with God. *I don't accept God!*'" In his first book, *Spirits in Bondage*, and well before his conversion, we find this cold-blooded verse expressing his anti-God state of mind:

Come let us curse our Master ere we die,
For all our hopes in endless ruin lie.
The good is dead. Let us curse God Most High.[11]

During his Oxford days, Lewis lived a double life as a student and also had some kind of intimate relationship with Mrs. Moore, a relationship covered in systematic deceit. The biographers of Lewis are accurate: Lewis was an unknown, arrogant Oxford don.

In his journey, Lewis became aware of how arrogant he really was. In a letter to Leo Baker, his friend, Lewis comes clean with a minimal concession to God: "I have stopped defying heaven: it can't know less than I." God exists, but God is still an "it." He recognizes the iceberg in his path: "The old doctrine is quite true you know — that one must attribute everything to the grace of God, and nothing to oneself." With candor, Lewis confesses: "Yet as long as one *is* a conceited ass, there is no good pretending not to be." Few books are as insightful into human nature as his *Screwtape Letters*. When it was suggested that he had studied morality deeply to write such a penetrating book, Lewis admitted the source of his moral insights was his own proud heart. In a letter to his friend Arthur, he reveals what he finds in his inner world: "Depth under depth of self-love and self-admiration."

From arrogance, however, he moved to surrender. A famous passage in *Surprised by Joy* divulges his awareness that God was becoming present to Lewis:

> You must picture me alone in that room in Magdalen [his college at Oxford], night after night, feeling, whenever my mind lifted even for a second from my work, the steady, unrelenting approach of Him whom I so earnestly desired not to meet. That which I greatly feared had at last come upon me.[12]

His reading, rich with imagination and mythology and a yearning for "Northernness" and "Joy," chipped away at his atheism:

> A young man who wishes to remain a sound Atheist cannot be too careful of his reading. There are traps everywhere.[13]

With Lewis, we have no story of a person seeking God. Instead, he sensed God visiting him, and he cracked the door to let the light of faith enter:

In the Trinity term of 1929 [after Easter] *I gave in, and admitted that God was God*, and knelt and prayed: perhaps, that night, the most dejected and reluctant convert in all England.[14]

On September 19, 1931, Lewis entered into a late-night discussion with his friends J. R. R. Tolkien and Hugo Dyson that took him one step closer to Christian faith. When they revealed to him that his love of myth should have led him to love the Story about Jesus' dying and rising, Lewis took another step. God had become present in Lewis's inner world, but that night Christ knocked on his door. During a trip to Whipsnade Zoo, Lewis opened the door to Jesus Christ as the true Son of God and let him in. All at once life made sense. Or, as Lewis put it later in his inimitable way: "I believe in Christianity as I believe that the Sun has risen, not because I see it but because by it I see everything else."[15]

Lewis "gave in," and his whole life both unraveled and came together at the same time, leading him to be one of the greatest converts of the twentieth century and a great example of pride undone before the rule of King Jesus. The Lewis we love is the Lewis transformed by the presence of God's grace.

WHAT HAPPENS WHEN GRACE TAKES ROOT?

You can read Paul's life or you can read the life of C. S. Lewis. Or you can look straight to the life of Jesus, and the first thing you will see when grace takes over a person's life is a life shaped by love. Let us remind ourselves that a local church shapes the Christian life. Let us remind ourselves that the challenge is to establish a grace-created and grace-creating fellowship of differents. But a Christian life shaped for that kind of fellowship will require not only grace but also love.

PART 2

LOVE

5

Love Is a Series of Prepositions

Over and over Paul *explicitly claims* that love is the center of the whole Christian life:

> For the entire law is fulfilled in keeping this one command: *"Love your neighbor as yourself."* (Galatians 5:14)
>
> But the fruit of the Spirit is *love.* (Galatians 5:22)
>
> *Do everything in love.* (1 Corinthians 16:14)
>
> And over all these virtues put on *love, which binds them all together in perfect unity.* (Colossians 3:14)
>
> And this is my prayer: *that your love may abound more and more* in knowledge and depth of insight, so that you may be able to discern what is best and may be pure and blameless for the day of Christ, filled with the fruit of righteousness that comes through Jesus Christ — to the glory and praise of God. (Philippians 1:9–11)
>
> For in Christ Jesus neither circumcision nor uncircumcision has any value. *The only thing that counts is faith expressing itself through love.* (Galatians 5:6)

Take Paul at his word. Love is the "only thing that counts," and counts way more than circumcision — which is a good thing for Gentile males! And in a deft, revolutionary claim, Paul radicalizes love when he announces publicly that loving your neighbor is the "entire law."

Response from the right side of the synagogue: "There are 613 commandments in the Torah, so how can one of the commandments be the *entire* law?"

Paul's response: "Because love expresses the totality of God's will for us."

In making love central, Paul stands next to Jesus, who said all the commandments were derived from loving God or loving others (Matthew 22:37–40).[1] Paul echoes this when he says that just as the first fruit of (life in the) Spirit is love (Galatians 5:22), so we are "to do everything" in love.

For Paul, love is central. It was central because he knew the challenges of the Christian life for those who were in fellowship with one another in house churches dotting the Roman Empire. The *only* way they would make it is if each person learned to love the others. Roman slaves and workshop owners were not used to sitting down at table and praying with Torah-observant Jews, and kosher Jews were not used to reading Scripture with prostitutes or migrant workers — yet Paul believed this was God's greatest vision for living! Which brings us back to the need to love one another.

LOVE IS A GREAT IDEA UNTIL...

Love is a great idea until the one you are called to love happens to be unlike you. Love is a great idea until you discover who your neighbors actually are. Love is a great idea until you see who actually attends your church. Love is a great idea until your kids go ballistic. Love is a great idea until your house floods because someone left the sink running. Love is a great idea until you see who sits next to you at church on Sunday morning. I could go on, but, yes, love is central and good and civil and breeds tolerance. No one wants to dispute love.

BUT WHAT EXACTLY IS LOVE?

Everyone thinks they know what love is, but few can define it well. Some will back down and simply say, "I can't define it, but I know when it see it — or when I feel it." So here are two rules for defining what love means in the Bible.

Rule 1. Do not define the Bible's words by looking up "love" in a modern English dictionary. The dictionary defines how words are used in English today, not what words meant back in the Bible days. Notice what dictionaries say: love is "an intense feeling of deep affection." Yes, emotions and affections are what our culture thinks when the word "love" is used. But that dictionary definition, which is 100 percent shaped by our Western culture, is a pale shadow of what the Bible means by love.

Rule 2. Define love in the Bible *by watching God love Israel, his Son, and the church — in fact, the whole of creation.* God shows us what love is, and we can't answer our question until we turn away from the dictionary's emphasis on emotions and affections and go to the Bible's special way of revealing what love is. Before we go to the Bible, though, we need to spend some time dabbling in what love means in our culture, because it is the air we breathe, the movies we watch, the books we read, and the news we consume. Culture hands us a definition of love that we need to set back down.

LOVE IN AMERICAN CULTURE

Our culture defines love by emotional experience, by pleasure, and by satisfaction.[2] Brain researchers constantly point to dopamine, a neurochemical released that gives us the sense of pleasure. They tell us that orgasm, satisfaction in a relationship, the taste of chocolate, and the stupor of alcohol are on the same spectrum of neurochemical experience. Most of us have absorbed the view of love that defines it as an emotional experience, by which we mean something that gives us a dopamine rush. Many today speak of "falling in love," which is our culture's way of saying "falling into dopamine's pleasure zone." Or we speak of "chemistry," equating love with the pleasures of a neurochemical flourish. But dopamine rushes are not what the Bible means by love.

Because our culture — and many Christians — are so enculturated into this sense of love, we struggle with love in our marriages, in our families, and in our relationships with close friends and with one another in what should be our salad bowl churches. Why do we struggle? Because we've got our hearts wrapped around the wrong ideas about love. Does the Bible's sense of love begin with dopamine bliss? No. It begins in a spot most in our culture want to ignore, so let's turn now to the first of four elements of love in the Bible.

Element 1: Rugged Commitment

The Bible begins telling us what love is with the thoroughly unexciting idea of God making a covenant commitment with Abraham. (Read Genesis 12 and 15.) God loves by entering into the rugged commitment of a covenant with Abraham, a covenant commitment that finds new expression in the promise to David, discovers a brand new future in the new covenant prophecy of Jeremiah 31, and then lands on the final covenant God makes with us in Jesus Christ (what we call his "new covenant"). Love then is not primarily emotion or affection, but rather a covenant *commitment* to another person. Commitment does not deny emotions; commitment reorders emotions.

I use this word "rugged" alongside the word "commitment" in expressing what a covenant is for obvious reasons. Love is often hard work. American theologian Stanley Hauerwas once said that no two people are fully compatible.[3] If he's right — and I tend to think he is (and who argues with Texans anyway!) — love is about the rugged commitment to another person who may shift from being compatible to being annoying — which can certainly be true of church folks in God's grand social experiment. No wonder Paul talked about love so much!

Element 2: Rugged Commitment to Be "With"

God's central covenant promise was that he would be *with* Israel: "I will be your God, and you will be my people."[4] How was God *with* humans?

God was with Abraham in a smoking pot. In Genesis 15 God sealed his commitment with Abraham in an action as strange to you and me as it was common and expected to Abraham: animals were cut in half and each party walked between them to announce legally, "You can do this to me if I am not faithful to my commitment." The big difference with God and Abraham, though, is that *only* God walked between the pieces — in the form of a smoking pot. This was God's way of saying to Abraham, "I'm with you." As the Bible unfolds, God expresses his presence with Israel in a pillar of cloud and fire, then in a mobile shrine called a "tabernacle," and then in a huge, immobile temple. All along, God's presence was known through his leaders, Israel's kings and priests and prophets.

But God's deepest commitment to be "with" was expressed through the incarnation. When Jesus was born, Matthew tells us Isaiah's prediction was fulfilled. Jesus was "Immanuel ... God *with* us" (Matthew 1:23), and this theme of with-ness continues: Jesus, after his resurrection, sends the Spirit to be *with* us. The final book of the Bible sketches a vision of the new heavens and the new earth in the new Jerusalem, where "God's dwelling place is now *among* the people [of God], and he will dwell *with* them" (Revelation 21:3). God's covenant is a commitment to be *with* us.

ON AN ALASKAN ISLAND

In her splendid memoir about summer fishing in Alaska, Leslie Leyland Fields opens up some windows on love as with-ness.[5] As newlyweds, she and her husband moved to an Alaskan island to fish salmon all summer to make funds for the rest of the year. It was exciting and hard and challenging for her relationship with Duncan, who in the evenings and nights was her husband and soulmate and lover, but who on the boat during the workday was her boss who sometimes raised his voice in the heat of scrambling to pick salmon from the nets. Salmon fishing is all-consuming and their business grew. Soon Duncan and Leslie had children, and it was impossible for her to care for them and to fish, so they hired some workers, who lived with them. Leslie spent more time on shore, leading her to ponder love:

There was a cost to this new, more balanced life, though. Since we weren't fishing together regularly, our only face-to-face conversation time was at the meal table.

Now comes a powerful line expressing the necessity of with-ness for love to be sustained and flourish:

> The essential adhesive to our relationship, what had drawn us together in the first place, thinned to near silence.

Love cannot be love without presence, which Leslie and Duncan learned during that tough summer when their love was in jeopardy:

> We had barely talked for more than ten days. How much longer could I do this? Not just now, but how many more years?
>
> So much was given up to live here — it felt to me that we had relinquished our lives to the lives of the salmon, who were themselves swimming to their own deaths.

Beside that piercing analogy of salmon to their love is her witness to the absolute necessity of presence for love to exist:

> Seven years into this I knew unequivocally that marriage was not a vehicle, nor could human hearts be put on ice without freezing.

They struggled to restore love.

> Reconciliation that summer was not inevitable; I did not expect it, but slowly it came. Duncan listened to me.

Those last words, "Duncan listened to me," contain one of the secrets to love. To be *with* means being attentive enough to the other person to listen and genuinely hear what their heart is saying.

In one of those rare transitional moments in marriage, Duncan years later asked a question that led to a deeper covenant: "Do you ever wish you hadn't married me and come to Alaska?" After the ice-breaking joke and Leslie's response, "Of course! Lots of times!" she realized she and Duncan were about to express their deepest selves and said:

> Duncan, I'm glad I'm here. I'm glad I'm here *with* you.... I do know that
> you are the one God gave me, and this is where God has brought me.

Men aren't always good at expressing the heart, but his next words tell the
story of love and the biggest fear of genuine love, falling from with-ness
into apart-ness:

> I know, too, Leslie. But sometimes I think back to that summer — I'm
> afraid I'll lose you again.

She counters:

> You won't. A lot has changed since then, Duncan. I'm afraid you're stuck
> *with* me. I promise.

Not only are those words all the way from Alaska; they are what the
Bible means by love — a promised, rugged commitment to be *with* another
person, no matter what. "Friends," C. S. Lewis said, stand "side by side,
absorbed in some common interest." But love wants more. "Lovers," he
declared, "are normally face to face, absorbed in each other."[6]
Love isn't just for married folks. Some people are single because they
want to be, some even though they don't want to be, and some because of
divorce or death. Single people love others too. (I have to say this because
some married people cannot think of love in terms other than marriage.)
Jesus was single and probably Paul was too. Love is a rugged commitment
by one person, married or not, to another person, married or not. The
relationship may weather stormy waters, but love hangs on through the
storm. It is the hanging on — married or not — that illustrates what love
is. Person A says to Person B, "I'm here *with* you through it all."

Element 3: Rugged Commitment to Be "For"

Love in the Bible is also a rugged commitment to be *for* a person. To love
someone means you are their advocate, on their side. Kris's mother's name
was Betty and her father's name was Ron. Ron and Betty routinely drove a
hundred miles from Freeport to Libertyville to watch our son, Lukas, play
baseball. Lukas knew their love through their presence.

Betty had a way of saying things that drove home that she was Lukas's biggest fan and advocate. I remember one time after a long, hot-weather baseball game, marked by two things: we lost and Lukas had a good game at the plate. In our living room, cooling off, we talked about the game and the good moments and the bad moments, when Betty suddenly declared, "Lukas, I wish your coach could arrange it so you would be the only one who could bat." Of course that arrangement would be more golf than baseball, but it was one of those moments when our son internalized that his grandmother was his biggest advocate and fan. Luke had some bad days at the plate too, but the one thing he always knew was that his grandma had his back.

With that in mind, we need to remind ourselves of *Rule 2*: Christians define love by how God loves us. What we learn is that God's rugged commitment is to be with us and for us. God's for-ness is something that is expressed over and over in the Old Testament covenant formula, "I will be their God and they will be my people." We could translate this as "I've got your back" or "I'm on your side" or "I'm with you as the God who is for you." That covenant formula is found throughout Scripture, from the first books in the Bible to the last book, where in Revelation 21:7, God says, "I will be their God and they will be my children." God's love is a covenant of supporting strength; he is our proponent; he is our advocate. He's on our side.

It is hard to believe that two of the greatest writers of the twentieth century, at least for Christian readers, were close friends. Both were professors at Oxford who often met at a local pub or in a university room to chat about what they were thinking and writing. J. R. R. Tolkien struggled to get his ideas onto paper and then into print, and Lewis was a with-and-for kind of friend throughout the process.

Here are the words of Tolkien about Lewis: "Friendship with Lewis compensates for much, and besides giving constant pleasure and comfort has done me much good from the contact with a man at once honest, brave, intellectual — a scholar, a poet, and a philosopher — and a lover, at least after a long pilgrimage, of Our Lord." Tolkien spoke, too, of Lewis's support for his work, and this is how he described Lewis's for-ness: "Only from him did I ever get the idea that my 'stuff' could be more than a private hobby." When Lewis died — and after they had experienced some envy-shaped fracture in their relationship — Tolkien said this of losing his friends as he himself aged, "So far I have felt the normal feelings of a man of my age — like an old tree that is losing all its leaves one by one: [but the death of Lewis] feels like an axe-blow near the roots."[7]

Now I have to back up and back off from this positive and hopeful sketch of love, because sometimes a relationship collapses. Sometimes one person is abusive. When abuse happens, the commitment has to be changed, if not ended. For some there may still be hope of reconciliation; there may be hope for healing, but we need to emphasize that in this broken world the best of intentions may not always achieve the harmony needed for love to continue or to flourish. Not all relationships last, even among Christians and even when our Lord's grace is present.

Element 4: Rugged Commitment "Unto"

We learn love by watching God, who loves in a rugged covenant commitment to be with us, to be for us, and — here is the fourth element of love — *unto* his perfect design for us. If "with" is the principle of presence and "for" the principle of advocacy, unto-ness is the principle of direction.

God loves us, *and God's kind of love transforms us into loving and holy, God-glorifying and other-oriented people in God's kingdom.* God's with-ness transcends simple presence and advocacy; his with-ness and for-ness are a transforming power.

How does this happen? God's gracious presence transforms us because it is, to use the words of theologian Leslie Weatherhead, a "transforming friendship."[8] Our love of others does the same. When we love others, we indwell them and they indwell us, and personal presence makes space for others that influences us to become like them. Genuine friendships, which are two-way, are always transformative. One reason, then, we don't love those unlike us in the church is because we don't want their presence rubbing off on us, or because we can't control our influence on them.

All biblical love has direction *unto* the one to whom we surrender our love. If the other person is good, we have the potential to become good; if the other person is bad, we can become bad. Here's a light illustration: Kris is tidy, and by nature she likes to keep the kitchen counters clean and uncluttered. I love Kris, and she offers her love to me, and I echo back across the valleys of life my love for her. We indwell one another. Her presence transforms me unto her; it's that simple. When we got married, Kris didn't give me a list of expectations, nor did she ever tell me that "in this house we will keep our counters tidy." But her indwelling of me has made me — over time (hint, hint) — tidier in the kitchen. In my most recent trip through the kitchen, I noticed a few breadcrumbs on the counter. I don't eat toast for breakfast, but I grabbed the kitchen cloth and cleaned up the breadcrumbs. Our mutual indwelling of one another is transformative.

We can use various terms for the direction of God's transforming love: Christlikeness, holiness, *shalom*, love itself, and the kingdom. I will use these terms interchangeably, but perhaps the best shorthand is to say God's love is "unto" kingdom realities.

Now let's get theoretical for a moment as we address perhaps the most important thing I have to observe about love.

Order Matters

The order of these prepositions matters: first, *with*; second, *for*; and third, *unto*. Or, put another way, presence, advocacy, and then direction. What this means is that our presence communicates to the one we love our advocacy, and that combination of presence and advocacy empowers the one we love to internalize that we love them. Many parents want the direction (the "unto") for their daughter or son. Many friends, too, want the direction of Christlikeness in the person they love, but some are unwilling to be "with" often enough to communicate being "for" to that person or child.

An alarm: wanting direction *without* presence or advocacy is experienced by that other person (child or friend) as coercion. In other words, pastors behind pulpits and parents on the other side of the table and friends sometimes have not earned the connection required to be a person who can mentor a person "unto" kingdom realities. It is presence and advocacy that create the opportunities for genuine kingdom direction. God transforms us in grace by being present as the one who is for us, and that presence of his transforms us unto God's design of Christlikeness.

BACK TO THE CHURCH AND THE CHRISTIAN LIFE

God's love communicated to us in the Bible clearly reveals that love is a covenant, a commitment to be *with* someone, to be *for* someone, and to be *with* and *for* them *unto* the kingdom. To love another person means we are committed to them even when it is demanding and difficult, if not seemingly impossible. I hear friends clapping for anyone who says love is hard, and I see hundreds of parents nodding their heads in agreement and others shouting, *Amen!* I won't even begin with how hard it can be to love neighbors or opposing coaches on soccer teams or the weirdo in that small group.

Again, to love a person means we are committed to being *with* them, to our presence with them. To love a person also means they know that we are *for* them; they need to know our hand is on them and behind them. And to love a person means that together in our mutual indwelling we strive *unto* kingdom realities, or Christlikeness, or holiness, or love, or full maturity in Christ.

These divine codes for love drove the apostle Paul to a new kind of people of God, the church, and we have compared the church to the salad in a bowl. Just a short time spent in the salad bowl reveals that God's kind of love is not bliss. It's far harder than bliss, in fact. It's relatively easy to love people just like us (though even that can be challenging), and it's hard to love people unlike us or who don't even like us. But the gospel calls us to love everyone in the fellowship. Truth be told, sometimes we can be put off or surprised by what we find.

MY FRIEND DAN

I was surprised when I met Dan Kimball.[9] He was totally retro, with a pompadour haircut like that of Little Richard, Elvis, Johnny Cash, Jerry Lee Lewis, and The Ramones. If you don't know their haircuts, Google them or Google "pompadour." When we first met, Dan was wearing a black leather jacket, another light jacket under that, a vintage 50s shirt, a white crew neck T-shirt, cuffed blue jeans, and Doc Marten shoes. I was a college teacher at the time and like to think that nothing surprises me when it comes to dress, so I just thought, "Cool, that's unique." And, if I were a little more forthcoming, I'd also add, "That pompadour's a bit odd." What I also observed, however, was that under his 50s hair and clothes was a humble, charismatic servant of God whom I have grown to love and admire.

Dan is a rockabilly fan and played in a rockabilly band in London, where he gave his heart and mind and life to Jesus Christ. After returning to northern California, he almost cried out of joy when his church asked him to participate in the youth ministry, especially since he had grown up totally outside the church culture. Dan had had only an atypical experience of deep Christian fellowship with some elderly saints in London, and he was grateful others were affirming his yearning to serve the Lord, so he said yes.

Then one of the pastors called Dan into his office, affirmed him in a way that communicated, *I'm with and for you, but let's get the unto taken care of,* saying, "First, you really need to get a haircut." His pastor gave Dan a twenty-dollar bill and said the haircut was on him. Then he pointed to Dan's shoes (the yellow threads on his shoes were too flamboyant) and recommended Dan dress like a pastor who knew how to get along in churchland.

So Dan tried. He got some gray khaki double-pleated puffy pants and a crew shirt — and quickly realized he was being pushed against his sensibilities and beyond the Bible. So he pulled his '66 Mustang (he's the real deal) into the Goodwill store and slapped all those clothes on the counter and went back to being Dan Kimball in that same dress, pompadour and all, and the good hand of God's transforming grace has been upon Dan Kimball.

Not only that, but the experience of having been judged on the basis of what he wore and how he combed his hair has formed Dan into a leader who both senses judgmentalism and who strives to create loving acceptance of those who are different.

THE FELLOWSHIP OF DIFFERENTS

The church God wants is one brimming with difference, and that will mean the Christian life is all about loving whoever happens to be with you in this fellowship of differents. As sure as you are sitting there, someone's going to sidle up next to you in your fellowship — and it might be someone dressed rather odd. So the million-dollar question for you and me and how we do church is this:

How diverse is your love?

or

**How ready are you to love the differents
in your fellowship?**

Now that we know what love means, the words *diverse* and *differents* become clearer. But to love everyone in our fellowship is a work of God's grace, the kind of grace that transforms us into a fellowship that welcomes and loves all.

6

Love Works

On paper, the church works. On paper, the church is perfect. (Who'd not want to be involved?) On paper, it is a loving fellowship for everything that knocks out sinful lives and creates holy ones, as each person grows into Christlikeness.

It all seems so good, until you arrive on Sunday morning or at Bible study on Thursday evening, or your dad gets out of hand or your sister becomes bossypants, or someone gets mouthy about what everyone ought to believe. No wonder Paul believed in transforming grace; he knew that love was needed for the church as God designed it.

Love works, but you have to work at it. To love the folks in your church is taxing and trying and testing. Loving others creates all sorts of tension, which is why we need to work at love.

PAUL, AN EXAMPLE OF LOVE

To observe how to love others in the church, one exasperating person after another, the apostle *Paul can be our example*. Why choose Paul? A friend of mine once asked me what was the *one thing* Paul taught in all his churches. I thought the answer was, of course, the gospel. He said, "No. Check out 1 Corinthians 4:16 – 17." So I did. Here's 1 Corinthians 4:16:

Therefore I urge you to imitate me....

That takes some *chutzpah*! But it takes more to say what follows in verse 17:

Timothy [Paul's best friend] ... will remind you of my way of life in Christ Jesus, which agrees *with what I teach everywhere in every church.*

Paul's words are packaged tightly enough that we need to unpack them a bit. Here's what he is saying, and I have arranged it so you can see how repetitive it is:

A   What I teach in every church is

  B   my way of life.

  B'   Because my way of life agrees with

A'   What I teach everywhere in every church.

Paul's claim is that *his life embodies the gospel so clearly one can learn the gospel by observing him* — and he claims he teaches this everywhere. If we believe him, his life provides a template of how love works, and I see three ways Paul worked at love:

+ Paul mothered and fathered others
+ Paul ached for others
+ Paul formed friendships with others

LOVE WORKS LIKE A PARENT'S LOVE

No image is more tender about how Paul worked lovingly for the formation of others than when he describes himself as a mother or as a father. Perhaps he had learned "teaching as mothering" in Jerusalem when he was studying under Gamaliel, the famous rabbi. A later rabbi pointed out that "Resh Lakish [a rabbi] said: He who teaches Torah to his neighbor's son is regarded by Scripture as though he had fashioned him [as a mother]."[1] Wherever he learned to see pastoral ministry as mothering, Paul's love was like a mother giving birth or a mother nursing children at the breast.

Each of these expressions emotes the love of Paul for his church families, and everyone knows that giving birth is, well, "labor":

> My dear children, for whom *I am again in the pains of childbirth until Christ is formed in you.* (Galatians 4:19)

Once I was preparing to teach about how longing for spiritual maturity in others was like giving birth, so I explained my ideas to Kris, who promptly said to me, "Scot, you have no idea what giving birth is like. Your only time in the delivery room you passed out."

Teaching new Christians, Paul observed, was also like nursing infants:

> *Just as a nursing mother cares for her children, so we cared for you.* Because we loved you so much, we were delighted to share with you not only the gospel of God but our lives as well. (1 Thessalonians 2:7 – 8)

I have no experience on this one either, so I will move on to an analogy I can relate to, his fatherly love for his churches:

> For you know that we dealt with each of you as a father deals with his own children, *encouraging, comforting and urging you* to live lives worthy of God. (1 Thessalonians 2:11 – 12)

The good parent works at mothering or fathering a child into mature adulthood, and Christian parents work in their love toward Christlikeness. Paul spiritually parented Christians in the church, one Roman after a Jew, one woman after a man, one freed Roman after an enslaved Roman.

Parenting, of course, can be suffocating, so notice Paul's aims. He labors in his love "until Christ is formed in you" so that those he's writing to will "live lives worthy of God." Our dictionary definition of love has, to use theological words, no eschatology. That is, it has no final goal other than perhaps the personal happiness of the one loved or the one who loves — as long as that lasts. But Christian love has direction. It aims at one person helping another to become Christlike. One of our grace assignments in the church is to be mothers and fathers of others in the faith. How are we to accomplish this? The single, most powerful influence of parents on children is *the dynamic of presence*. Likewise, we work at love for others in a parental way through the dynamic of our presence.

The church has always affirmed its responsibility to mother and father others along in their faith. Listen to these historic words of the church from *The Book of Common Prayer*, asked of those who are present when someone is baptized: "Will you who witness these vows [of commitment] do all in your power to support these persons in their life in Christ?" Some may find the words too formal, but hesitations about formalities aside, part of loving others in God's grand social experiment in the church is working at the kind of love that guides others up and into our faith.

In thirty years of teaching, my favorite class of all time was a college course on Women and the Bible, with about a third of the course devoted to a theology of relationships. This particular class always came prepared to talk not only about the reading, but also about their own relationships. The unofficial leader in the class was Kellie Carstensen, and when the course finished, she suggested we hold a twice-monthly event in my office at 8:30 a.m. on sexual purity and relationships. And for the next school year, "The Group" (as I called them) traipsed into my office and collapsed in various states of stupor into my chairs and a couch. (You've got to admit a voluntary gathering of college students at 8:30 a.m. is special.)

Kellie and I communicated recently about The Group, and she said, "This to me is the true picture of discipleship, which Paul himself advocated: as adolescents we got to receive advice from elders, then we were able to take that knowledge to our peers in discussion, wrestle with it together, and finally claim it as our own belief." Some parents and leaders complain about young adults when it comes to relationships, but if they take the time to listen to them, they might just hear them saying what Kellie wrote to me: "We want your wisdom, and we'll listen, but let us work this stuff out for ourselves."

Read again those passages about Paul as a parent, and you will see the same dynamic acted out: wisdom given, freedom given, response required — all in the work of love as we all strive to become more Christlike.

LOVE WORKS IN ACHING FOR OTHERS

Mothering and fathering others sometimes generates pain and aching for love to accomplish its kingdom designs. C. S. Lewis wrote these words in his famous book *The Four Loves*:

> There is no safe investment. To love at all is to be vulnerable. Love anything, and your heart will certainly be wrung and possibly be broken. If you want to make sure of keeping it intact, you must give your heart to no one, not even to an animal. Wrap it carefully round with hobbies and little luxuries; avoid all entanglements; lock it up safe in the casket or coffin of your selfishness. But in that casket — safe, dark, motionless, airless — it will change. It will not be broken; it will become unbreakable, impenetrable, irredeemable. The alternative to tragedy, or at least to the risk of tragedy, is damnation. The only place outside of Heaven where you can be perfectly safe from all the dangers of perturbations of love is Hell.[2]

Because Paul worked at love, he also emoted the pain (and joy) of love. I came of age as a professor and theologian when pastors were not to show their affections or give off the scent that they were, after all, human — which was also a way of giving off the scent that they didn't read the Bible about love.

Love works only if we work at love, and part of that work is aching emotionally. Nonemotive "love" flies in the face of the apostle Paul, who opens his heart so wide so often we wonder at times whether he was insecure or too vulnerable — or that we've got the wrong idea about love.

There are two episodes in Paul's letters — one in 1 Thessalonians 2:17 – 3:3, the other in 2 Corinthians 2:1 – 4; 6:11 – 13; 7:2 – 16 — where Paul's love aches so much for others that we can just picture him wringing his hands, tears flowing. I will do my best to reproduce the story of 2 Corinthians, because it perfectly describes what it means to work at love.

Paul experienced tough times with his "children" at Corinth, including dealing with one man who was shacking up with his father's wife (not his own mother). This was Corinth, after all. Paul rebuked him and the church — wanting them to repent because he ached for kingdom realities. He begins by revealing that his heartbroken love shapes his strong language:

> For I wrote you out of great *distress* and *anguish* of heart and with many tears, not to grieve you *but to let you know the depth of my love for you.* (2 Corinthians 2:4)

A few chapters later he expresses his vulnerability to their response, all but ripping open his chest to show them his motherly-fatherly heart, a heart that aches for love in return:

> We have spoken freely to you, Corinthians, and *opened wide our hearts to you. We are not withholding our affection from you,* but you are withholding yours from us. As a fair exchange — I speak as to my children — *open wide your hearts also.* (6:11 – 13)

So achingly hard does he work in his love for their spiritual formation that he lives and dies with their response!

> Make room for us in your hearts. We have wronged no one, we have corrupted no one, we have exploited no one. I do not say this to condemn you; I have said before that you have such a place in our hearts *that we would live or die with you.* (7:2 – 3)

As he waits for their embrace, he is incapable of sleep and comfort. The only thing that will relieve his anxiety is good news from Titus, who is paying a visit to Corinth, and here is Paul's description of that news:

> For when we came into Macedonia, *we had no rest, but we were harassed at every turn — conflicts on the outside, fears within.* But God, who comforts the downcast, *comforted us* by the coming of Titus, and not only by his coming but also by the comfort you had given him. He told us about your longing for *me,* your deep sorrow, your ardent concern for *me, so that my joy was greater than ever* (7:5 – 7).

Friends, your ache for the conversion or maturation of a friend is just like Paul's. Parents, your ache for your discontented and indecisive teen is a godly imitation of Paul. Pastor, your yearnings for formation among those in your church reveals your love for them. As Paul does, work at love.

LOVE WORKS AT FORMING FRIENDSHIPS

Another dimension of Paul's working at love is this: to love others is to form committed friendships. Kris and I became friends as children, but our friendship turned into dating when we were fifteen-year-old sophomores. We had the all-too-dreamy, but nonetheless true belief that we would get married someday and live happily ever after, singing Beatles and Beach Boys songs and wearing love beads and bell bottoms.

In 1973, some five years later, we got married, so if you are the calculating sort, I was twenty and Kris nineteen. Ours is a marriage of friendship, and by that I mean that we are committed to being "with" one another. I hear or see something interesting, I text Kris, and she (more often) does the same to me. When I have lunch at a new place, I want to take her there when we get a chance. Some elements of our covenant love commitment of presence include spending our evenings together as much as possible.

We have always spent our weekends together, and when I am asked to speak away from home, I ask if Kris can come. Often, if they say no, I say no right back. This not a law in our house, but rather a guiding light we walk by. Sometimes I do travel without Kris, and we then fly out to that location later together, so that I can show her where I was. We walk together every day, chatting and discussing issues that concern us. Sometimes we turn to books like this one, and other times we chat about our children or our parents, who have more issues as they age. Another way of putting this is that we don't have separate rooms in the house to which each of us retires. We are with one another because we believe love is about presence, and we work at this kind of love.

In spite of what churches sometimes communicate, one doesn't have to be married to experience love. From Jesus to Paul, one of the dominating themes was turning invisible people into neighbors, something done by all kinds of Christians, married or not. Jay Pathak and Dave Runyon, two Christian leaders devoted to neighborhood and church renewal in Colorado, decided that the biblical scribe's famous question — "Who is my neighbor?" — would become the question propelling their ministry. Jesus' parable in response to his question, the Good Samaritan, is even more famous, in which the Samaritan showed love for the beaten man left for dead.

Answering that question, in fact, created a neighboring movement in Jay's and Dave's community. They tell their story in *The Art of Neighboring*,[3] but they press Jesus' question into the most important form I know. How so? By expanding the question to include more than the beaten-down-and-outers of this world. As they put it, "Today as we read the parable, we go straight for loving the neighbor on the side of the road. Thus we make a metaphor of the neighbors — a metaphor that doesn't include the person who lives next door to us" (who is a literal neighbor). So they urge us all to get real, grab a piece of paper, make nine boxes on the piece of paper, put your home in the middle, and then write out the names of the people in each of the eight homes closest you. Easy enough? (Nope, we didn't know all of them by name.) Then write out identifying information about each person, and then — if you know it — deeper information about what's going on in each person's life. If you don't know their names, ask them. If you don't know anything about them, get to know them. Over time you can fill out all three levels for your neighbors.

That's what it means to love someone — to make them a neighbor.

PAUL'S BEST FRIEND

Recently I read the entire book of Acts and all the letters of Paul in just two sittings to get the big picture. You know how sometimes watching an old favorite movie evokes a forgotten theme? In the same way, when I finished reading, I was struck by the number of friends Paul had. Paul worked hard in his mission to reach Gentiles with the gospel, but notice how often he expressed a desire to be with his coworkers. One of them was Timothy, and Paul's special relationship with him surfaces in one particular verse in 1 Corinthians 4:17:

> For this reason I have sent to you Timothy, *my son whom I love*, who is faithful in the Lord. He will remind you of my way of life in Christ Jesus, which agrees with what I teach everywhere in every church.

Before I list the facts of their "with" relationship, notice that Paul calls him "son," reflecting Paul's motherlike birthing and fatherlike mentoring. Paul expresses his love for Timothy, he affirms him, he knows Timothy can accurately tell about Paul's life, and he trusts him. Paul had spent gobs of time *with* his friend Timothy as an expression of their love for one another.

Timothy is one of those people in the New Testament who is always in the background. Fortunately, he lurks in the shadows so often that his story can be told (but rarely is). So I want to bombard you with the facts of his life, and you can go to the endnote to find the Bible references:[4]

+ Timothy's father was a Gentile, but his mother a Jew.
+ He was probably converted to following Christ during Paul's first missionary journey to Lystra, where Timothy surely saw Paul being stoned.
+ Timothy's mother was a believer.
+ Paul chose Timothy to be "with" him on his second missionary journey, and Timothy received a special endowment of the Spirit through the laying on of hands.
+ To regulate his "status," Paul had Timothy circumcised (delicate, delicate).
+ When Paul traveled to Athens, Timothy stayed with Silas in Berea and then joined Paul in Athens.
+ Timothy encouraged the Christians in Thessalonica and reported good news about the Thessalonians to Paul later, part of that good news being expressed by a gift of money for the poor saints in Jerusalem.

+ Something often ignored: Timothy helped Paul write both 1 and 2 Thessalonians, helped evangelize Corinth, and helped write 2 Corinthians and probably also Romans.

+ He traveled with Paul to Jerusalem as Lystra's delegate to the Jerusalem church.

+ He helped Paul in writing Colossians, Philemon, and Philippians.

+ Timothy was imprisoned for the gospel and eventually released.

Were the two inseparable or what? Paul gets all the credit, Timothy lurks in the background, and no one yet has argued that we should start calling Timothy the author of Philippians. But here's what the opening lines say: "Paul and Timothy, servants of Christ Jesus, To all God's holy people in Christ Jesus at Philippi" (Philippians 1:1).

Paul is an example of love, but what perhaps surprises us the most about Paul's love is how hard he worked at it. His aim was to form relationships with one person after another, and to love them unto Christlikeness. Some days went well; some days were a disaster — but Paul worked hard regardless of circumstances.

For us to get along in the salad bowl of God's grand fellowship of different sorts of people, we need his grace to create in us the kind of love Paul had for others. The only way we can become the church of God's design is for us to imitate Paul in love.

And as we do, there's yet one more element of love to see in church life.

7

Love Shares

Have you ever wondered what the apostle Paul did all day long? When Christians in the churches of Asia Minor, Greece, and Italy went to work, what did Paul do? It is too easy to assume Paul was like a modern pastor, which means — proceed to stereotype — he got up, said his prayers and read his Bible, had his cup of coffee, ate some grainy toast and cleaned up the crumbs, did his morning exercises, made another cup of coffee, checked his emails, then went off to the office to study and prepare sermons and drink more coffee and do a funeral or a wedding, and then get ready for meetings and take a call from someone who didn't like the choice of music in the last worship service, and then prepare for some more meetings and then actually meet people, and then have meetings about how to get better at meetings.

Is that what Paul did? No. And neither do most pastors.

During the day Paul made tents, which is how he is described in Acts 18:3 ("because he was a tentmaker"). The most influential post-Jesus Christian in history labored daily making tents in some sweaty, hot, dusty location with his fingers worked raw from bone-needles, knives, and awls.[1] Truth be told, Paul seemed fond of reminding others how hard he worked. Hear him out, and I italicize for emphasis:

> Surely you remember, brothers and sisters, our toil and hardship; *we worked night and day* in order not to be a burden to anyone while we preached the gospel of God to you. (1 Thessalonians 2:9)

His next letter to them says much the same:

> For you yourselves know how you ought to follow our example. *We were not idle* when we were with you, *nor did we eat anyone's food without paying for it.* On the contrary, *we worked night and day, laboring and toiling* so that we would not be a burden to any of you. We did this, not because we do not have the right to such help, but in order to offer ourselves as a model for you to imitate. For even when we were with you, we gave you this rule: "The one who is unwilling to work shall not eat." (2 Thessalonians 3:7 – 10)

More than a half-decade later, he seems to be cranking out the same Country and Western complaint:

> Are they servants of Christ? (I am out of my mind to talk like this.) I am more. *I have worked much harder.... I have labored and toiled and have often gone without sleep*; I have known hunger and thirst and have often gone without food; I have been cold and naked. (2 Corinthians 11:23, 27)

We can just about hear Paul yelling out, "I did this all for you, dagnabbit!" — with a little "Give me some love!" as the chaser. But I suspect we are missing the whole context if we think Paul is complaining. *It cost Paul immensely because he loved his churches so immensely.* He had covenanted to be with them and for them and wouldn't allow them to carry any of his financial burdens from being with them.

He labored for his churches, and his love cost him physically, emotionally, psychologically, and financially. "Besides everything else, I face daily the pressure of my concern for all the churches. Who is weak, and I do not feel weak? Who is led into sin, and I do not inwardly burn?" (2 Corinthians 11:28 – 29). Why? Think about it: Paul was founding house churches across the Roman Empire, and some of those in the churches — probably most — were poor and often on the edge of ruin. These new churches were known for generosity, but Paul had a trade that could keep him afloat, so he chose to work so as not to burden his churches. Love — and this is one of the most notable features of Paul's entire life — shares with others as generously as possible. If the church is what it is supposed to be, it will have needy people, and for the church to be what God designed it to be means learning to share with others.

LOVE BENEFITS OTHERS

I said above that Paul didn't ask for money, but that's not entirely accurate. He didn't ask for his churches to provide room and board, but he did ask them to support others. Let's remind ourselves again of the heart of Paul's mission. He ached for unity *and* diversity in a fellowship of differents. To express the unity of his Gentile churches with the Jewish believers in Jerusalem, Paul spent bundles of energy raising funds for the poor saints in Jerusalem. Many readers of the New Testament fail to see how often Paul's collection for Jerusalem appears.

In Paul's earliest letter he refers to an event where he was asked to report to the Jerusalem pillars (led by James, brother of Jesus, which gave him an advantage) about his preaching. Paul explained his gospel to them, and they affirmed him and all shook hands. But they did so with one important proviso: Paul was asked to remember the poor saints in Jerusalem (Galatians 2:10), and remembering the saints in Jerusalem became Paul's mission within his mission. Now grab your Bible and read the following verses: 1 Corinthians 16:1 – 4, then skip around in 2 Corinthians 8 – 9 (these two chapters are concerned with the collection for the poor), and then read Romans 15:25 – 32, where Paul says that spiritual benefits among the Gentiles indebt them to provide material gifts to the poor in Jerusalem. Notice in Romans 15:31 that Paul worried "that the contribution I take to Jerusalem may be favorably received by the Lord's people there." Raising funds for the poor in Jerusalem so dominated Paul's life that he brought up the collection during his trial (Acts 24:17).

Alongside Paul's tentmaking day job and his gospeling and teaching ministries — two full-time jobs — Paul had another. His second and third missionary journeys, roughly from AD 49 to 57, involved constant collections and the gathering of representatives from each of his churches to accompany him to Jerusalem with the financial gifts from Gentile Christians. That's a ten-year fund-raiser — yikes!

For Paul, this collection symbolized unity. The funds for the poor saints both made the Gentiles visible to the Jewish believers in Jerusalem, and it made the Jewish believers visible to the Gentile churches. This third full-time job as a fund-raiser led to a myriad of lessons about supporting one another (financially) in the Christian community, all based on one wonderful principle.

EACH ACCORDING TO MEANS

Believers in Paul's churches soon learned the principle of giving *according to means*. You can't give if you don't have, and there were plenty in Paul's churches who did not have. We too easily associate generosity with the millionaire's extravagant gifts, but whether we look to Jesus, who pointed out the "widow's mite" as a genuine expression of giving, or to Paul's teachings in 2 Corinthians 8 – 9, the limit of our costly love is our means. Give generously of what you have, and if you don't have much, give little generously.

No better example of this care and provision — whatever your situation in life — came home to me in the splendid example of Mary-Ann Kirkby in the memoir of her life as a Hutterite girl in Manitoba, Canada.[2] Hutterites, who descend from the radical side (the Anabaptists) of the Protestant Reformation in Europe, to this day settle into mutually-providing communities of about one hundred, where the focus seems to be the kitchen, from which springs delightful community meals. Hutterites live a simple lifestyle, but they have enough. They have family and security, and they take care of one another *according to their means*. Mary-Ann's large family, the Ronald Dornn family, was originally part of the New Rosedale and Fairholme Colonies, but their family broke away to create a new and separate life. Their story in the community and after they left illustrates generosity according to means.

Most in the Fairholme Colony refused to help the Dornn family when they chose to leave the community, but that did not stop Sana, one of the members of that community: "I'm going to da kitchen," she said, because it's "not right dat you're leaving empty-handed."

Another time, Mary-Ann's younger sister, Rosie, got seriously ill and ended up in a hospital. During her week-long stay, she turned nine — but because she was a Hutterite, Rosie had never had a birthday party. So the hospital celebrated with a birthday cake. Rosie, true to her Hutterite life of providing for others, went from room to room with pieces of cake speaking broken English, "Want some, take some."

Mary-Ann, too, was generous. During her time at the Fairholme Colony, she earned nine dollars by giving tours of the colony, only to surprise the visitors with a little plea for them to donate some quarters, with which she planned to buy a pair of skates. But realizing her family was poor, she approached her father.

"Dad," she said, "I think I have more money than you do. You are working so hard, and I feel you should have this money so we don't go broke."

"I think you do have more money than I do," he said, and accepted her gift with gratitude, continuing the cycle of generosity according to means among the Dornns.

Mary-Ann later reflected on her mother's custom of prayer, evangelism, and hospitality: "Our home was continually crowded with people who needed a place to stay, a hot meal, or a word of encouragement. We never locked our doors.... No one was ever turned away. 'There's always room for one more,' was Mother's motto."

Each family member was generous in his or her own way — and according to his or her own means. "Generosity according to means" is both the limit and the challenge to the cost of love.

FUNDS FOR THE FELLOWSHIP

The Dornn family's approach to generosity springs from what the Bible, especially the apostle Paul, says about loving others with generosity. Right here we encounter something we (Americans) must face — we are not generous.

In *Passing the Plate*, a book on this topic, authors Christian Smith, Michael Emerson, and Patricia Snell examine "how and why it is that the wealthiest national body of Christian believers at any time in all of church history end up spending most of their money on themselves rather than generously sharing it with other people and for other needs, or what they consider good causes, including the strengthening of the ministries of their own churches."[3]

The point is clear: the Bible teaches generosity, and we are not generous. Paul was, however, and he urged his churches to be generous too. The church will only be what God designed it to be — a genuine fellowship of all sorts — when it also becomes generous according to its means.

One could write chapters about this topic, but I will reduce it to eight principles of Christian charity that surface in Paul's reflections, found in 2 Corinthians 8 – 9. At the very heart of these teachings of Paul regarding believers taking up a collection is a simple idea: love shares.

Christian love involves sharing our resources with needy Christians. Such sharing symbolizes our unity in Christ, loving fellowship in Christ, and special love for the needy. One of Paul's great statements comes at the end of the first letter he wrote: "Therefore, as we have opportunity, let us do good to all people, *especially* to those who belong to the family of believers" (Galatians 6:10). Christians are to share funds with all, especially with those in need in their local church.

Sharing resources is shaped by generosity. One of the more striking features of the New Testament is the absence of tithing. Why? Kingdom realities created new possibilities for the community of faith, and the operative word for those first Christians was *generosity*. Paul describes how God's work in Macedonia led to "rich generosity" (2 Corinthians 8:2; 9:5). He even says that "they gave as much as they were able, and even beyond their ability" (8:3).

Sharing resources is an act of love. Paul walks a tightrope when he raises funds for the poor, doing everything he can to make sure it is not a new law or simply a dutiful obligation. For him, sharing is about love: "I want to test the sincerity of your love," he says in 8:8. This is not guilt, but rather a realistic expectation of what love looks like — it shares.

Sharing resources is modeled on the life of our Lord King, Jesus. Paul makes this abundantly clear: "For you know the grace [gift, sharing of resources] of our Lord Jesus Christ, that though he was rich, yet for your sake he became poor, so that you through his poverty might become rich" (8:9). Jesus was rich and became poor for others so that they might in turn become rich. Paul followed that template for his own life, giving sacrificially to invest in others for their good.

Sharing resources is about the intentional act, not the amount. The apostle Paul lived in a world every bit as unequal as ours, so he wisely instructed Christians to give "according to your means" (8:11; see 9:7). But "intent" is not enough, he said. Determine how much you can give, and then give that — or, as Paul puts it, "so that your eager willingness to do it may be matched by your completion of it" (8:11).

Sharing resources aims at equality. Surely one of the more radical statements made by Paul was that the generosity of one person would balance the lack in others "that there might be equality" (8:13). He is not thinking of a national or global economic system here, but rather of timely generosity — when you have abundance, you give to those suffering, so that when they have plenty, they can benefit others in poverty — perhaps even you. This sense of timely balance shapes Paul's rule that those who give sparingly will benefit sparingly, while those who give generously will experience generosity (9:6). Yet we are not off the hook, for Christians living in abundance when others are living in poverty contradicts the very heart of the gospel.

Sharing resources is for any in need. In the churches of Paul, and we hope in ours, there were all sorts of people: craftworkers, homeless, slaves, ex-prostitutes, an occasional elite, some educated, but most uneducated. The resources of the Christians were available to one and all: Jews and Gentiles, slaves and free, males and females. Generosity does not restrict itself to identity politics, but expands itself to those in need. Ask yourself this simple question: Are you willing for your resources to be distributed to those in need, or do you want them to go to the needy most like you?

Sharing resources results in God's glory. As Paul begins to close the shutters on his instructions about sharing, he realizes all of this results in people thanking God and praising God as they all experience the Lord's blessings. He writes that "your generosity will result in thanksgiving to God" (9:11) and "others will praise God" (9:13).

The good hand of God's generous grace — the preeminent word for giving in the New Testament — gives us hands of reciprocal generosity. When the Dornn family was reduced to an insecure future because the farm they were renting was sold, Mary-Ann said these words about her father's hands:

> That night we all knelt in a circle in the living room to pray. I caught sight of Father's folded hands. I remembered those hands on the steering wheel of the truck as he and I drove to Deerboine Colony to collect Mother and Rennie [who tragically died before they returned]. They were the hands once fine enough to do delicate calligraphy, the hands that rested on Mother's shoulder in a moment of tenderness, the hands that shook in anger over Jake Vetter's unreasonableness [to whom he offered his hand of forgiveness]. I saw not just my father, but a man of conviction and principle, willing to do whatever it took to support a family.[4]

Those hands were like the hands of the tentmaking apostle, hands of generosity shaped by God's generous and gracious hand of love.

Working and giving love, empowered by God's Yes of love and grace for us, takes shape in God's way in this world — the church. For the church is designed by God to be the space in this world where we find love and grace. But while these are great ideas, the problem is that the church too often is simply not the real thing.

PART 3

TABLE

8

Tomatoes versus Maters

The only way I can believe store-bought tomatoes are tomatoes is to pretend. Store-bought tomatoes are a tasteless invention I call "maters," and maters can be used to add some color (almost red) to an otherwise colorless dish. Maters are nothing more than (almost) red pulp that evokes the hope of tasting the real thing, but never delivers. Those who manufacture store-bought maters pick them when they are green, knowing they will "mature" a bit so that in the store it will look plump red and potentially juicy. But we now know it's an act of trickery. A "mater" is not a tomato. Can I get an Amen?

During August and September — and sometimes in July — our garden produces the real thing: juicy, tasty, and fully red. Garden tomatoes are so good I'm tempted to put them on my morning steel-cut oats. The worst part is that we've got maters from early fall through early summer, and that makes for a long winter longing for real tomatoes.

ONE CHURCH?

Most Sundays, when leaving a worship service to come home, we pass other churches, such as Lutheran, Presbyterian, Roman Catholic, Eastern Orthodox, Baptist, Evangelical Free, and Evangelical Covenant. Then there are the nondenominational churches with cool names like The

Branch or Jacob's Well. Truth be told, many of these denominations have locked horns in the past. The reality of church divisions, differences, and disputes is the "mater" of individualism and separate-but-equal Christianity. We choose maters instead of the tomato — genuine unity.

Jesus prayed that we would be one. He actually prayed for more than that because he asked that we "be brought to *complete* unity." Then he ramped up the request a bit more, stating that the credibility of his followers' witness would be rooted in their unity. Then he anchored unity even deeper — in the unity of the Son and the Father (John 17:21 – 23).

We must stop right here to ask ourselves two questions: Is the lack of power in our witness because the church is so divisive, so un-unified, so out-of-step with Jesus' prayer? Is it because we've spread out the items in the salad onto the plate in separate piles instead of living together as a mixed salad in God's salad bowl of unity?

This theme of unity is so important to Paul that he brings it up early and then again late in his mission. There is one Spirit and one Lord and one Father, he points out (1 Corinthians 8:4 – 6), and *therefore* there is "one body … just as you were called to one hope when you were called" (Ephesians 4:4 – 6). Paul uses "one" seven times in those three verses in Ephesians, and a Three-in-One God — a God whose difference is brought into glorious unity — means a many-but-one body.

But the church today is more like a mater than a tomato, more like a tasteless experience of the real thing Jesus prayed for, Paul taught, and God *is*! When we worship apart on Sundays, when we fellowship apart during the week, and when we follow Jesus apart from one another, we mock the unity of God! If God can keep it together in the Trinity, then we who are filled with the Spirit ought to keep it together too.

A PROBLEM TO CONSIDER

We tend to think of the Christian life with personal questions:

How am I doing with God?

How is my walk with Christ?

Am I growing?

We tend not to ask these questions of the Christian life:

How is my church doing with God?

How is my church walking with Christ?

Is my church growing?

Our "personal relationship with God," as we often put it, is good, and the church without personal faith is a rotten mater. But thinkers across the spectrum today, from those who study the Bible to those who study culture, all agree that too many of our personal questions arise from our Western culture and not enough from the Bible itself. In fact, selfishness is so natural to us that many Christians don't even care about the unity Jesus prayed for and Paul taught. But it's bigger than that, for the unity Jesus prayed for and Paul taught is the unity that God is! Choosing life as a mater instead of a tomato means turning from God's own unity. Mater Christianity elevates individualism while tomato Christianity enters into the challenge of fellowship with all the saints.

The story of the Bible is not simply about the salvation of individuals. The story of the Bible is about the creation of *one* faithful, saved people of God, Israel. That story for Christians means the *expansion* of that one people of God to include Gentiles, for what God is doing in this world is *creating one universal people*. Paul's entire mission is about expanding God's people by including Gentiles into the one people of God, the church.

Think of it this way: if Genesis 11 scattered the people at Babel by creating languages, the miracle of Pentecost overcomes our many different languages with *one* language to form a new unity among people. Amazing, isn't it, that the first thing that happens at the birth of the church is *many diverse peoples become unified and one through the Spirit*! One Spirit, one Lord, and one Father of us all. It is no wonder that Jesus prayed for unity. Sadly, we're still eating the maters of disunity in Christ instead of the tomato of genuine unity in Christ.

What can we do? Paul gives us two potent strategies for church unity, if we will be open to the grace of God's transforming Spirit. But first we need to learn to dance.

LEARN TO DANCE

My niece Kari married Jonathan Williams. Both were athletes at the University of New Hampshire — Kari in track and field, and Jonathan in football. They got married at a wonderful location on one of the Finger Lakes in New York, and then, after the ceremonies, we all went to the reception room to dance.

Now I know John Travolta put on a bit of a show in the movie *Saturday Night Fever*, but that was nothing compared to what I saw on the dance floor at Kari's wedding. Jonathan is African American, and now a stereotype — black people can dance. The music transcended differences — Jonathan and his football friend and seminary student at Regent University, John McCoy, and his wife, Jesse, and Ray, whom I call Mr. Smooth, and some white people mixing it up with black people, and some young and some old and some ladies and gentlemen. But when they turned on the music that led to a dance called Electric Slide, I sat down to watch the whole dance floor turn into unity in dance I have never seen before.

You can settle for maters or you can have the tomato, but if you want the real tomato of unity, you have to get onto the dance floor, turn on the music of God's Yes for all, and learn to dance together.

STRATEGY #1: GET A NEW MIND

Every day Paul stared at the colossal problem of getting Jews and Gentiles, from across the whole spectrum of Roman society, to dance together in the church. How did he think unity could be achieved? Listen to these mind-boggling statements of Paul's, this first one from his earliest letter:

> There is neither Jew nor Gentile, neither slave nor free, nor is there male and female, for you are all one in Christ Jesus. (Galatians 3:28)

Nearer to the end of his ministry, he has slightly expanded this:

> Here there is no Gentile or Jew, circumcised or uncircumcised, barbarian, Scythian, slave or free, but Christ is all, and is in all. (Colossians 3:11)

What Paul is teaching is not that Jews have been removed from the family, but that *everyone now has the chance to be promoted into the family of God alongside faithful Israelites*. This message challenged the Jews' pride of their heritage as much as it challenged Gentiles to cross the line into a new kind of family.

Paul wants us to think differently, to know, believe, and embrace that "in Christ" there is neither "slave nor free." In the workshops, in the Roman agora, in the belly of ships, and in the villas of the citizens there were clear societal distinctions. Romans were obsessed with status, and their clothing reflected their status — marked for some with thin or thick purple stripes. Citizens were not slaves, and slaves were not citizens (whose rights were protected). Martin Goodman, one of the leading scholars on the Roman world today, puts it this way:

> On the public level, Roman society was highly stratified on the basis of birth and wealth. The social and political status of each adult male citizen was fixed at irregular censuses.... On the domestic scale ... the only fully legally recognized persons ... in each family unit was its male head, the *paterfamilias*.[1]

Hierarchy, status, reputation, and connections were the empire. The church, though, was not the empire! So when the Christians gathered to worship, to fellowship, and to meet and eat, the ruthless, divisive, and status-shaped backbone of the empire snapped. There would be no slave and no free in the church. There would be no Roman, no Greek, no Egyptian, and no barbarian. This was God's grand social experiment, and the Romans — from elites to the slaves — experienced the church as nothing short of a wild revolution of equality.[2] This idea, that Paul's mission was a mixed assembly of differents, lies at the core of my own beliefs about how the whole Bible works, and I am committed to believing this until the day comes when they take away my mustard-slathered hotdog.

There's even more to what Paul is saying, for when Paul speaks about males and females, he is quoting Genesis 1:27. In creation, God "gendered" us into a male and female, but in the new creation, God makes us one. In the church, we discover a fresh empowerment of women to exercise what God calls and gifts them to do. I think of Priscilla, who taught Apollos; I think of Phoebe, who was a church leader and probably read the letter of Paul to the Romans, and who therefore had to answer questions about what Paul meant; I think of Junia, who is called a superlative apostle/missionary; I think of Euodia and Syntyche, who were "co-workers" with Paul in his gospel work; and I think of the daughters of Phillip, who were prophets. Invisible women in the Roman Empire become visible in Christ. Of the fellow missionary workers named alongside Paul, 20 percent were women — no small number in a male-oriented, hierarchical, women-can't-vote society.

Brady Boyd, pastor at New Life Church in Denver, in his new book *Let Her Lead*, asked a series of questions that can shed light on Paul's vision of equalizing men and women:

> Last week, I was on a flight home after a speaking engagement in Texas, piping Adele as loudly as my ear buds would go. Whatever song she was singing stopped my multitasking mid-task and made me take notice. I shook my head reflexively and thought, "I can't imagine what this world would be like without the voice of women." What if we had never heard Alicia Keys, Beyoncé, or Adele? What if we'd never read J. K. Rowling? What if we'd never seen the likes of Condoleezza Rice and Hillary Clinton rise to some of our nation's highest offices? I'm not endorsing 100 percent of everything they say, of course. I'm just endorsing the liberty they enjoyed in saying it.[3]

Think about it. What if the world of social work had never known Jane Addams, the world of fashion known Coco Chanel, the world of cooking known Julia Child, the world of medicine known Marie Curie, the world of entertainment known Aretha Franklin, the world of cosmetics known Estée Lauder, the world of cultural anthropology known Margaret Mead, the world of domesticity known Martha Stewart, the world of justice known Sandra Day O'Connor, the world of compassion known Mother Teresa, the world of television known Oprah Winfrey, the world of literature known Virginia Woolf, or the world of humanitarianism known Eleanor Roosevelt?

What if we'd never heard from Rosa Parks?

Yes, these questions — *what if?* — lead us straight back to Paul, to life "in Christ," to realizing that diversity is God's design. Are we willing to embrace the diversity of the church as *the very thing God most wants?* If so, the first strategy for Paul is to get a new mind about ethnic, class, and sexual differences. In Christ, they have all been transcended. God says Yes to all kinds.

STRATEGY #2: LIVE IN THE SPIRIT

My doctoral professor, James D. G. Dunn, is a world-known scholar of the New Testament. I cannot think of a better statement of his than when he described what the Spirit can accomplish: "*The Spirit of God transcends human ability and transforms human inability.*"[4] Write that on your desk or mirror and tweet it, and follow the tweet with #boom. The Spirit gives us power to do things we could never do, and takes what we can do and makes it even better.

When Paul looked at the situation — including roughneck, adulterous, powerful, and idolatrous Gentiles in the family of God meant to be one — he knew it was impossible. Gentiles had their views of Jews, and their views were as viscerally contemptible then as anti-Semitism is now. Jews had their issues with Gentiles too and often referred to them simply as "sinners." But Paul believed both could hop out of their well-worn ruts of segregation by living in the Spirit. Here's how Paul puts it: "Neither circumcision nor uncircumcision means anything" — and here many of his own ilk would not agree, but he goes on — "what counts is the new creation" (Galatians 6:15), which is Paul's theme of the presence of the Holy Spirit, who makes all things new in the church. When I read that, sometimes I just shake my head in amazement.

How does God accomplish this? By giving us spiritual gifts. Ask yourself why God chose to give to the church spiritual gifts — then ask how Paul saw them. If "the Spirit of God transcends human ability and transforms human inability," then perhaps the most significant strategy for building unity is to let the Spirit guide the whole body of Christ in its assignment of gifts. In the heat of battle, when his churches were cracking and creaking with disunity, Paul reminded them of the gifts of the Spirit.

People talk a lot about spiritual gifts in churches today, but far too much of the discussion focuses on the question: What is *my* gift? Paul, by contrast, asks, *Why* the gifts? His answer? Unity. As each person's body has different parts, so the body of Christ has different parts. The "parts" of the body of Christ are the "gifts" of the Spirit. To repeat Paul's question, *Why?* "So in Christ we, though many, *form one body*, and each member belongs to all the others" (Romans 12:5). Paul will bring up gifts again near the end of his ministry, where once again we learn that gifts are given to *create unity in the church* (Ephesians 4:16). God's gifts are given to make us one, and, in fact, they do make us dependent on one another. How ironic that spiritual gifts today — God's gifts — have become a source of division! A better word than "ironic" would be "tragic," or "sad," or "disgusting"!

If we live in the Spirit, we are one. If we are settling for "maters," however, it is because we are not living in the Spirit. The one God, the one Spirit, and the one Lord — he makes us one. Those who are most filled with the Spirit dwell in unity with the most Christians, and history has plenty of examples.

THOSE WHO FOCUS ON THE SPIRIT

Let us assume that unity — not just in our hearts, but "complete" as Jesus said it and in actual practice — is God's design for the church, and that the Christian life flows out of God's grand vision. When I look at that goal and think about who most often breaks through the boundaries and achieves unity, I think of the Spirit-shaped movements often called Pentecostal or charismatic. No groups have achieved unity between African Americans and whites more than Pentecostals; no groups have achieved more unity between the sexes; and no groups are more characterized by a mix of poor and rich. Those who surrender to the Spirit have the capacity to transcend their inabilities and transform their abilities.

Take William J. Seymour,[5] who was born in 1870 to ex-slaves in the state of Louisiana, a state that prior to the Civil War existed with a sense of tranquility and peace, but afterward became far more racially divisive. Seymour found his way to Cincinnati and was on the verge of death from small pox when he had a conversion/call experience. Seymour partook in a kind of charismatic Christian faith, but without the personal experience of speaking in tongues. He learned some theology at the hand of a powerfully influential leader, Charles Parham, whom many credit as the founder of the American charismatic and Pentecostal movement. In Texas, in order for Seymour to listen to the teacher, he had to sit outside Parham's classroom with the door cracked open — just because he was black. That sort of experience — and far worse — was typical for William Seymour, who then turned the very faith being used *against* blacks to become the source of unity *among* all, white or black.

Seymour was invited to a church in Los Angeles, and though there were some early rocky days, the story of the three-year long Azusa Street Revival at Seymour's church, the Apostolic Gospel Faith Mission, can be laid — humanly speaking — at the feet of Seymour. Therefore, in some sense, the Pentecostal and charismatic movement, numbering today more than 275 million, can be laid at the same feet. Though Seymour was black and partly blind in one eye, God used him to achieve unity between the races in a time in American history that was more racially charged than any other time.

The church in Azusa was unimpressive with its dirt floors, boxes fitted with wood planks for seating, and sawdust on the floor. The pulpit was made of two large wooden shoe crates covered with cotton cloth. A humble man, Seymour spent far more time on his knees praying than he did standing in front of the congregation teaching or preaching. But God met them, the Spirit fell, and they too experienced a Pentecost. Just like the original Pentecost, ethnic and racial lines got blurred, and "within a few days the congregation had shifted from being solely black to representing something of the mix of the city." Social and economic status, too, had to go. At Azusa Street, there was not "ostentatious hierarchy, and the breadth of the power contradicted a set of social conventions," said his biographer. Some of the finest words ever written about the power of the Spirit are those of Seymour in his newspaper: "God makes no difference in nationality, Ethiopians, Chinese, Indians, Mexicans, and other nationalities worship together."

What happened at Azusa Street became a national story. Gaston Barnabas Cashwell, a white North Carolinian ex-Methodist minister who had become charismatic, took a train to Los Angeles to witness the revival. When he saw the mix of races, he almost climbed back on the train for the return trip. Seymour's message challenged him to pray for a deeper, personal revival. While kneeling, Cashwell observed a "black hand place itself upon his own fair head. His reaction? It caused 'chills to go down my spine.'" A few more meetings and Cashwell confessed that he had "lost his pride." One journalist said the "color line was washed away at Azusa." Simply put: *the more Spirit, the more unity; the less unity, the less Spirit.* As Seymour put it, "Pentecost makes us love Jesus more and love our brothers more. It brings us into one common family."

TRANSCENDING DOES NOT MEAN ERADICATING DIFFERENCES

Recently I have been teaching a course at Northern Seminary called "Letters to the Early Churches." I looked around at this satisfying class of church leaders, paused, and then said, "This is much closer to what the church is supposed to be than ordinary Sunday churches." Why so? In our class we have five African Americans, one Indian, ten white Americans, two Latin Americans, and one Asian American. Thirteen are men, six are women, with some in their mid-twenties and at least one (I won't give his or her name) topping sixty. Some own Macs and some PCs. Mo's a golfer, Stanley ministers to those who have been incarcerated, Gail's a minister as is Mattie, Eric played professional baseball and is now a pastor of discipleship, Ming works on computers, and Rajmani is pastoring. If you were to attend the class, you'd see that though we are often different, we come together around the Word of God, around prayer, and around fellowship as we are learning. A unity transcends our differences when we spend this amount of time together, and come the dismissal of class at the end of the semester, we'll miss one another because we've grown together.

But transcending differences in Christ does not mean *eradicating* differences. Eradicating differences is what happens when we're tempted toward uniformity — that is, when we swamp the salad with dressing. It happens when we separate from one another into separate locations for separate ideas and ethnicities. One in Christ does not mean Ya'akov (Jacob) is no longer a Jew, nor does it mean Theodore is no longer a Gentile; one in Christ does not mean Fortunatus is no longer a Roman and wealthy, nor that Publius is no longer a slave and poor. One in Christ does not mean Paul ceases being male, nor does Junia cease being a female. One in Christ does not mean African Americans have to be white. Getting a new mind and living in the Spirit mean we transcend our differences *while remaining different as we live with one another.* Our difference is not eliminated, for difference is the vitality of our fellowship.

The oddest thing happens when we think about our fellowship more. The very gospel is all about creating a new kind of people in this world, and this fellowship begins at the table.

9

The Table
of Connection

Imagine "going to church" in the first century. If you were in a major Roman city, such as Rome, Ephesus, or Pompeii, you'd leave your home and walk in your leather sandals (or barefoot) through the city on paved roads. The pavers in your city are large stone blocks, not as smooth or as square as the ones we find in our driveways or walkways today, and it is hard not to stub your toe or trip.

You enter a house church where everyone gathers, and you immediately encounter some "church kids" playing hide-and-seek, someone's slave passes you carrying a spit with some already roasted meat dangling on the end. You also see that the household's former shrine to Apollo has been desecrated — better yet, liberated from idols. You walk through an atrium, where the evening sun gently falls on you, and then a few steps beyond the atrium you enter into a large room where others are sitting. Some lounge on the floor while others are on sofas with pillows. Someone — a slave — is fanning what appears to be an important leader. It is the "elder" (what we call "pastor" or "priest"), who has a small scroll open, and he's chatting with someone about what it says.

Outside the room on the veranda are low tables, and some have already taken their seats for dinner. There are flasks of wine and some pots of water and some trays of food — chicken and fish — and some "veggies" and some baked bread. There you sit at table, eating next to a Roman magistrate whom you had not met other than in a legal case some time back, but he doesn't remember you. He does "pass the peace," however, with a handshake and a kiss to the cheek. You also meet a young Jewish man who not only follows the Torah, but believes in Jesus, and you observe that he's eating what he calls "kosher."

Across the room, you observe that a slave, instead of serving others, is sitting next to a Roman citizen, their different statuses identified by their clothing, and they are praying together with their hands clasped. The conversation is going wonderfully with others around you when someone — the elder — stands up and says a prayer to lead the group into the Eucharist. The elder reads from the great apostle who had been to this city some years back, and what he reads about is Jesus' betrayal and death and the resurrection to the throne of God. You hear about bread and body and about wine and blood, and then he passes bread and wine around the room.

You snap off some bread, eat it, and then take a deep gulp of wine. You pass these to the magistrate next to you, and the table grows silent. Your thoughts wander to what has happened to you because of what happened to Jesus — dying so that you now are saved from a life of sin. You recall your own liberation as you sit with a few dozen liberated people. Your world has been turned upside down, your husband tolerates your "superstition," your oldest son thinks you're stupid, while your daughter and younger son sometimes accompany you. You hope your husband will join you too someday, and you have begun to notice an urgency in your prayers for your eldest son, sometimes moving into tears or anxiety. He's becoming far too Roman in his ways, and you know Roman ways lead to slavery to sin and grasping for status and uninhibited sexual expression.

The elder speaks about the cup and announces it is God's love and grace and Yes for everyone. He reports a sad story he heard about a church in Greece (you thought he was referring to Corinth but he didn't mention the city), where some of the wealthier followers of Jesus were eating before the poorer ones arrived. The elder makes it clear that Roman ways stop at the door, and that everyone, men and women, slaves and free, Jews and Greeks, and rich and poor are all one family in Christ. The elder then says this Passover-meal cup is a cup of thanksgiving (*eucharistia*), and that by drinking from that cup each person is participating in the death of Jesus, the Jewish Messiah who can liberate the Romans, and you realize how personal this is to you. He then says that eating the bread means you have just partaken in the body Jesus gave for us, a body that made you all one, whether you are Jewish or Roman, man or woman, a slave or a Roman citizen (which you are).

The elder then warns about dancing with the demons by engaging in worship in the Roman shrines. Your husband keeps one in your own residence near the front door, and previously the elder spoke with you about the host's conversion and how he tore down and destroyed the shrine to Apollo in this home. The elder urged you to be very, very careful about eating food offered to idols because the host was still struggling with his commitment to Jesus as the one true Lord.

As the sun is fading over the Italian countryside, you lose yourself in a reverie as you both listened to the elder teach and at the same time thought about your unbelieving husband and your older son. You began to pray for them both as you listened to him — and back and forth you went between them and him, for quite a while as the elder spoke, and you prayed for God's good hand of grace to fall on your family as it had fallen on you. Throughout the evening, the elder has connected the whole of life to the Eucharist because the church begins at that table. What you experience in the villa is an amazing fellowship, a new kind of family.

WHAT A DIFFERENCE!

Ordinary Romans now in Christ would have been struck by how equal everyone was in such a setting. We have a harder time grasping this today, so I will provide a letter from a period slightly later than the New Testament, but still illustrating the norm for evening banquets in the

Roman Empire. The letter is from Pliny the Younger, who tells a story about eating at a wealthy man's home:

> It would be a long story — and it is of no importance — to tell you how I came to be dining — for I am no particular friend of his — with a man who thought he combined elegance with economy, but who appeared to me to be both mean and lavish, for he set the best dishes before himself and a few others and treated the rest to cheap and scrappy food.
>
> He had apportioned the wine in small decanters of three different kinds, not in order to give his guests their choice but so that they might not refuse. He had one kind for himself and us, another for his less distinguished friends — for he is a man who classifies his acquaintances — and a third for his own freedmen and those of his guests.[1]

Everyone was ranked by status in the Roman Empire, with the wealthy getting the best dishes, the best food, and the best wine. Not that this happened always, and Pliny tells this story of a man who thought this was wrongheaded, but eating according to rank was often enough the case. Against this background, the gatherings of the Christians reconstructed everything from the bottom up: everyone was welcome, everyone got the same meal, everyone was equal, and everyone had one Lord, King Jesus. At the new family's table they were one.

At this meal they were connected to God and to one another, for the Eucharist dramatizes God's social experiment as it connects God to everyone, and everyone to everyone else and God. How can Eucharist do this, you wonder? Let's turn to the powerful connections that begin at the table.

EUCHARIST CONNECTS US TO ROUTINE MEALS WITH JESUS

Jesus turned routine meals into kingdom realities, which means a new society was being formed around evening dinner tables and people got converted at the table with Jesus. Moreover, Jesus' disciples learned more about him and the kingdom every evening sitting down together with him. If you were invited for dinner, you probably would have heard Jesus respond to questions by telling stories, which we call his parables.

What would have struck any Roman higher-ups was that Jesus' tables were mixed. Jews of status sat with Jews of no status; saints sat with sinners, the former learning they were the latter and the latter learning they could become the former. Tax collectors sat with zealots, for the table with Jesus was a place of grace.

At the Last Supper, Jesus connected that meal to the dinners they had been having and to the dinner they would eventually have. He said, "I will not drink again from the fruit of the vine until that day when I drink it new in the kingdom of God" (Mark 14:25). The routine meals of the past became a meal of memory, and that last connecting supper was to be remembered whenever Jesus' followers gathered ("Do this in remembrance of me," so we read in 1 Corinthians 11:24–25).

The early Christians celebrated Eucharist in connection with dinners in homes. So we need to convert our imaginations today, learning to eliminate the fancy cups and plates and white linens and tasteless portions of bread and drips of wine/grape juice and the solemnity and oddity of how we "do" Eucharist. We also need to convert our practice, learning to let our table fellowship with one another morph into remembering the Lord.

Ponder How Eucharist Connects Us to Passover

Often our Eucharist is a solemn, somber, and sober service that barely reveals the connection of the Last Supper to Passover. The Lord's Supper occurred during the week of Passover, an eight-day, joyous, festive celebration in Jerusalem. It was a holiday remembering the original Passover in Egypt (Exodus 12 tells the story), which means that Passover was first and foremost a celebration of liberation from oppression. Anyone who misses the liberation theme in Passover misses what it was all about, and our solemn services rarely excite hope of liberation.

When Jesus told his disciples to eat his body and drink his blood, he was transforming the bread and the wine of Passover from food to be eaten and blood to be daubed on doors into something profoundly new and disturbing. He was saying that he himself was the Passover bread and blood. Paul says this very thing in 1 Corinthians 5:7: "For Christ, our Passover lamb, has been sacrificed." So when his followers ate that bread and drank that wine, they were ingesting what would protect them from God's judgment (now, similar to the children of Israel in Egypt, against Jerusalem at the hand of Rome); that same bread and wine would now liberate them unto new life together — all of them — in the kingdom of God.

Ponder How Eucharist Connects Us to the Gospel

When Jesus said, "This is my body," and "This is my blood," and when he said, "Do this in remembrance of me," he made the story of Passover a story about himself. Jesus is rightly and utterly self-centered. We proclaim — or "gospel" — when we partake in the Eucharist because we turn our focus toward Jesus, toward his life, his death, his resurrection, and his return. Paul couldn't have made this more clear: "For whenever you eat this bread and drink this cup, you proclaim [*gospel*] the Lord's death until he comes" (1 Corinthians 11:26).

Celebrating and participating in the Eucharist declare what the gospel declares — that he died for our sins (15:3). "This cup is the new covenant in my blood," Jesus said (11:25). The Eucharist — as an action, as symbols, as an event — gospels to all those who observe and to all those who participate. It announces that sins are forgiven and sinners liberated by ingesting the bread and wine of Jesus. When we eat and when we drink, we accept and receive and participate in the atoning death of Jesus, the liberating power of the resurrection, and the expectant return of the Lord to establish his kingdom. The Eucharist is intimately connected to the gospel itself.

Ponder How Eucharist Connects Us to Personal Faith

One of the more dramatic features of Israel's Passover was how personal and individual it was. Passover was not like attending a professional football game; there were no spectators at the Passover. Everyone had a job to do, and everyone participated. Some gathered wood for roasting the lamb, some prepared the herbs and spices and bread, some got the rooms ready, and the males went to the temple to sacrifice the lamb and returned home with the lamb waiting to be roasted and eaten. The father guided the family through the story of the Exodus, but *each person responded and ate the meal.* Each person was expected *to remember.* Each person, then, was expected to relive the exodus from Egypt each year. This is why Paul repeats what Jesus revealed at his Last Supper: "Do this …" and "Do this …" and "eat" and "drink," and "proclaim" and "examine." This was so sacred, and at the same time so personally connecting, that those who did so lightheartedly were warned that they would "eat and drink judgment on themselves" (1 Corinthians 11:29).

When you sit or walk to eat and drink at the Eucharist, it is you and God. You are to do business with God as God does business with you. Prepare in advance. Examine your heart to eliminate the noise. Recollect the great story of the exodus. Read the passage in one of the Gospels (Matthew 26; Mark 14; Luke 22), or in 1 Corinthians 11:17 – 34. Or ponder a great salvation passage, from Abraham's covenant story to the great celebrations of redemption in Revelation. Pray in the presence of God. In and through it all, *reaffirm your trust in the saving acts of God in Jesus: his life, his death, his burial, his resurrection, and his exalted rule and return.*

The word *Eucharist* means thanksgiving, so do just that. *Thank God* for salvation, justification, reconciliation, redemption, forgiveness, sanctification, and the coming kingdom of God.

Ponder How Eucharist Connects Us to Church Worship

I want to step forward just a bit in time to the second century, where we encounter a weekly service in which Eucharist is celebrated. This excerpt is from the early Christian apologist Justin Martyr, and what we need to observe is that Eucharist is the center of the church's worship. I have highlighted the Eucharist in italics:

> And we afterwards continually remind each other of these things. And
> the wealthy among us help the needy; and we always keep together;

and for all things wherewith we are supplied, we bless the Maker of all through His Son Jesus Christ, and through the Holy Ghost.

And on the day called Sunday, all who live in cities or in the country gather together to one place, and the memoirs of the apostles or the writings of the prophets are read, as long as time permits; then, when the reader has ceased, the president verbally instructs, and exhorts to the imitation of these good things.

Then we all rise together and pray, and, as we before said, when our prayer is ended, *bread and wine and water are brought,* and the president in like manner offers prayers and *thanksgivings,* according to his ability, and the people assent, saying Amen; *and there is a distribution to each, and a participation of that over which thanks have been given, and to those who are absent a portion is sent by the deacons.*

And they who are well to do, and willing, give what each thinks fit; and what is collected is deposited with the president, who succours the orphans and widows and those who, through sickness or any other cause, are in want, and those who are in bonds and the strangers sojourning among us, and in a word takes care of all who are in need.

But Sunday is the day on which we all hold our common assembly, because it is the first day on which God, having wrought a change in the darkness and matter, made the world; and Jesus Christ our Saviour on the same day rose from the dead. For He was crucified on the day before that of Saturn (Saturday); and on the day after that of Saturn, which is the day of the Sun, having appeared to His apostles and disciples, He taught them these things, which we have submitted to you also for your consideration.[2]

The wisdom of the church was quickly established, so that when they gathered, they celebrated the Eucharist. The Eucharist was connected to worship, and worship was connected to teaching the gospel, and teaching the gospel was connected to — you guessed it — church unity.

Ponder How Eucharist Connects Us to Church Unity

If you read beyond the italics, you will have noticed that the worship service, which came to its focal point in Eucharist, connected the believers to charity for the poor, to orphans, and (the most neglected group in churches today) to widows (and widowers). Everyone in the church gets connected at Eucharist. Everyone.

Once when I had finished preaching at a church in Connecticut, and having observed in the sermon that widows are the most neglected group in many of our churches, an elderly man approached me with tears running down his cheeks and said to me, "We widowers are neglected too." Reconnecting with the disconnected, making the invisible visible — all because of God's Yes to all of us — is what the Eucharist is all about. "The gifts of God," we say in liturgical services, "for (all) the People of God."

But we don't have to go to the second century to see this concern about giving to the poor. Besides the obvious — namely, that Jesus' table fellowship invited the poor and hungry to the table — the apostle Paul gets after the Corinthian Christians because they are neglecting the poor in their love feast meals that often preceded the Eucharist. To them Paul said, "So then, my brothers and sisters, when you gather to eat, you should all eat together" (1 Corinthians 11:33). That is, the meal that flowed into the Eucharist was for all to share equally.

A major element of Eucharist then is found in the word *connected*. At the Eucharist you are connected to other followers of Jesus to focus on him together and to share food together and to worship together. *Together* we embody the unity of the body of Christ. This is such a splendid idea — and on paper it works perfectly — but everywhere I go, I hear challenges to the importance of the church that is connected at the table.

Let's look now at two of those challenges.

10

We Is Bigger than Me

My friend Dan Kimball wrote a book with a title that haunts me. His book is called *They Like Jesus But Not the Church*. I'm a Bible guy kind of theologian, and we theologians know it is impossible to love Jesus and not love the church. After all, it's his body! Yet, not only do I understand the possibility of this impossibility, I sympathize with the expression because, truth be told, so many churches and denominations are wobbly today.

Not long ago, I was speaking in Pennsylvania. Early in the morning I was picked up to be taken to the church for a "mic check," and on our way we passed a half-dozen churches that were shut down — one now a school, one now a business, and the others now nothing but echoes of worship and fellowship long ago. I got to wondering if the same fate would strike the church where I would speak, which were not pleasant thoughts prior to a full day of preaching, teaching, and answering questions from God's good people.

Churches are shutting down all over the nation because lots of people think following Jesus and fellowshiping at a church are disconnected. I disagree because the New Testament teaches that the Christian life occurs primarily in and through a local church. So how did we get to this point where some good Christians think church is entirely optional — even an obstacle to the Christian life? American Christians disappearing from the

105

church have encountered two major challenges when it comes to thinking about the church's importance — and the two challenges come from two important figures in our country's story. I call them whisperers.

FIRST WHISPER: FIND THE PERFECT CHURCH

America pioneered an idea that has become a Western world assumption and law: the church and the state are separate. Westerners assume both freedom of religion and the "wall of separation" between church and state. The earliest Americans pioneered this, and no one was more responsible for the robust idea of religious freedom from state interference than the seventeenth-century's Roger Williams. His contribution to America, indeed to the entire Western culture's belief in the separation of church and state, is a remarkable story even if many today know little about him.

England's church and state were intertwined, and over the centuries had shifted at times toward the Roman Catholic Church and finally toward a Protestant (Anglican) Church. One group of Protestants, the Puritans, were intent on purging the Anglican Church of all traces of Catholicism. But when it didn't happen as they wanted, some of them pulled up stakes, piled into a boat, and became America's Pilgrims. Edwin Gaustad, one of the finest American church historians, sums up the Puritan aim: "Far from England's intruding and persecuting bishops, protected from the nation's nosy and arresting sheriffs, the Puritans, taking only the New Testament as their pattern and guide, could fashion a pure, nonpolitical, uncorrupted, noncompromised church."[1]

When Roger Williams landed on America's shores — not long after the first Puritans set the dream for an uncorrupted church in motion — he saw problems, so his intent was to purge the Boston Anglican church of its problems and establish a church based on the New Testament and the New Testament alone. Eventually he pulled up stakes from the Boston area entirely, moved south, and established a new colony, Providence Plantation (today's Rhode Island) marked by freedom of religion. Williams believed, for example, that there was no warrant for infant baptism and therefore insisted on baptism only for the true believer (hence, the Baptists).

If I love Williams' contribution to the relation of church and state in American society, I am not excited about the patterns he established that continue to whisper in the Christian's ear. Williams sought the perfect expression of the New Testament church and, even if one has to give him credit for courage and zeal, Roger himself became the problem — every church he started he eventually pulled out of because it was never committed enough to his own views of what the New Testament taught. The one who wanted to separate church from state to create a pure church became the solitary church of one. He was the first American who loved Jesus but not the church.

Roger Williams's example still whispers these thoughts to each of us today:

Read the New Testament carefully.
Discover the glories of what the church should/could be.
Start all over again with a new vision for the church.
Experience problems achieving the vision.
Get discouraged.
Withdraw from church.
Start another church with new-and-improved vision.
Soon find fewer and fewer like-minded souls.
Do church home alone.

We are given in America the power of choice, and religion has become a smorgasbord to choose your own church based on its ability to live up to your own preferences. This leads to the first thing we need to observe about the actual New Testament pattern, one Williams managed to avoid and one many today do not want to acknowledge: *we are a messy family.*

There never was a golden era when the church "did church" perfectly. Sometimes well-meaning people suggest the first-century was a golden era, but anyone who reads the New Testament knows there were problems within weeks! In Jerusalem, ethnic rivalries meant Greek-speaking widows were neglected, and at Corinth its members were forming personality cults. Strife emerged quickly in Paul's messy house churches. Many regard the book of Romans as the highest plane of New Testament theology, but in that letter Paul had to put gospel pressure on the "weak" and the "strong," subtle terms for Jews and Gentiles, who were struggling to fellowship with one another in Rome (Romans 14:1 – 15:13). Paul's strategy for the Roman church problems was "love," once again. Right there in Rome, right away, problems surfaced among the Christians.

Roger Williams wanted a pure and holy church.	Paul wanted a church for the impure and unholy who could be made pure and holy by Christ.
Roger Williams wanted a church for the lovable.	Paul wanted a church that loved the unloved.
Roger Williams wanted a church of likes.	Paul wanted a church of differents together in fellowship.

Whenever I hear about people who say they love Jesus but not the church, I pull out Dietrich Bonhoeffer's famous little book, *Life Together*, and point to chapter 1. There he shows that many are disillusioned because they've created a dream-image of the church that doesn't exist. Then Bonhoeffer offers these stunning words:

> Those who love their dream of a Christian community more than the Christian community itself become destroyers of that Christian community even though their personal intentions may be ever so honest, earnest, and sacrificial.[2]

If smaller families with histories of love and kinship struggle, what happens when you toss together in a church a bundle of folks with all their differences and dysfunctions? C. S. Lewis once observed that we are called to love those who happen to be in the church with us, but he made the fair observation that they may well be "odder than you could have believed and worth far more than we guessed"![3]

The church is a hospital for sinners, not a retirement center for the perfect. Looking for perfect Christians in a perfect church is failure to understand what the church is. Roger Williams's model is to find solid Christians in order to build the solid church. Paul, however, told us to find the most difficult ethnic tension you can — Jews and Gentiles — and see if you can build a church! The church was and is today the most radical social experiment in history.

SECOND WHISPER: YOU ARE ON YOUR OWN

Sitting next to Roger Williams is Henry David Thoreau,[4] yet another American whispering similar messages in our ears. When we think of Thoreau, we think of his short stay in his solitary hut on Walden Pond and of his solitary walks and life. Thoreau's hut and life express a powerful and penetrating character-theme for Americans: we take care of ourselves, we work for ourselves, we answer to ourselves — and that means we often attend church for ourselves. At the heart of the American psyche is the Self, and Thoreau helped form the American Me so that it is bigger than the American We or the church We.

Thoreau's stubborn individualism is expressed boldly in this set of lines: "Do what you love. Know your own bone; gnaw at it, bury it, unearth it, and gnaw it still." His sympathetic biographer, Robert Richardson, summed up Thoreau in these words: he "stands as the most attractive American example … of the ageless Stoic principle of self-trust, self-reverence, or self-reliance." Richardson also wrote, "In death as in life the principle of individuation reigns."

So difficult did Thoreau's individualism make his life that he struggled to engage in long-term, meaningful relations with others. Later in his life, he can only say these sad words of his best friend, Ralph Waldo Emerson: "There was one other with whom I had 'solid seasons,' long to be remembered, at his house in the village and who looked in upon me from time to time." He won't even mention the man's name. Perhaps Thoreau's most influential image and words come from the conclusion to his famous *Walden*, where he said, "If a man does not keep pace with his companions, perhaps it is because he hears a different drummer. Let him step to the music which he hears, however measured or far away." The one who drinks the Me-beer of Thoreau will not find the We-wine of the Eucharist to his taste.

For all the good Thoreau has done for Americans in spurring us all to find ourselves, his life embodies a kind of American individualism that cuts sharply against the grain of the church. His message is whispered in the ear of each American, and when one of us combines Roger Williams with Thoreau, we've got bigger Me's than most We's can contain.

CHURCH WISDOM: WE IS BIGGER THAN ME

The most important term in the Bible is God, and we can break that one term into three: Father, Son, and Spirit. The second most important term in the Bible is People (of God), and we can break that into three as well: Israel, Kingdom, and the Church. In other words, God and We. As I've mentioned, far too much of Christianity is obsessed with that which is personal, individual, intimate, devotional, and private. In other words, the Me.

Nothing expresses this more than today's grandiose razzmatazz slogan: "I'm spiritual, but not religious." What this slogan means is two things. First, I don't like the institutional church or institutional religion. Second, I compose my own way of spirituality, and it's between God and me. But "Me" is not one of the most important words in the Bible. You don't get "Me" until you pass through God and People, and if you move in that order, Me morphs into We. The slogan "I'm spiritual, but not religious" is what happens when Thoreau merges with Roger Williams.

The Me posture turns the Bible upside down and inside out. The Bible's focus — read it from beginning to end and you will see this — is on what God is doing in this world *through the people of God*. Page after page, chapter after chapter, book after book — sixty-six of them in all — the Bible tells the story of Israel that morphs into the story of the Kingdom and the story of the Church. That story of People finishes in Revelation with God creating a new Jerusalem in the new heavens and new earth, where the focus again is on the people of God. No one's name is even mentioned; there is no "I see Donald and Sherry and Cathy and Bud." Yes, of course, there is an intensely personal and individual element within the story of the People, but the Me-story is contained *within* the We-story.

WE SHARE LIFE

The best word for the church in the whole New Testament is not the word *church*, a word for a gathered assembly. The best word for the church is *fellowship*, which simply means that we share life with one another. That is precisely what happened to the first Christians when the Spirit of God plopped them all together in those house churches across the Roman Empire. Such an odd box of differents.

Some look at the early church as if it's wearing a Mona Lisa smile and think those early chapters in Acts describe a failed experiment in communal living. But Acts is not describing a golden age when everything was perfect; rather, it was describing how those early Christians, drenched as they were with the Holy Spirit and feeling the glow of their new lives at work, learned to live with one another in *fellowship*. All they wanted was for the We to be bigger than Me.

Here are the two sets of verses from Acts 2:42 – 47 and 4:32 – 35, reduced to the basics:

> They devoted themselves to the apostles' teaching and to fellowship, to the breaking of bread and to prayer. Everyone was filled with awe at the many wonders and signs performed by the apostles. All the believers were together and had everything in common. They sold property and possessions to give to anyone who had need. Every day they continued to meet together in the temple courts. They broke bread in their homes and ate together with glad and sincere hearts, praising God and enjoying the favor of all the people. And the Lord added to their number daily those who were being saved.

All the believers were one in heart and mind. No one claimed that any of their possessions was their own, but they shared everything they had. With great power the apostles continued to testify to the resurrection of the Lord Jesus. And God's grace was so powerfully at work in them all that there were no needy persons among them.

What are the marks of our shared life in our new fellowship?

We listen to the apostles.
We share meals with one another.
We sing, pray, confess our sins, and worship God together.
We share resources with one another.
This happens through God's power at work in us.
New people enter into this fellowship through gospeling.

The We of fellowship, then, is spiritual, it is social, and it is financial. But fellowship is not something we create; it is the result of God's work in us. When God's people live in fellowship with one another, when they "do life" together, the church embodies the gospel about King Jesus and people respond to the gospel about him. When they live in fellowship, the Me finds its joy in the We. It's messy, believe me, very messy, but no matter what the mess, the gospel is at work to turn messy people into holy people, even if it takes a lifetime (or more).

PART 4

HOLINESS

11

Holiness as Devotion to God

The word *holiness* makes some think of old black and white lithograph images of men in suits and women in long dresses at summer camps, while for others it sends shivers up and down the spine. For still others, the word *holiness* ignites their deepest religious affections. In one day at Northern Seminary, one student told me she was "a holiness girl," and ten minutes later another said that "holiness always becomes legalism." Many of us grew up under the famous "Thou shalt not's" of the Bible, and as the list lengthened, pastors, parents, and siblings expounded on the evils of R-rated movies, beer, girls and guys, curfew times, skinny jeans, and half-sleeve or full-sleeve tattoos (or "tats").

The best way to ruin holiness is to turn it into a list of Don'ts (with no Do's) or to pull out Leviticus and point it at the on-fire football player who just got a cross tat on his muscular shoulder. Flannery O'Connor once called this picayune attentiveness to every possible peccadillo measuring "your sins with a slide rule."[1] Because holiness is an utterly beautiful and glorious attribute of God and because we are summoned to be holy, we aim to convert our shivers and eye rolls into affection.

For the Torah-devout Jewish apostle Paul, leaning as he was every day into a mission to the (demonstrably sinful) Gentiles and the (not quite as demonstrably sinful) Jews, holiness was the air he breathed and the challenge he saw for the churches. There wasn't a day that he was not aware of the opportunity for each of his churches for a life devoted to God. The Bible's big idea about holiness comes to expression in Leviticus 11:44–45:

> I am the LORD your God; consecrate yourselves and be *holy*, because I am *holy*. Do not make yourselves *unclean* by any creature that moves along the ground. I am the LORD, who brought you up out of Egypt to be your God; therefore be *holy*, because I am *holy*.

Here we see the two major elements of holiness in the Bible:

1. God is holy.
2. Therefore, God's people are to be holy.

Our holiness is grounded in God's prior holiness, which means we have to figure out what it means to be holy in this messed-up fellowship called the church. No one experienced the challenge of holiness more than the apostle Paul, because those Roman Empire house churches were filled with folks who didn't have a clue what "holiness" meant.

BEYOND "SEPARATE"

Many people say holiness means "separated." In other words, some define *holiness* as no longer sinning the way they used to. Here's Paul's list of sins from which they are to be separate, and I'll ask you a question before you read it: What happens to your church if everyone who does these things gets kicked out?

> The acts of the flesh are obvious:
>   sexual immorality, impurity and debauchery;
>   idolatry and witchcraft;
>   hatred, discord, jealousy, fits of rage, selfish ambition, dissensions, factions and envy;
>   drunkenness, orgies, and the like.
>   I warn you, as I did before, that those who live like this will not inherit the kingdom of God. (Galatians 5:19–21)

Paul orders his list into sins of desire, sins of worship, sins against one another, and sins of extreme desire. *Is holiness just not doing these things any longer?*

Think about this at a theological or even philosophical level: God *is* holy. God doesn't *have* holiness the way we have an iPhone. No, *God is in his being holy.* Now another question: If God *is* holy, and if God is *prior to all creation*, and if some say holiness means being different from or separate from something or someone else, *when God was "all alone" and there was nothing else, was God holy then?* Yes, in fact, God was and is and always will be holy. This leads us to an important point: holiness cannot be reduced to separation or difference. At a deeper level, holiness means "devoted." In the Do's and Don'ts approach, holiness should focus on the Do's. In other words, if separation focuses on differences *from* the world, the deeper level of devotion focuses on a life devoted *unto* God. The two belong together, and we need both.

Let me illustrate this with something ordinary. One day I was messing around with a piece of wood and saw a nail poking out. I thought of my curious grandchildren grabbing that board, so I looked for a hammer — but there was no hammer in the garage. I was tempted to whip out one of my golf clubs, like my wedge, and give the nail a little knock and be done with it — but those are my Ping Eye 2 irons, and they're not cheap. I love those irons, and they are made for golfing. I'd hate to damage a golf club hammering a nail.

That sense that golf clubs are special and reserved for — or devoted to — one task and withdrawn from hammering a nail illustrates what "holiness" means in the Bible. It means devoted, and almost always in the Bible it means *devoted entirely to God.* (I've been tempted to use a hammer on a golf course, but not for redemptive purposes.)

WHEN I THINK OF HOLINESS, I THINK OF...

A. W. Tozer's two books *The Pursuit of God* and *Knowledge of the Holy* deserve to be read — scratch that — deeply pondered by every Christian.

Tozer said that the Christian life begins right where the Bible says it does — with God — and that the only path to holiness is time in God's presence. Tozer was ordained in the Christian and Missionary Alliance Church, and he was so devoted that "after the laying on of hands at the conclusion of the ordination, Tozer refused to linger for niceties, fellowship, and celebration. Instead he slipped away from everyone and found a place of solitude. There he prayed alone to the Lord who set him apart and called him to a preaching ministry."[2] In his prayer, a record of which has been preserved, Tozer asked simply God, "Lay thy hand upon me." The pattern of Tozer's entire life was that when others wanted to talk about God or with one another, he wanted to talk to God. When others wanted to debate about God, he wanted to spend time in God's presence.

So his life was devoted to God in prayer and he spent so much time in prayer that he had a habit worth telling. "Most of his prolonged prayer time … took place in his church office on the back side of the second floor [in Chicago]." That's not so unusual, but this is: when he got to his office in the morning, he "would carefully hang up his suit trousers and don his sweater and raggedy old 'prayer pants.'" Why? Because he spent so much time on his knees he wore out pants and needed a "raggedy" pair so he could afford to pray.

"Tozer's preaching was affected by his praying" so much that, as a contemporary said of his sermons, one can say his "preaching was a declaration of what he had learned in prayer." He himself admitted this: "I never go to the Bible for a sermon, I go to the Bible to see God. Then I get words for sermons." Time in God's presence led him to be a critic of the superficial prayers and theology in the church. "No one," he announced, "who has ever bowed before the Burning Bush can thereafter speak lightly of God." Reading the story of the über-devoted Tozer raises the question: How can we be holy? Or to frame it bigger ways, how can a local church — our church, your church — become more holy?

There are three elements to holiness. First, we don't make ourselves holy; holiness is the inner work of God. Second, holiness means learning to live a life that avoids sins. Third, holiness means learning to live a life devoted to God. We'll combine the second and third because Paul does so often.

HOLINESS AS THE WORK OF GOD

Holiness can't be manufactured or purchased. Sometimes we listen to some of the spiritual formation experts and get the impression that if we do enough of the spiritual disciplines, we will become holy. Then we listen to the social justice activists and wonder whether becoming more active will make us become more holy. Then we listen to the theological debaters, and it seems the more we know, the more holy we will become. Then we listen to some pastors, and it seems rather obvious that if we want to become holy, we need to join or imitate their particular church. We listen to my Catholic and Orthodox friends, and they suggest that what we need is more Eucharist. Then there are the "pietists," who seem to teach that holiness is the product of more prayer and Bible reading. Fasting, activism, knowledge, church participation, Eucharist, and prayer feature in a holy life, but they are not its source. The apostle Paul points us directly to the spring of the spiritual life, and *it is the work of God's Spirit in us that produces holiness.*

Let me quote a few lines from Paul to make this abundantly clear, and I have italicized those words that draw our attention to God as the source of holiness:

> May *God himself*, the God of peace, *sanctify* you through and through. (1 Thessalonians 5:23)

> … because God chose you as first fruits to be saved through the *sanctifying work of the Spirit* and through belief in the truth. (2 Thessalonians 2:13)

From Paul's earliest letters to some of his latest, the theme remains the same: holiness is the work of God in us. So if we want our church to become holy, we need to learn to spend time in God's presence, basking in the light of his holiness.

THE DON'TS BECAUSE OF THE DO'S

We are all in the habit of thinking "Do's and Don'ts" are shallow religion, but the Bible is filled with lists of Do's and Don'ts. The most famous law code in history is the Ten Commandments, which could be called the Eight Don'ts and the Two Do's! (Three Don'ts, Two Do's, and then five more Don'ts.) Why do we have the Don'ts? Isn't this all negative and primitive?

No, in fact, it's not. God wants us *not to do* some behaviors, and God wants other behaviors to mark his people. But because holiness is about devotion, it is best not to talk about "Do's and Don'ts," but rather about "Don'ts because of the Do's." That is, because we are *doing* devotion of God, we *don't* want to do sin.

I can think of no passage in the Bible that teaches holiness better than Ephesians 4 and 5, which we could call Paul's version of the "Don'ts because of the Do's." In this passage we have to imagine Paul's house churches filled with shop workers, slaves, migrant workers, and males struggling with what they were learning in the church. Paul wanted the churches to be holy, and that for him meant a life devoted to God. But Paul did not begin the Christian life with a list of Don'ts. He began it with a vision for each of us to be fully devoted to God. Here's one of his lists, and I've marked it with a + and a - to make the Do's and Don'ts obvious (we begin with Ephesians 4:24):

> (+) ... put on the new self, created to be like God in true righteousness and holiness.
>
> Therefore each of you (-) must put off falsehood and (+) speak truthfully to your neighbor, for we are all members of one body....
>
> (-) Anyone who has been stealing must steal no longer, (+) but must work, doing something useful with their own hands, that they may have something to share with those in need.
>
> (-) Do not let any unwholesome talk come out of your mouths, (+) but only what is helpful for building others up according to their needs, that it may benefit those who listen....
>
> (+) Be kind and compassionate to one another, (+) forgiving each other, just as in Christ God forgave you....

(-) But among you there must not be even a hint of sexual immorality, or of any kind of impurity, or of greed, because these are improper for God's holy people. (-) Nor should there be obscenity, foolish talk or coarse joking, which are out of place, but (+) rather thanksgiving. (-) For of this you can be sure: No immoral, impure or greedy person — such a person is an idolater — has any inheritance in the kingdom of Christ and of God. (-) Let no one deceive you with empty words, for because of such things God's wrath comes on those who are disobedient. (-) Therefore do not be partners with them.

For you were once darkness, but now you are light in the Lord. (+) Live as children of light (for the fruit of the light consists in all goodness, righteousness and truth) and find out what pleases the Lord. (-) Have nothing to do with the fruitless deeds of darkness, (+) but rather expose them....

(+) Be very careful, then, how you live — not as unwise but as wise, (+) making the most of every opportunity, because the days are evil. (-) Therefore do not be foolish, (+) but understand what the Lord's will is. (-) Do not get drunk on wine, which leads to debauchery. (+) Instead, be filled with the Spirit, (+) speaking to one another with psalms, hymns, and songs from the Spirit. Sing and make music from your heart to the Lord, (+) always giving thanks to God the Father for everything, in the name of our Lord Jesus Christ.

This kind of pure devotion to God is what Paul has in mind, then, when he begins to think about the moral messiness of his house churches. He wants those churches to be holy, but he knows that God's work in them will lead them away from sins and toward the greatest virtues running through the Roman Empire — love, justice, peace, compassion, and forgiveness.

But right in the middle of many of his concerns about holiness — and you knew this was coming — he expresses a concern about sexual sins and sexual purity. It is impossible to talk about the church then or today without addressing sexuality, including what the Bible says about one of our culture's most pressing social issues — homosexuality. But these sexuality issues need to be addressed from where Paul himself addressed them:

holiness and salvation as a lifelong process and struggle — all within the context of a local church.

We've looked briefly at three elements of holiness. In the next chapter we'll look at sexual sins, and then we'll remind ourselves to be welcoming and patient as God's process of redemption works its way in our churches.

12

Sexual Bodies
in a Church

In any given local church in the Roman Empire it was almost certain that you'd have converted Romans who had lived a life of sexual experimentation, exploration, and exploitation — or who were involved in and perhaps were seeking liberation from enslaved prostitution. I have been to Pompeii, and as we walked up the path into the city, what we saw, well, it is not an exaggeration to say the city was swamped with erotic images. I noticed to my right a bathhouse with a fresco of a woman climbing onto a reclining, naked ready-for-action man. Inside the bathhouse is a mural of a man penetrating a man, while the man he is penetrating is penetrating a woman. The sexual reality across the Roman Empire, of which Pompeii was a typical example, was a total lack of sexual inhibition.

Converts to Christ came from this circle of people. Paul's churches were made up of many people who began their Christian journey in places most Christians would not even recognize today. These were the people gathering, the people praying, the people at the dinner table, the people longing for grace in the Eucharist, the people longing for redemption (of the body) and eternal life, and the people the pastors were pastoring. Same-sex sexual relations,[1] which were one well-known element of the

Roman sexual life, was the story of more than a few of Paul's converts, and what Paul says about this topic can serve us well in learning what it means to live in a fellowship of differents and also what it can mean to grow in grace. Sexual redemption, holiness, and purity are part of the ongoing church life both then (and today).

THE ROMAN CONTEXT

Studies of the sexual lives of Roman (or Greek)[2] men reveal a typical pattern: males had "procreational" sex with their wives, with whom they shared a home, children, and a family life, and had "recreational" sex with others. This was normal sexuality for a Roman male, and to a lesser degree for Roman females. Yes, that's right. This was the norm. Those recreational others included young boys (pederasty),[3] prostitutes (the percentage of prostitutes in Roman cities staggers the mind), and slaves. It is a sad fact of Roman history that when a female slave is mentioned, as she is in the New Testament several times, there is the likelihood that she was used for sexual gratification. Sex outside marriage was not a moral issue for most in the Roman Empire.[4] Here are words from Rome's greatest orator, Cicero, about the custom of sexual relations with prostitutes:

> If anyone there thinks that young men should be forbidden association even with prostitutes, he is certainly very stern; but he is also in disagreement not only with the permissiveness of this century, but even with the custom and indulgences of our ancestors. When was such a thing not done, when was it censured, when not allowed, when finally was that which is now permitted not permitted?[5]

Romans believed in uninhibited sexual exploration, married or not. Sexual relations for males, then, occurred at two levels: at home with one's wife, who was expected to be faithful, and in the public realm with others. At the center of sexual relations among the Romans and Greek was dominance, for in penetrating another one exercised dominance and status over the other person. (That theme of domination, to be sure, was occasionally countered by descriptions of admirably vulnerable, mutual, and intimate relations of a man with his wife and a wife with her husband.)

In their sexual recreations, some husbands participated in sex with women while some of these husbands also engaged in same-sex relations on the side.[6] Paul is describing this sort of relationship in 1 Corinthians 6:9, which reads "men who have sex with men" (NIV), but the explanatory footnote clarifies that the words "refer to the passive and active participants." Less discreetly, these words describe Roman husbands who have heterosexual relations with a wife, but who recreationally may prefer males — either penetrating them or being penetrated by them. When we ask, "Who were those who engaged in same-sex relations in Paul's day?" we are then to think mostly of married males engaging in same-sex relations recreationally. Since committed same-sex relations were known in the Roman world, 1 Corinthians 6:9 – 11 could be describing faithful same-sex couples, but this is less likely than a Roman husband's recreational sex with other men.[7]

Lesbianism existed but was not nearly as pervasive as same-sex relations among males. Lucian, writing in the century after the apostle Paul, says, "They say there are women like that in Lesbos, masculine-looking, but they don't want to give it up for men. Instead, they consort with women, just like men."[8]

While this might give the impression that Greek and Roman males in particular were a bit like dogs spritzing here and there to mark their territories, which sadly is not entirely inaccurate, what we need to focus on is that uninhibited sexuality in the Roman Empire was as far as one could get from the Jewish world. The Jewish world was marked notably by sexual restrictions.

THE JEWISH TRADITION

Paul grew up in the Roman Empire, in Tarsus, where he would have observed typical Roman male sexuality on a daily basis, where murals and frescoes depicted Romans' sexual lives, where he would have encountered the common presence of prostitutes and slaves, and where he would have no doubt also heard about same-sex relations and pederasty. But Paul's Bible, our Old Testament, established the norm and the law for the Torah observant Jew, and Paul was observant. That norm was sexual fidelity — husband and wife, and husband and wife alone. That was the biblical ideal, though the Bible has more than its share of descriptions of broken sexuality. Israelite sexuality, for example, involved polygamous relationships among the leading elites. There are all sorts of explanations for polygamy, concubines, and sexual infidelities such as David's — and who needs to be reminded of old randy Solomon? The fact remains that the Bible's core ideal is sexual fidelity between husband and wife.

So, running from the front to the back of the Old Testament is the prohibition to engage in sexual relations outside or before heterosexual marriage, which means the Torah was against same-sex relations. Whether one looks to the attempted violent rapes at Sodom in Genesis 19:1 – 14, to the debauched sexual violence of the Levite and his concubine in Judges 19:22 – 30, or to the laws of Israel that prohibited homosexual relations as an "abomination" that is seen among the pagans (Leviticus 18:22; 20:13), the biblical tradition established sexuality for the husband-wife relation alone.[9] Any other form of sexual relation was "out of order."[10] So Jesus,[11] but especially Paul, grew up in a sexually charged Roman culture with a sexually countercultural way of life. Yet Paul's mission was to mix it up with the Gentile culture, and he knew his mission would create all sorts of challenges.

PAUL'S TEACHINGS

Not surprisingly, when Paul began to establish house churches across the Roman Empire, his Jewish sexuality tradition and the Roman sexuality practices came into immediate conflict. As a Torah-observant Jew Paul no doubt believed Roman recreational sexuality defiled humans and flaunted the will of God; he also knew the same was possible among Jewish citizens, and he knew it was unfortunately a part of his churches. But in spite of these realities, Paul was a pastor seeing both conversions and holiness. In speaking into such churches, here are some of the most famous words about sexuality ever uttered by Paul:

> Or do you not know that wrongdoers will not inherit the kingdom of God? Do not be deceived: Neither *the sexually immoral* nor idolaters nor *adulterers* nor *men who have sex with men* nor thieves nor the greedy nor drunkards nor slanderers nor swindlers will inherit the kingdom of God. And that is what some of you were. But you were washed, you were sanctified, you were justified in the name of the Lord Jesus Christ and by the Spirit of our God. (1 Corinthians 6:9 – 11)

Once we understand the context of the Roman male's sexual practices, we are encouraged to interpret Paul's list here of sins[12] not so much as a list of who is in and who is out but more as a list of the "notorious sins of notorious sinners" Paul saw in every city in the Roman Empire. When "vacationing" Torah-observant Jews returned home to Jerusalem and someone asked them, "What are the Gentiles like?" this is the kind of stereotyped list they might produce.[13] The most important element here is that Paul says, "And this is what some of you *were*. But *you were washed, you were sanctified, you were justified.*"

Paul's basic teaching was countercultural in two regards. First, what these Gentile Christians did in the past should be in the past; second, sexual relations for his churches were designed by God for a man and his wife, a wife and her husband. Remember what we read in the previous chapter from Ephesians: "But among you there must not be even a hint of sexual immorality, or of any kind of impurity, or of greed, because these are improper for God's holy people" (Ephesians 5:3). Paul called the folks in his churches to "flee from sexual immorality" (1 Corinthians 6:18). So the apostle to the Gentiles makes it clear — and this is radical in his day — that one has only two options: celibacy or faithfulness to one's spouse. What may be most important for us to hear is that *fidelity* was almost certainly more of a challenge to the typical Roman male than *celibacy*.

We need to observe that one chapter earlier in 1 Corinthians, Paul said something similar, but in that text we are tipped off to the bigger picture Paul has in mind:

> I wrote to you in my letter not to associate[14] with *sexually immoral people* — not at all meaning the people of this world who are [*sexually*] *immoral*, or the greedy and swindlers, or idolaters. In that case you would have to leave this world. But now I am writing to you that you must not associate with anyone who claims to be a brother or sister but is *sexually immoral* or greedy, an idolater or slanderer, a drunkard or swindler. Do not even eat with such people. (1 Corinthians 5:9 – 11)

That bigger picture is that 1 Corinthians 5 aims at all instances of sexual immorality, while 1 Corinthians 6 gives a concrete example, including same-sex relations. While it is possible Paul has faithful same-sex relations in mind (and we'll say more about that below), he is more likely speaking about the far more pervasive recreational same-sex relations. Paul's holiness mission, then, is to rescue notorious Roman sinners from the sinful life of the Roman world and to establish them in a life of sexual holiness among God's new people, the church. This could take time, and that theme is what our next chapter is about.

Importantly, Paul says in Romans 1 that same-sex relations are "unnatural" because they are against the divinely created order (compare Romans 1:26 – 27 and Genesis 1:26 – 27). In Romans 1 Paul evokes or quotes from Genesis 1 a number of times: notice the terms "creation of the world" (1:20) and "images" (1:23) and "created things rather than the Creator" (1:25). By speaking of "unnatural" or "natural," Paul refers to God's created order, including anatomical design: thus, men are designed by God for women as women are designed by God for men, and males fit with females as females with males.[15] Paul's language here about what is "natural" is as wide as it can get: he sees all same-sex sexual relations as outside the divine, created order and inconsistent with life "in Christ."

Paul speaks into and against the Roman world's sexual practices, and in this he establishes a fundamental vision for life "in Christ" or for life "in the church." Everyone in the fellowship is on a journey toward full redemption, including redemption of the body and sexuality. There is every reason to think Paul would welcome everyone who wanted to eat at the table and enter into communion with Christ, but there is also every reason to believe Paul would have emphasized that Christians were to abandon uninhibited and recreational sex outside marriage as well as sexual relations prohibited in the Bible. From Paul's letters, we read routine reminders of the need for sexual purity, which reveals not all were resisting the temptation to "act like a Roman." But as long as one was on the journey toward sexual redemption, Paul was encouraging. At the house churches they didn't put up a sign that said "For the Morally Kosher Only."

To sum this up: Paul was addressing the sexual immoralities of Romans in general, and he saw same-sex relations as an example of the sorts of things Roman males and females engaged in. His appeal was for the converts to come out from that kind of world into the world of faithful, monogamous, heterosexual relations or into the world of celibacy, even if they struggled to learn the way of holiness. One can argue that Paul's concern was not what is being discussed today — the appropriateness or inappropriateness of same-sex, faithful unions and marriages (see below). Yet even if that was not his central focus, his words in Romans 1 about "unnatural" apply to all same-sex sexual relations. There was no better news Paul had to offer his churches than the news of God's grace, love, forgiveness, and transforming Spirit at work among them and available for eating and drinking at the Eucharist. At the door of Paul's house churches the sign read "Welcome," but Paul's word for it was "Grace," as in God's transforming power unleashed through the Spirit.

FINDING A CHURCH-SHAPED SCRIPT

Some call the passages in the Bible I mentioned above the clobber passages, and in some ways they are right. If all we do is say, "The Bible says 'No!'" we have only part, the smaller part, of a message. I began this theme in the last chapter by looking at holiness, and we will move on to see that redemption is a process in the next chapter. But there's more within these two themes — we need a church-shaped script, which begins with this: we are called to love everyone. What this means, in light of our earlier chapters about love, now takes on new dimensions: we are called to a rugged commitment to all, including those who experience same-sex attraction. Because of how the church has historically treated those who experience same-sex attraction, we need to say a few more words directly.

If we are called to love one another, we are called to be "with" gays and lesbians (this means physical presence over time), and we are called to be "for" in the sense that these folks will know they are loved, and we are summoned to walk with gays and lesbians toward the kingdom of God and toward sexual holiness. Love does not mean "I will love you if you do what I want," or "We will accept you in our church if you live our way." That's not love; that's coercion. But neither does love mean toleration: you do what you want and I'll leave you alone, and I'll do what I want and you leave me alone. Love is a rugged commitment to someone, which involves presence, advocacy, and a companionship over time as we walk toward the kingdom of God — which means growing in holiness, love, and righteousness together.

There's much to be said about our own redemption in a church-shaped script, and I turn here to someone who knows better than I do. Nick Roen,[16] someone who has known only the experience of an exclusive same-sex attraction (SSA), exhorts our wonderful fellowship of differents to offer a holistic script:

> What the church needs is an alternative script. And it must be a holistic script that accounts for the real emotions and desires of those with SSA. We can't live a life of only saying, "No!" to our desires. We need to be able to say "Yes!" to something greater, something better.
>
> The most basic — and the most glorious — thing that I have said "Yes!" to is Jesus [what I called in the previous chapter "devotion"]....
> However, following Jesus does not make my yearnings for human intimacy and companionship magically disappear. What does Christianity have to say to those areas?

Nick contends this script involves a new self-identity: gays and lesbians are in the church, and they are not "them" but "us." As he puts it, "We belong in the Body just as much as any other sinner who trusts Jesus. The church must be a place where those wrestling with SSA feel welcome, included, and safe to work out our salvation in the Lord." He also urges us to develop a script that takes singleness seriously, and I find this to be one of the most important observations he makes. The church's basic "script" is for the married. Singleness, however, cannot be reduced to a stage people pass through; it too can be a calling. Perhaps more important, and this is true in my own experience in churches, it can also be a stage of lonely longing for the one who wants to be married.

Finally, Nick Roen calls us to a script that permits — and this is where the theme of this book comes to the fore — depth in community. In other words, he is calling us to a fellowship of differents — and one of those "differents" is those experiencing same-sex attraction. Here's how he puts it: "What if they heard not simply, 'Don't have that relationship!' but, 'You are welcome in the church, and ... we will seek to support you in your walk of faith with community, loving relationships, and hospitality'?" Maybe we could ask it this way: What happens to the "they" when they are one of "us"? In other words, when it becomes a relationship of with, for, and unto?

Holiness, yes. What the Bible teaches, yes. Redemption as a process, yes. But all in a community marked by the transparency of a loving commitment to one another and pursuing holiness together in a way we all flee sexual temptations.

THE CHURCH'S MOST RECENT CHALLENGE

I am of the view that Paul's strongest words about same-sex relations were most likely directed at married males carousing with boys, prostitutes, and slaves, even if Paul's terms "natural" and "unnatural" sweep across the entire spectrum of same-sex relations. What Paul does not raise, and what complicates the picture for those who experience same-sex attraction, is that research now shows that some of us only know same-sex attraction.

Most who emerge sexually as adolescents with same-sex attraction are shaken to the core, endure secrecies that haunt and often lead to anxiety and depression, long for heterosexual desires but cannot find them, pray to God for healing and transformation but rarely have their prayers answered, and are wounded daily by the insensitive remarks of Christian leaders intent on being as faithful to the Bible as possible.

A pastor who has a ministry to and with many who experience same-sex attraction told me over the phone that if the stories do not break your heart, you have no right to speak about the matter. What I am saying, then, is that those whom Paul had in mind — let's call them the Typical Roman Male — were not so much compelled by same-sex attraction as by sexual indulgence. The Typical Roman Male is not the same as the person who has always experienced same-sex attraction, and today we are talking far more often about the latter than the former. This is the church's most recent challenge.[17]

One of the best memoirs by a Christian who is both gay and celibate is that of Wesley Hill, who is now an evangelical New Testament professor at Trinity Episcopal School of Ministry. He has told his story in *Washed and Waiting*.[18] He knew from his own adolescence that he was gay; he never experienced desire or attraction to a woman; he prayed for transformation; he consulted with godly, loving friends and counselors; he once danced at a wedding with a beautiful woman but nothing was ignited in his system until, looking over her shoulder, he saw an attractive man dancing with another woman; and Wes has remained celibate — and at times very, very lonely. Painful loneliness. Carpet-soaked-with-tears kind of loneliness.

Three of Wesley's words describe the journey: struggle, loneliness, and shame. All along surrendering his heart and life to God, striving daily to be obedient, and taking up the cross of self-denial as a way of life. Yet, yet, yet ... he has not found that God has granted him a desire for heterosexual relations. As he puts it, "Since that time of self-discovery [in high school], I have struggled week in and week out to know how to live faithfully as a Christian."[19] Wesley Hill has more to tell us, but for now he stands as a noble example of the difficult, lonely journey of celibacy.

This is the church's most recent challenge; this is the story of Nick Roen in our previous section, Wes Hill, and countless others. What does the church do when all of its people want to be obedient and want to be transformed?

A THIRD WAY: TOWARD REDEMPTION

There was a flare-up on the internet among some Christian leaders making strong claims that there is no "third way." Listening to the stridency, one could think this has become a creedal test case issue on both sides. There are only two ways, both sides have announced loudly: a Strong For or a Strong Against. I'd like to propose that there is a Third Way, the way of redemption in the context of the fellowship of the church. That is, the Third Way focuses not on which view one holds to firmly but the divine end for each of us: holistic redemption. The Third Way knows salvation takes time. It knows that transformation is transformation *toward* redemption. It knows that it may wait until the kingdom for the kind of liberation redemption brings. The Third Way also believes the context for this redemption is the local fellowship, the church.

It is impossible to talk about sexual redemption without talking about salvation as a process, which we will discuss more in our next chapter. But before we turn to that theme, a few observations are appropriate. Paul, as well as we, undoubtedly knows some who are seemingly instantaneously transformed. But Paul's letters reveal that not all experience sudden sanctification. So let this be the standard posture we take in our local church: *Christians are in a process of transformation, all of us without exception.* Some are more mature in one area than in others, but *no one is perfect* — and that means we both desire mature Christian living and know maturity takes time.

Furthermore, it has been made clear by statistics that a low percentage of men and women who experience same-sex attraction are in for deep change. So many, like Wesley Hill, contend that they will need to be prepared to "wait" until the kingdom of God to discover complete redemption. Put more directly, redemption simply does not mean that even those who experience same-sex attraction will become "straight" prior to the kingdom of God.[20] Here are Wesley Hill's words about his own approach to waiting as a celibate Christian:

> My homosexuality, my exclusive attraction to other men, my grief over it and my repentance, my halting effort to live fittingly in the grace of Christ and the power of the Spirit — gradually I am learning not to view all of these things as confirmations of my rank corruption and hypocrisy. I am instead, slowly but surely, learning to view that journey — of struggle, failure, repentance, restoration, renewal in joy, and persevering, agonized obedience — as what it looks like for the Holy Spirit to be transforming me on the basis of Christ's cross and his Easter morning triumph over death....
>
> I am learning that my struggle to live faithfully before God in Christ with my homosexual orientation is pleasing to him. And I am waiting for the day when I will receive the divine accolade, when my labor of trust and hope and self-denial will be crowned with his praise.[21]

A pastor told me that the most common question he is asked by same-sex participants in church is, "What can we do in the church?" My operative principle is this: the last thing we want anyone to do is to leave the church. That same pastor also told me if everyone in their church was as engaged as the same-sex participants, they'd turn their city upside down! The second one is this: if we present Jesus and grace and holiness in our churches, then we want those who experience same-sex attraction to belong in order to become what God wants them to be. To be sure, for many leaders at the denominational and local level will have to struggle with answers to this question.

Perhaps we need to turn this question around to ask what we can learn from how the celibate, struggling, same-sex Christian is learning to live. Again, I have learned from Wesley Hill. Our theology leads us to believe that the kingdom has broken into this world already, that new creation is already underway, but that kingdom is not yet fully here. So we can expect transformation, growth, and change, but we cannot expect full redemption or perfection now. Wesley Hill calls same-sex attraction as a kind of "thorn in the flesh" and that from Paul we can learn that suffering ushers us into the suffering and cross of Christ. Listen to these golden questions of Hill:

> Could the suffering that goes along with being gay (for a Christian who is committed to celibacy) not be seen primarily as some result of the fall to be "prayed away" but rather as the occasion for finding one's identity in the cruciform story of Jesus? The cross of Christ, writes J. Louis Martyn, "is in one sense followed by the resurrection, [but] it is not replaced by the resurrection." The life of the new creation breaking into the present doesn't so much cancel out the suffering of the cross as it gives that suffering its true, redemptive meaning. Likewise, I wonder, isn't it legitimate for gay Christians to speak of their homosexuality not simply as their share of the world's fallenness but as their way of joining Jesus on the Calvary road — for the sake of sharing Jesus' life with others, for the sake of *love?*[22]

On top of his questions I ask this: What can we learn of the cruciform life in fellowship with those who experience and suffer from same-sex attraction? Our posture cannot be one of pity; it must be one of mutual fellowship in the cross and resurrection of Christ, the kind of fellowship where we minister to one another.

The two principles of the Third Way then are: the progressive nature of our own growth in redemption and the importance of the local church as the context for that growth. Let us remind ourselves that Jesus did not require someone to be kosher to eat at table with him. In fact, he created table fellowship for all sorts in that first fellowship of differents. If some said, you must be kosher to eat with us, Jesus said, eat with me and I will make you kosher. Furthermore, he expected those at the table to grow into holiness and love, but that came through fellowship. So too with the apostle Paul, whose house churches were filled with sinners in need of grace, which they found at the table that led them to Jesus. So too with our churches today: we invite all to the table and pray for God's Spirit to be unleashed for transformation, even if that transformation does not occur until the kingdom of God. We are washed, we are waiting, and in the meantime we are striving to be holy and loving.

What is perhaps most needed is for us to understand how Paul sees the Christian life as a journey through the meaning of the word *salvation*. For salvation is not something that happens once and for all — salvation is a process.

13

Salvation as Process

Every fall the church I grew up in had a revival, a weeklong set of evening services designed to get our neighbors saved. In order to do so, we first had to invite them to church, which took more pluck than I usually had. When they got to our church service, they encountered an enthusiastic church, sacred music ramped up to its best, and a revivalist or evangelist who could tell stories that would make your hair frizz and scare the be-jeezus out of you. To give folks plenty of time to respond to the evangelist's invitation, we often sang the famous Billy Graham song *Just As I Am*. At least once, we sang through all six verses twice.

I had a friend who sometimes went forward as soon as the music started because, knowing how long the invitation could last, he thought he'd be released from the service faster if he just went forward, cooperated with the counselor who led him through the Sinner's Prayer ("Lord Jesus, I am a sinner, I invite you into my heart ..." and so on), and then left through the back door. More than once, I held out only to find him already outside and laughing up a storm about how long it had taken the rest of us.

Sadly, those emotion-packed revival sermons have made me uncomfortable with the words *salvation* and *saved*, and I've spent much of my professional life trying to regain a love for them. The first thing that helped me appreciate the terms was learning — and I can't remember from whom — that salvation has three tenses in the New Testament. Biblical salvation is salvation times three.

> *Past:* We have been saved (Romans 8:24).
> *Present:* We are being saved (Philippians 2:12).
> *Future:* We will be saved (Romans 13:11).

Add these together and you come up with something vitally important for life in a fellowship of differents: *salvation is a process, not a one-time, one-and-done event.* It takes, one might say, a lifetime and beyond to get saved, but there is an idea behind all uses of the term *salvation* that turns it into a story.

SALVATION AS MINI-EXODUS

The first element is easy: the word *save* or *salvation* means to "rescue." In the Bible, the first and most important salvation event is the exodus,[1] and because it was so important, from that time on *every salvation event was seen as a mini-exodus leading God's people to liberation.*

Salvation is exodus. John the Baptist's dad saw his and his wife's salvation as everyone else in the Bible did: a mini-exodus rescue. Here are some of Zechariah's words from Luke 1:

> He has raised up a horn of *salvation* for us. (Luke 1:69)
> *Salvation* from our enemies [Rome]. (1:71)
> To *rescue* [exodus] us from the hand of our enemies [Rome]. (1:74)

Near the end of his life, the apostle Paul told Timothy that Jesus, the only mediator between God and humans, had given "himself as a ransom [the word used for rescue-for-liberation at the exodus] for all people" (1 Timothy 2:6). At the heart of the apostle's mission is God's mission to rescue both Gentiles and Jews, males and females, slaves and the free — and the mini-exodus, or personal-exodus, for each leads them into a kind of "promised land" called the church. The church is a fellowship of liberated differents, a community that has gone through a mini-exodus designed to liberate its people.

STORY OF A MINI-EXODUS

My favorite place on Planet Earth is Assisi, in the heart of Umbria in Italy. That great little man, St. Francis, lived there.[2] Here is the story of this influential, exemplary figure who was liberated from a kind of slavery to opulence and sensuality to a life of nothing less than joyous holiness. Francis, or Francesco, began life with a dainty silver spoon in his mouth. He was baptized in March of 1182 at the beautiful duomo of San Rufino in Assisi. His father, Pietro di Bernardone, was a wealthy businessman who traded often in France, so calling his son "Franky" or "Frenchy" set the young man on a path that only God would set straight.

At first, Francis was a refined and winsome salesman, the sensuous partier of the well-to-do of Assisi, a noted singer and joker, and one who dressed every bit the attention-seeking dandy. A military battle against neighboring Perugia in 1201 led to his capture and year-long imprisonment. His former nightlife gave way to suffering and depression, and the experience shook him so deeply that after his release, Francis could no longer live as he had lived. He broke free from his depression for a brief spell, contemplated returning to a military life, but saw the end of that kind of life and returned home determined to live a Christian life.

His friends found him listless for parties; his father found him lifeless for business. To deepen his newfound love for Christ, Francis spent hours in a small church, San Damiano, contemplating an image of the suffering Christ. He left home and began to live in this small chapel, much to his mother and father's consternation. Driven to rescue him from his madness, his parents sought to bring him home, but Francis could not go back on his newfound faith. He went into hiding, but then, in an extravagant gesture, came public in a way that frightened his parents so much they took him home and locked him up. Here's the story of his mini-exodus.

Francis' father became absorbed with the financial implications for his business if he were to die and business were to fall in part into the hands of his crazy son. So he sued his uncooperative, free son. The church and court systems were so connected that a bishop was also the judge, and he convinced Francis to renounce any claim to his family's business, which Francis did with glee. In an act of sheer liberation, he removed his clothes and laid them at the feet of his father. "From now on," he said, "'Our Father who art in heaven,' and not 'My father, Pietro di Bernardone.'"

The liberated Francis spent his time in the woods, singing, praying, praising, serving the poor, and pondering what God would have him do. Later stories tell of him being robbed in the woods around Assisi. When asked to identify himself, he replied, "Herald of the Great King." His compassion for the poor is synonymous with the brown robe of the Franciscans to this day. The words of his biographer, Augustine Thompson, put this best: "What before was ugly and repulsive now caused him delight and joy, not only spiritually, but also viscerally and physically.... The startled veteran sensed himself, by God's grace and no power of his own, remade into a different man."

Francis experienced at the personal level the biblical story of the exodus. The exodus took the children of Israel from Egypt to the Promised Land, and that leads to the questions, *What's our Egypt? What's our promised land?* But first questions first.

WHAT'S OUR EGYPT?

Jesus Christ is our own Passover sacrifice (1 Corinthians 5:7), which means that we who are in Christ have experienced an exodus from the Egypt of three things. First, we are saved *from systemic oppression.* Paul revises this exodus-from-Egypt theme into being rescued from cosmic principalities and powers. After close to two decades of traveling the Roman Empire, preaching the gospel and feeling the forces of evil in systemic opposition from high places and seeing that displayed in sexualities beyond description, Paul says this:

For our struggle is not against flesh and blood, but against the rulers, against the authorities, against the powers of this dark world and against the spiritual forces of evil in the heavenly realms. (Ephesians 6:12)

What does this look like for life in the church? We are to drive out, by the power of the Spirit, the Egypt of oppression, ethnic divisions, gender hierarchies, and the creation of other such boundaries, to name but a few. Then, from among us, we are to establish in the church a community painted with the colors of peace, love, justice, reconciliation, holiness, righteousness, and wisdom. For Paul, Egypt was the ways of the Romans, and the Promised Land, in part, is new life in the church.

Second, we are saved *from "Egypt's" cosmic, Satan-driven assault of death against us*. As Pharaoh wanted to put the children of Israel to death, so Satan's design is death from the moment we are born until the moment we die. In Christ, however, we are liberated from the Egypt of death. Paul sums this up when he writes to Timothy:

He has saved us and called us to a holy life — not because of anything we have done but because of his own purpose and grace. This grace was given us in Christ Jesus ... who has destroyed death and has brought life and immortality to light through the gospel. (2 Timothy 1:9 – 10)

The Bible's major enemy — from Genesis 3 on — is death. At the heart of our Egypt is death, and our Passover lamb, the one who died in our place and for our forgiveness, has liberated us from that death.

Finally, we are saved *from a life of sin*. Here is how Paul talks about our past life of sin (Titus 3:3 – 7), and I've italicized "Egypt" words and emboldened "exodus" words and, to anticipate the next section, underlined "Promised Land" words:

At one time we too were *foolish, disobedient, deceived and enslaved by all kinds of passions and pleasures. We lived in malice and envy, being hated and hating one another.* But when the kindness and love of God our Savior appeared, he **saved** us, not because of righteous things we had done, but because of his mercy. He **saved** us through the washing of rebirth and renewal by the Holy Spirit, <u>whom he poured out on us generously</u> through Jesus Christ our Savior, so that, having been **justified** by his grace, <u>we might become heirs having the hope of eternal life.</u>

As Israel left Egypt, and as St. Francis left his own Egypt, so we've left the Egypt of sin and systemic injustices by the power of our mighty deliverer, and we are headed for the Promised Land. God is on our side. Ringing in my ears is God's promise to the children of Israel: "The LORD will go before you, the God of Israel will be your rear guard" (Isaiah 52:12). God's mission was to rescue and to escort Israel safely home to the Promised Land.

ONE CHURCH'S STORY

One Sunday, at Cookman United Methodist Church, a man for some reason came forward to announce publicly that he was a new believer in Jesus Christ.[3] "I need help," he said. Then this man poured out his soul before the congregation about his past life and how he had been incarcerated for five years. He then began to weep. The worship leader put her hand on the man's shoulder and the minister, Rev. Donna Jones, came to his side to lead him to kneel at the altar. An elder anointed the former prisoner with oil. Then the worship leader, attentive to the church's responsibility to lead folks out of Egypt into the Promised Land, said, "The church is the place to get the kind of help you need" and to "love you to wholeness."

That is what Paul has in mind from the moment he began to talk about holiness and redemption in all ways, including the body, and about salvation as a process.

WHAT'S OUR PROMISED LAND?

As God liberated the Israelites from Egypt so they could live in the land as God's holy people, so God rescues us so we can live in a new kind of promised land. What is that? In brief, it is living a life of liberation in the church. Realize that it took the Israelites forty long years to get from Egypt to the Promised Land, and that is perhaps the parable we need — that redemption is a process over the journey of a life. The children of Israel didn't pass through the Red Sea to hear the Ten Commandments and then immediately achieve sanctification. That took time, and we are in that time right now, the time where new creation life begins to bubble up into us and into our church fellowship. That new life is the subject of our next section.

The revivalists sold us short at times in focusing so much on the past tense of salvation, that is, on rescue from Egypt, as well as the future tense, eternal life — but not enough on the present: kingdom life in the church. But we have seen salvation is a lifelong process — liberation from Egypt so we can live in the land God prepares for us. It is time for us to restore the beauty of the word *salvation* to the borders of the Bible's big vision, the way Francis restored beauty to broken-down chapels around Assisi. He made those chapels brand new.

PART 5

NEWNESS

14

A New Freedom

Freedom, like the Statue of Liberty in the middle of New York Harbor, stands up and greets us as we enter into the church and into a church-kind of Christian life. Some readers may have already raised a hand of protest before the period on that last sentence because they have experienced anything but freedom or liberation in the church. Others raised their hand the moment the word *freedom* appeared, because they're worried that this so-called freedom will lead to the ways of the Romans! So we've got some clearing to do before the wondrous freedom of the gospel can greet us on our way into the new body of Christ, the body where Jews and Gentiles, slaves and free, and males and females are tossed together into a fellowship of differents. Also, what one group — say the Jews — thinks is free, the Gentiles might think is slavery. So the differences multiply as soon as freedom becomes the church's new way of life.

Everything about this early-church life was new for everyone, including Paul. They were trying out a new kind of community under a new Lord with new people around them with all kinds of new ideas about how to live under the new Spirit with new assignments and new gifts and new morals. What God was doing was so full of promise, so altogether ... well ... new, which is why Paul said the following:

Therefore, if anyone is in Christ, the new creation has come: The old has gone, the new is here!

This line from 2 Corinthians 5:17 says that if we are "in Christ," no matter who we are or what we have done, it's all brand new. At the heart of this newness of the new creation is freedom.

Christian freedom is not shaped by major political documents of the Western world. Neither do we discover freedom in major thinkers. What the Bible means by freedom was not defined by Thomas Paine, the American advocate for liberty, or Jean Jacques Rousseau, the French thinker to follow him. Nor is it defined today by either the Tea Party or the Democrats. Even church leaders are not always reliable when it comes to freedom, for a Do's-that-focuses-mostly-on-the-Don'ts kind of church destroys freedom. But Paul wanted a new kind of freedom; that meant he raised the ire of plenty, though it was worth the fight to enter new territory.

PAUL'S MAGNA CARTA ONE-LINER

In the first letter Paul wrote that survives in the Bible, Galatians, Paul went toe-to-toe with a group he calls the "circumcision party," which ought to be self-explanatory (#ouch). The circumcision party claimed connection to the Lord's brother, James, and to the Jerusalem church, and they no doubt represented the pro-Torah group of Christians (#intimidating). After attempting to demolish the circumcision party's arguments for four chapters, Paul finally lands on his feet with something altogether practical for how to live. Here's the great line:

It is for freedom that Christ has set us free. (Galatians 5:1)

Only four words in the original Greek, but this single line about freedom is the most radical statement Paul ever made. I will lay down free coffee that there were four responses:

Strong Pro-Torah group: "Heretic! Dangerous! Toss da bum!"
Sensitive Pro-Torah group: "Free? From what? Clarify please! Paul's
always saying crazy, over-the-top stuff. He needs to be more
balanced. James is now our official apostle."
Sensitive No-Torah group: "Free? What about our Jewish believer
friends? Should we get them a ham sandwich? Paul certainly has
his moments."
Strong No-Torah group: "Paul, youdaman! Get me a beer and some
BBQ pork!"

The fact is that Paul uttered that great claim of freedom because he
meant it. Yes, a life of freedom means exploring new ideas and new ways
of living, which requires *discernment*. Discernment about how freedom
means fellowship, godliness, holiness, love, justice, wisdom, and peace,
and how it does not mean indulgence, greed, vindictiveness, and narcis-
sism. But it still remains freedom, and for many in the churches this kind
of freedom was brand new.

When my daughter was fresh into high school, I was working on a
commentary on Galatians, and I was totally tanked up on Paul's teaching about freedom and life in the Spirit (the two belong together). When
Laura was going out the back door on a Friday evening, she turned and
asked Kris and me, "What time should I be home?" I said immediately,
"When the Spirit leads you to come home. You are free." Kris looked at
me and then at the confused face on Laura, and then said clearly, "Eleven
o'clock." (As a parent of a teenage girl, I agreed with Kris that freedom
and life in the Spirit meant 11:00 p.m.!) After Laura closed the door, Kris
turned to me and said, "Why in the world did you say that?" Precisely,
I thought, as I turned to the apostle Paul and asked the same baffling
question.

Okay, she was too young in her faith to discern what time to come
home, but the ideal Christian life is not a life of "rules and regulations,"
but rather a life of irresistible, Spirit-shaped, new creation freedom to do
all God calls us to be. This new kind of freedom has two sides, just like

salvation's Egypt and the Promised Land: freedom involves a freedom *from* and a freedom *for*. Again, both are important, and we need to look at each.

A NEW FREEDOM FROM ...

Only those who are enslaved want to be liberated, which means we are driven by Paul's wonderful word *freedom* to see that we *were* prisoners (in our own Egypt). And if we were prisoners, we ask what are now free from.

New Freedom from Social Boundaries

The Roman Christians were prisoners to the Roman way of status and hierarchy where only equals were equals and most people were unequal. We need to hear this message about freedom in a Roman world where Paul was suddenly announcing — rebellious and revolutionary it may have sounded — that everyone in the church was now free. A Roman history scholar once told me Paul's words were "just plain irresponsible" and "were destined to get his churches in trouble." Paul was not about to worry what the Romans were thinking, nor did he care that some of the more kosher-oriented Jews thought he'd jumped the shark. He openly declared the age-old and biblically-rooted wall between Jews and Gentiles was torn down, and no verse says this more graphically than Ephesians 2:13 – 16:

> But now in Christ Jesus you who once were far away have been brought near by the blood of Christ. For he himself is our peace, who has made the two groups one and has destroyed the barrier, the dividing wall of hostility, by setting aside in his flesh the law with its commands and regulations. His purpose was to create in himself one new humanity out of the two, thus making peace, and in one body to reconcile both of them to God through the cross, by which he put to death their hostility.

Briefly, in Christ, Gentiles — those who were "far away" — and Jews are tossed together, with Christ as our "peace." Even more dramatically, the dividing wall in the temple that once divided Jews from Gentiles has been torn down. The Strong Pro-Torah party wanted Gentile believers in

Jesus to go all the way and get circumcised to show they were fully converted. Any honest Bible reader knows how important circumcision was to the Strong Pro-Torah group, so their concerns were understandable. But Paul, who had seen the freedom of the Promised Land, declared "No! No! No! We are all justified by *faith*. Gentiles do not need to add Torah to faith to be fully converted." Here's how Paul put it: "Neither circumcision nor uncircumcision means anything; what counts is the *new creation*" (Galatians 6:15). The guy had some nerve.

What Paul says here can easily be extended to what he says about slaves and free and men and women: those boundaries have also been knocked down. In Christ we are one, but the church is even more radical by calling us to knock down all social boundaries to create an equal fellowship of differents. Sadly, I repeat, churches today have raised the very walls that the cross of Jesus tore down, but we have to move on. We are also to see that we have a ...

New Freedom from Shackles to Sin and Death

The past life for those in the fellowship of differents was often a life of turmoil, and I want to put several words together, so be patient as we read these texts together. Paul said in Romans 6:18 that "you have been set free from [the prison of] *sin*." He expands the prison two chapters later when he writes "through Christ Jesus the law of the Spirit who gives life has set you free from the law of sin and *death*" (8:2). Sin leads to death because sin leads to *accusation*.

Three words: *sin*, *death*, and *accusation* — the accusing stare of the judge. In Ephesians 3:12, however, Paul writes, "In him [Christ] and through faith in him we may approach God *with freedom* and confidence." Again, in Colossians 1:22, he speaks about being "free from accusation." For prior to Christ we were shackled to sin, death, and God's accusation — but now in Christ we have freedom from all that. That's theology, and it helps to see it in action. To do so, I can think of no better story of this kind of turmoil and the freedom of Christ beyond it than the recent story of a favorite pastor of mine.

New Freedom Found: Greg Boyd and His Body

Greg Boyd is known for his honesty. Unlike so many leaders, he doesn't worry about shaking the boat. Boyd, in fact, seems to like shaking the boat to see if we can get stronger sea-legs for our faith. He came to faith out of a troubled background, including addiction to pornography, a story he tells about in his new book *Benefit of the Doubt*.[1] He was converted through a charismatic, Pentecostal-type church, where he both found a family and got confused theologically. After encountering intellectual challenges beyond his capacity at the time to answer, Boyd's faith began to fall apart and he walked away. After a Sunday night service Boyd unloaded to his friend Brett his fear, his doubt, his vulgarity, his inability to straight-arm his sinful habits, and his utter refusal to believe in God.

It was nothing less than a vulgar torrent of anger at God, self, the church, and anyone else in his path. He had struggled with porn and intellectual doubts, and nothing — not the Bible, not leaders, not friends, not the church — could provide the deep assurance he craved. His late-night rant went something like this:

> You [God] say you love me, but it's a f***ing lie — and you know it! *You know it!!*
>
> You don't love *me*! You don't really love *anyone*! What you love is your G*d-d***ed rules! Well guess what? I've never been able to keep your f***ing rules!...
>
> I never had a chance! I'm not the one who packed my body so full of hormones I can't handle it.... And I didn't choose to be born in a home with a dad who thinks porn is as normal as breathing!...
>
> So I'm going to go to hell while you enjoy the bliss of heaven.

And in one desperate profanity-laced last scream at God, Greg Boyd signs off:

> I tried. I *really* f***ing tried! You know I f***ing tried! But now I'm just f***ed.

But something happened then that has to be explained as a revelation from God. His buddy Brett began to talk to him, and they pondered what it was that they were missing in their addiction to porn and incapacity to find freedom and holiness. Boyd threw open his Bible and began to read, mocking the inability of the Bible and God to respond to his issues, but he came upon this verse: "Therefore, there is now no condemnation for them which are in Christ Jesus." To make a long discussion short, that text shone God's searching light of revelation on Boyd's soul. He confesses in admiration and wonder the discovery that he could never do enough, and that doing enough was not even what God wanted. What God wanted Boyd to see was his grace and love. In that verse from Romans Boyd saw it, and his response was this:

> "Unbelievable!" I exclaimed. "Brett, do you get that? *Do you get that?*" I began to laugh as I continued. "If the almighty God declares us to be righteous and free of condemnation, no one can argue with him!"... Why have I never seen this before?... It's beautiful! It's unbelievably fantastic! It's the best news imaginable!

What Boyd found was free grace, and that free grace set Boyd free from the sins that shackled his desires to sexual images. He confessed:

> God responded to my outburst by revealing to me, through my reading of Romans 8, that I am unconditionally loved, that I have absolute worth, and that I am absolutely secure in his love. *This* is what I, like everyone else, had been desperately hungry for all my life.

Boyd's body was being set free from sin unto God's holy will:

> The love of God ... began to permanently break the stronghold of pornography over my life. It's not that I had a 100 percent victory over this sin from this night on. But this experience broke the chains, making it possible for me to move in the direction of total freedom.

Greg tells a story of being enslaved to sin and being set free from sin unto a glorious new kind of freedom, which is exactly what Paul taught in all his churches.

A NEW FREEDOM UNTO ...

The new creation has arrived, creating freedom in a number of directions, including that we have ...

A New Freedom to be the New People of God

Too often we think of freedom only in personal terms (can you hear Roger Williams or Henry David Thoreau?), but for Paul, "freedom" was a church word. We have a new expanded family because we are set free unto the *new People of God*. This new People of God is *precisely what new creation is all about.*

This grand social experiment of God's was doing something unprecedented in the ancient world, so Paul is particularly happy when the Jerusalem leaders laid the right hand of fellowship on him and his mission. Those leaders' hands meant that Paul could march ahead expanding the people of God by gospeling the Gentiles (Galatians 2:9). For Paul, this hand of fellowship meant — at the daily and practical levels — creating space to *eat with Gentiles at a common table.* Why? Because if there is one people, there is one table! Christians have been set free to embrace all of God's children.

If I may, who are our table companions? Do you enjoy this fellowship of differents at your table?

A New Freedom for New Love for All

This new People of God required a new power if God's design for the church was to get off the ground, and that new power was *a new love for all.* We can return to the theme of the earlier sections on love, where we learned that love was central to Paul. At the bottom of the word *love* is the word *neighbor.* When I think of neighbor and the new freedom to love all, I think of Wayne Gordon, one of Chicago's finest pastors in the Lawndale neighborhood, a pastor who loves God and has learned to love his neighbors and his neighborhood. I have been to Lawndale in Chicago, and I have seen the marvelous ministries stirred up by God's Spirit in a responsive pastor and leaders and congregation. Whether one begins at the old building or the newer church gym or the state-of-the-art recreation center and medical facilities, wherever one begins, one is looking at a concrete response to one's neighbors. Wayne ended up writing a book called *Who Is My Neighbor? Lessons from a Man Left for Dead.* Here's how he answers that question in short chapters with one story of rescue from the slavery of Egypt into the Promised Land of freedom in the church. "Who is my neighbor?" Wayne asks — and here's how he answers:

> My neighbor is someone hurting, who needs help, who cannot help themselves, who appears on my path, who has been robbed, who is half dead, who is naked, who is unable to ask for help, of a different race, who is a stranger, who has been stripped, who is a foreign traveler, who has been beaten up, who might require me to take a risk, who can't walk, who looks horrible, who is of a different religion, who is destitute, who is a victim of injustice, who has been passed by, who can't say Thank You, who has been wounded, whom nobody wants to help, who is lonely, who will cost me some time, who is visible, who is a victim, who has been violated, who is vulnerable, who is a human being, who feels humiliated, who feels helpless, who is poor, who is someone I'm afraid to help, who is dangerous to help, who is discouraged, who might cost me money, who needs tender loving care, who feels defeated, and who is someone I am able to help.[2]

Who is *your* neighbor? What I have seen in churches who ask that question and are genuinely willing to answer it is nothing less than new creation freedom to go places never seen, to welcome people never embraced, and to create a thriving, challenging fellowship of differents, one exasperating sinner after another! By responding to that question — *Who is my neighbor?* — we will discover a whole new kind of community that is shaped by ...

A New Freedom with a New Constraint of Love

Freedom ran rampant among the house churches of Paul, so much so that he had to apply the brakes at times. Freedom and love for all did not mean they could do whatever they wanted. Freedom does not mean moral chaos, nor does it mean trampling on another's ethnic identity or cultural heritage. "But do not use your freedom to indulge the flesh," Paul says in Galatians 5:13. But that statement becomes concrete when Paul goes to the mat with the Corinthians. Quoting someone who said, "I have the right to do anything," Paul responds with, "But not everything is beneficial." They retort, "I have the right to do anything," and Paul says right back, "But I will not be mastered by anything." They say, "Food for the stomach and the stomach for food, and God will destroy them both." In other words, *what difference does it make?* Paul replies, "The body, however, is not meant for sexual immorality but for the Lord, and the Lord for the body" (1 Corinthians 6:12 – 13). To be sure, we are free. But this does not mean we can do what we want. Liberty is not license. *No, in fact, Christian liberty is constrained by love.*

Our discussion of the meaning of love helps here. Love both guides us and constrains us. If we are committed to be with others and to be for others in such a way that we grow *unto* Christlikeness, *we will not live in a way that destroys the faith development of our brothers and sisters.* Love sets us free and at the same time constrains us within love, unleashing the ultimate future for us to enter into ...

A New Freedom for the New-Creation Resurrection Life

We are free unto *a new-creation eternal life.* Here is perhaps the best news of all. Resurrection life has been unleashed in the here and now, and that new creation life guides us toward full redemption in the kingdom. This is the secret to learning to live with others in the church. We see surrounding us some folks who are hard to love, and we see others who find us hard to love. We find some undeveloped characters and some poorly formed brothers and sisters. We see, as Paul did, both males and females whose sexual lives fall short of God's design. But this is where we make one of the most important decisions we can make when it comes to learning to live the Christian life in the context of life in the church: we are always tempted to shove the unclean out the door, but there's something in Paul's grand vision that prevents the temptation to ban others from our fellowship. If redemption is not complete until the kingdom, we will learn that we don't love others *for who they are now* but *for what God will make them in the kingdom.*

You can read this in Romans 8:18 – 39, but I will quote a few lines that show that our full freedom is yet to come:

> But we ourselves, who have the firstfruits of the Spirit, groan inwardly *as we wait eagerly for our adoption to sonship, the redemption of our bodies.* (Romans 8:23)

Surrounding us in the church are folks in whom God is at work and in whom God is doing a mighty work of redemption, but those same folks are not as free as they'd like to be. Whether we think of folks in Paul's house church, some of whom were slaves and abused by their master, or folks like Greg Boyd in the story above, all around us are the signs of God's freedom breaking in, giving us glimpses of the full freedom that is to come.

15

A New Faithfulness

What about those WWJD (What would Jesus do?) bracelets? In the U.S., this moral question about what Jesus would do in any given situation owes its origins to Charles Sheldon, whose life straddled the turn of the twentieth century.[1] Born on the East Coast in 1857, Sheldon moved with his family to the plains of the Midwest, where he learned the values of a life shaped by hard work, sacrifice, and the Christian faith from a dedicated Christian family steered by his father, Stewart, a Congregationalist pastor. He returned to the East Coast for an education at the esteemed Phillips Academy and Andover Seminary, where he became committed to what he called "untheological Christianity." That is, he came to the deep conviction that Christianity ought to result in a transformed life of love, justice, compassion, and equality. He remained an orthodox believer his entire life, but his focus was not on theological Christianity, but rather living the Christian life and encouraging others to do the same. Anything in the head that didn't shape feet and hands was of little interest to Sheldon.

As a young pastor at Central Congregational Church in Topeka, Kansas, Sheldon tried a number of new strategies to revive his flock, including spending one week of his daytime hours with each family in his congregation. His first breakthrough occurred through his experiences of living as a homeless man for a week to understand the realities facing those who were homeless and jobless. As a result, he decided that the Christian life was about following Jesus faithfully. The second breakthrough came when he wanted to enliven Sunday evening services by writing and then reading his own novels about the Christian life — and for thirty years his Sunday evening service was full.

The most famous of his novels, *In His Steps*, has become a Christian classic and has sold more than twenty million copies. *In His Steps* tells the story of a man who asked one simple question: "What would Jesus do?" Hence, WWJD. One of his best lines ever is this one: "It is, indeed, easier to give assent to the Westminster Confession than to love one's enemies."

What is perhaps the most important detail of his life is not his famous novel or even his simple question. What is most powerful is that Sheldon lived his conduct-creed his entire life. The man behind the pulpit, the man in the home, the man who sought to apply that question to the newspaper industry by editing a newspaper, the man who worked for freed slaves suffering in the Tennesseetown settlement in Topeka, the man who created a kindergarten at his church because he believed society would not change unless morality was anchored in faith, the man who tirelessly fought for prohibition, the man who at one time was writing seventy-five to a hundred personal letters per week to members of his church, and the man who relentlessly worked to create a church that broke down ethnic, economic, and racial barriers — that same man, day and night, decade after decade was Charles Sheldon. A poor (largely invisible) Christian black man once announced to Sheldon, "Brother Sheldon, your face may be white, but your heart is just as black as mine!"

Sheldon's faithful life illustrates new-creation faithfulness in the Christian life.

FAITHFULNESS: WHAT IS IT?

Look at the word itself. Faith*fulness* is a species of *faith*. In fact, the English word *faithfulness* in our Bibles is actually the word *faith* in Greek. Experts in translating this term seek to discern from the context in each case whether the word means "faith" or "faithfulness." For instance, in Galatians 5:22 Paul says one of the fruits of the Spirit is "faith" — or is it "faithfulness"? Sometimes we can't even tell. So we begin here: faithfulness is a species of faith.

Now look at the word again. Since faith means to *trust*, faithfulness means *trust over time* or *faith over time*. And since the term refers to trust over time, faithfulness can't be measured in the morning of faith, but only in the evening of a life. In what is perhaps the last letter Paul wrote we read these words: "I have fought the good fight, I have finished the race, I have kept the faith" (2 Timothy 4:7). Paul's life was one of "fight-fulness" and "finish-fulness" and "faith-fulness."

THE CHURCH NEEDS FAITHFUL FOLKS, NOT HEROES

What the church most needs is not heroes of faith, but faithful followers of Jesus. What your local church needs in order to live out the design of God for a church, that grand social experiment of bringing all sorts of people to the table and into the circle of one another's lives, is not great Christians, but faithful Christians.

Consider Randy Harris,[2] a servant professor at Abilene Christian University who focuses on discipling young men who need to see how to follow Jesus. Randy's vision is for a group of faithful young Christians to commit themselves — take a pledge in fact — to "do what Jesus says" in the Sermon on the Mount. First to read it and commit it to memory, and then to "live Jesus." He calls this group of Jesus followers the *Allelon Community* (the word *allelon* comes from the Greek word for "one another"). This is a group of people committed to follow Jesus with one another. Here's the point I'm making: you probably don't know Randy, but those around him certainly do (and I consider it a privilege to know him) — and what we know is the desire and struggle he demonstrates to live faithfully. We need more Randy Harrises in the church and not so many ... well, you can fill in the hero's name.

How can we be faithful? What can we do? Paul faced this question himself, expressing the joy of faithfulness in the evening of his life, but he saw the issue arise often in his churches. There are at least four themes for us to consider, and we begin exactly where Paul always begins — with God's grace at work in us.

WE HAVE GOD'S NEW CREATION POWER FOR FAITHFULNESS

God's grace locates us "in Christ," and God's grace is powerful enough to keep us there, but this new creation grace also creates faithfulness. Paul never wavered from the conviction that faithfulness happens by the power of God's gracious work in us:

> So then, brothers and sisters, *stand firm* (= faithfulness) and *hold fast* (= faithfulness) to the teachings we passed on to you, whether by word of mouth or by letter.
>
> May our Lord Jesus Christ himself and God our Father, who loved us and by his grace gave us eternal encouragement and good hope, encourage your hearts [= grace] *and strengthen you* [= grace] *in every good deed and word* [= faithfulness]. (2 Thessalonians 2:15 – 17)

Faithfulness is not our own strength muscled up by determination and discipline and grit; nor is it our strength combined with God's strength. Faithfulness happens when God's strength is unleashed in us as we look to, lean on, and love God.

So today, if you are discouraged about faithfulness, if you wonder if you've got what it takes, if you are wondering if the struggle with all these odd-shaped Christians in the church is worth it, if you are wondering if you can hang on, or if you are worried you could become like some of whom you have heard who checked out early, the message of Paul is *"You can't!"* Nor do you have to. The message of Paul is also, *"You can!"* Well, not so much "You can," as *"God* can, and *God* will!"

A friend of mine, Pastor Derwin Gray, wrote an experience-filled book called *Limitless Life* with a subtitle that says it all: *You Are More Than Your Past When God Holds Your Future*.[3] The theme of this book is that God's power is unleashed in us as new creation faithfulness.

WE NEED TO COMMIT OURSELVES TO FAITHFULNESS

I introduced 2 Thessalonians 2:15, in which Paul commands his readers to "stand firm and hold fast." But he can command faithfulness only because he knows about the daily commitment as a lifelong commitment — a radical commitment: "For to me, to live is Christ and to die is gain" (Philippians 1:21). I cannot imagine the apostle Paul's day beginning without imagining a prayer of commitment on his part.

A morning devotional prayer of commitment is wise because we are given the opportunity to remind ourselves of what matters most. For years I have prayed this prayer almost daily (it comes from *The Book of Common Prayer*):

> Lord God, Almighty and everlasting Father:
> You have brought me in safety to this new day. Preserve me with your mighty power, that I may not fall into sin, nor be overcome by adversity; and in all I do direct me to the fulfilling of your purpose.
> Through Jesus Christ my Lord. Amen.

The Celtic Book of Prayer, in its Morning Prayer, also directs our whole attention and life to a commitment to Christ:

> **Canticle**
> Christ, as a light
> illumine and guide me.
> Christ, as a shield
> overshadow me.
> Christ under me;
> Christ over me;
> Christ beside me
> on my left and my right.

This day be within and without me,
lowly and meek, yet all-powerful.
Be in the heart of each to whom I speak;
in the mouth of each who speaks unto me.
This day be within and without me,
lowly and meek, yet all-powerful.
Christ as a light;
Christ as a shield;
Christ beside me
on my left and my right.

Some are put off by recited prayers, and perhaps you are. I have for more than a decade started my day with a prayer of commitment, the Jesus Creed: "'Hear, O Israel: the Lord our God, the Lord is one. Love the Lord your God with all your heart and with all your soul and with all your mind and with all your strength.' The second is this: 'Love your neighbor as yourself.' There is no commandment greater than these" (Mark 12:29 – 31). This prayer of commitment reminds me that my two major obligations for the day are to love God and to love others. I recite this daily, and often many times throughout the day (because I need it).

Reading these prayers of commitment can perhaps encourage you to face Christ as you face each day. Faithfulness is not like the flu bug that you get because you happen to be in the wrong place at the wrong time, nor is it like winning the lottery where you happen to be in the right place at the right time. Faithfulness is the result of a lifetime of daily commitments, of what Eugene Peterson calls a "long obedience in the same direction,"[4] or, in the case of Charles Sheldon, a lifetime of asking a simple question — "What would Jesus do?" — and daily answering the question as Sheldon himself did, by responding with other Christians in his local community.

WE CAN BE FAITHFUL AND ORDINARY

When I was a child, an average student in my classes got a C for typical work. Most students got lots of C's. That's what "C" meant: average. After all, most people are average. Someone told me that a study was done of a recently graduated high school class, in which 90 percent thought they were above average. At least they've got great confidence. Grade inflation, shaped as it is by the desire to develop the ego strength of young adults, means average students now get B's. Today, "Excellent" (A) and "Above Average" (B) now mean "Good" and (almost as) "Good." But here are the facts: most of us are average because that's how the numbers work. In Christ, however, we learn about a new kind of faithfulness: ordinary is okay.

Most of us are ordinary Christians, and it's okay to be an ordinary Christian. The apostle Paul wanted ordinary Christians to do ordinary things the way the ordinary Christian life worked. Here's how Paul fashioned the life of the Thessalonian Christian:

> Yet we urge you, brothers and sisters, to do so [love all of God's family] more and more, and to make it your ambition to lead a quiet life: You should mind your own business and work with your hands, just as we told you, so that your daily life may win the respect of outsiders and so that you will not be dependent on anybody. (1 Thessalonians 4:10 – 12)

The ordinary Thessalonian follower of Jesus got up, said his or her prayers, maybe ate some breakfast, went to work (which may well have been farming at home or near the home), did his or her job well, took a couple hour oasis in the middle of the day in the heat, went back to work a bit, and came home to celebrate life in the joy of the Lord with his or her family in the context of that fellowship of Jews and Gentiles called the church.

FAITHFUL CAN BEGIN NOW, REGARDLESS OF THE SEASON IN LIFE

Ivan was born in Santa Isabel, Puerto Rico. Before the divorce of his father and mother, Ivan's family moved to Chicago. There, his mother struggled with financial assistance to raise four young males. The family was surrounded by gangs and drugs and experienced a number of home burglaries. His mother was, according to Ivan, "not much of a follower of Christ," but she permitted Ivan to participate in various youth groups at churches.

Decades later and not far from retirement, with children of his own, Ivan and his wife were at O'Hare Airport in Chicago on 9/11 when their flight was cancelled, so they drove to Fort Benning in Georgia to celebrate their son's graduation from basic training. "The tragedy," Ivan said about 9/11, "brought forth a sense of fear in my life. I hardly ever went to church and suddenly felt a spiritual need in my life. I started reading the Bible and began praying regularly. I developed an inner hunger to know more about God and about salvation.... I was simply a Christian by name."

Ivan's quest for resolution to his hunger to know God and God's grace and to enter into the power of the raised and ruling King Jesus led him and his wife to search for a "Bible-based church," which they found. "Soon thereafter I accepted Jesus Christ as my personal Savior," he said. Ivan was a seminary student at Northern Seminary, preparing to serve Jesus for the rest of his (ordinary) life. "Being Christian," he observes, "is a 24/7 commitment to Christ. Serving the Lord is not meant only within the four walls of a sanctuary but out in the real world."

Far too many Christians think the heroic is the norm. If the apostles Paul and Peter lived the heroic Christian life, the vast majority — 99.99 percent — didn't and don't. We live ordinary lives, and faithfulness is about learning that being ordinary is okay. The ordinary Christian life of the ordinary Christian is faithfulness. How does it happen? God's grace. One more line from Paul, from Philippians 4:13:

> I can do all this through him who gives me strength.

In the evening of life, I want God to say of me that I was an ordinary person who lived an ordinary Christian life empowered by the extraordinary grace of God my whole life long, just like Charles Sheldon and Ivan. How about you?

16

A New Guidance

In our home, I'm more spontaneous and Kris is more routine. It is not uncommon for me to call Kris in the morning and say, for instance, "Let's go to the Cubs game tonight." Kris will say back, "Scot, you're teaching a class at the church tonight." Routine people know schedules, while spontaneous people forget. I have over time come to value, more than I could ever have expected, routines and how once we find our schedule's sweet spot we can be both more tranquil and productive.

But one time Kris came home from work and said, "Let's go up to Lake Geneva tomorrow." She knew what went through my head before I said a word.

"Holy mackerel, where'd that crazy fun idea come from?" I said.

To which Kris said, "Pretty spontaneous of me, isn't it?!" We've learned that spontaneity can spice up the routine a bit, and routine can contain the spontaneity for a flourishing life.

Churches are of two kinds too. Not to be blunt, but charismatics and Pentecostals love, love, *love* spontaneity. (Surely you've noticed.) Some charismatic types don't even print out an order for worship on Sunday morning, while other churches write one, but they use pencil. Their motto: "This is where we are headed, but the Spirit may prompt us in another direction."

A friend was speaking at a charismatic church one day, and they got carried away during their worship time, leaving him with only ten minutes for his thirty-minute sermon. "Never mind," the worship leader informed him while sitting in the front row. "We also don't have a designated time to end our services. Go as long as the Spirit leads." Precisely the advice I tried to give my daughter Laura regarding her curfew!

At the other end of the spectrum, again to be direct, is the Anglican Church, which uses world without end *The Book of Common Prayer* (with sixteenth-century origins and some sixteenth-century prayers, majestic as sixteenth-century English can be). Any worship manual ratified by the government in something called "The Uniformity Act 1549" is likely to stabilize routine. An Anglican service is predictable, sometimes to the minute.

This spontaneous professor and author happens to love Anglican worship. The prayers are the same prayers they've always said, repeated in a cycle every year. The order of worship has the same elements every week, and all that varies are the announcements and the Scripture readings and the homily, a short version of what the charismatics call a "sermon" or "teaching time." That homily usually is derived from a text in the lectionary, not from something the preacher chooses. Evidently the Spirit's leading has already suggested the service is to finish at 11:30 o'clock sharp, maybe a little earlier but never after. I'm referring here to our church, Church of the Redeemer, led by our pastors, Jay Greener and Amanda Holm Rosengren.

A charismatic Anglican confuses all of us. I would like to suggest that Paul was a charismatic Anglican, who was a mix of routine and spontaneity, the former irritating the latter and the latter irritating the former. Welcome to the church of all sorts. Learning to make decisions with one another — guidance in other words — gets to the heart of what it means to be a church. Once again, Paul points the way.

PAUL AND HIS PLANS

Imagine you are in Corinth, and imagine you are an Anglican type gathered in Fortunatus's house church fellowship, when someone brings in

Paul's first letter to the church. Someone stands to read the whole thing. All kinds of problems are addressed and Paul's got reasons for everything he says, so it will be a long evening before it is time to go home. Finally we get to the last chapter (though there were no chapters in the original letter), and he starts out talking about the "collection for the Lord's people." Then he gets personal by talking about his travel plans: he's in Ephesus, thinking about getting to Corinth and then on to Macedonia and back to Corinth and then on to Jerusalem. By the time he's done, you have no idea if he'll get here or not, and — if he does — when that might be. Here are his words, and I've put his spontaneity in italics:

> Then, when I arrive, I will give letters of introduction to the men you approve and send them with your gift to Jerusalem. *If it seems advisable for me to go also*, they will accompany me.
>
> After I go through Macedonia, I will come to you — for I will be going through Macedonia. *Perhaps I will stay with you for a while, or even spend the winter*, so that you can help me on my journey, *wherever I go*. For I do not want to see you now and *make only a passing visit; I hope to spend some time with you, if the Lord permits*. But I will stay on at Ephesus until Pentecost, because a great door for effective work has opened to me, and there are many who oppose me. (1 Corinthians 16:3 – 9)

Stuff happened in Corinth — Chicago-politics-kind-of-stuff — so Paul wrote a second letter. The first chapter of that letter suggests the Corinthians thought Paul was unreliable, too spontaneous, living too much charismatic and not enough Anglican:

> Because I was confident of this, *I wanted to visit you first* so that you might benefit twice. *I wanted to visit you on my way to Macedonia and to come back to you from Macedonia, and then to have you send me on my way to Judea. Was I fickle when I intended to do this? Or do I make my plans in a worldly manner so that in the same breath I say both "Yes, yes" and "No, no"?* (2 Corinthians 1:15 – 17)

Evidently what Paul told them about his plans didn't work out, so he told them that was what he "wanted" to do. They must have been saying he was "fickle" and that he was "worldly" in how he made plans. That is, he would tell someone yes and it turned out no, or no and it turned out yes. Then he did what a million Christians have done — he gives God credit for his change of plans:

> I call God as my witness — and I stake my life on it — that it was in order to spare you that I did not return to Corinth. (2 Corinthians 1:23)

I've taken the side of the Anglicans at Corinth so far, but it's time to explain why and how Paul made his plans, the phenomenon called "Paul" or what we might call now a "charismatic Anglican." There were three guiding lights in Paul's life and mission, and these guiding lights can still guide local churches today.

In our local church, Church of the Redeemer, we make decisions about all sorts of things, but getting everyone on the same page requires listening to all sorts of people. Theologically, we've got Reformed and straight Anglican and Anabaptist and charismatic and not-so-keen-on-theology sorts, and we've got Africans and African Americans and Koreans and typical American Caucasians. We've got men and women and young and old(er), we've got marrieds and a good number of singles, and we've got husbands and wives and lots of little kids who make funny sounds when we sing. We've got career folks and students, artists, salesmen and executives, sound system analysts, and pastors. I could go on, but you see that a variety of interests and orientations are at work in our decision-making. How does a church of mixed-up sorts discern the will of God? (Carefully, obviously.) Paul points to some principles for new creation guidance, and while this applies to each of us as individuals, I'm thinking mostly about Paul and his churches, and how those churches needed guidance.

CHURCHES NEED TO BE SCRIPTURE-LED

Paul had some guiding lights in his life, the most important being faithfulness to the covenant that God established with Israel and God's new mission for him. Which is to say he was guided by the story of God and God's people, or to use our words, the Bible. In fact, it was because the apostle Paul was so soaked and saturated by that story that he could hear God when God began to expand the people of God into the Roman Empire.

Guidance begins with Scripture, or it will wander astray. How so? Some claim to hear God in such things as inner promptings or feelings of peace, or through prophetic utterances or the counsel of friends. Yet what they hear sometimes counters clear principles of God's Word, which means they are not hearing the God of this grand story. So we are quick to call our attention to the necessity of grounding all guidance in Scripture. This is where we begin, but it's not as simple as "just believe the Bible."

My friend David Fitch, a pastor-professor, tells a story about how his church discerned guidance on the basis of Scripture:

> One night a man in our church asked to speak with the pastors about his concerns with the direction of the church toward accepting women in pastoral ministry. Steve explained he was struggling with what had been going on. Two years earlier, our church had spent nine months reading Scripture together, listening to all sides of the issue and submitting to one another's gifts in order to discern how God was leading us in regard to calling women into pastoral ministry. We ended this time with a two-month-long church council to decide the issue for our congregation.... Steve was still not satisfied. For him, Scripture was clear, and it should be followed. Discerning the kingdom of God with the people of God guided by the Spirit of God is not what Steve wanted. He just wanted the "authority" of the Bible. Not finding it, he left.[1]

When faced with such issues, it is a temptation for many to call in an expert or rely on a professional, who often happens to be the "CEO pastor" of the church. But local churches are often driven to their knees on issues that for them — or at least for many in that church — are not clear.

CHURCHES NEED TO BE SPIRIT-LED

On his way to Jerusalem, Paul made a brief stop in Ephesus and created some theological controversy in the synagogue. Some wanted him to continue the discussion, but Paul said, "I will come back." That's firm. But Paul made his plans conditional: "if it is God's will" (Acts 18:21). He told the Corinthians the same thing: "I will come to you very soon." Again, that's firm, but again he had a chaser: "if the Lord is willing" (1 Corinthians 4:19). Paul made plans, but his plans could be rerouted if the Lord had other plans for him.

Think about Acts 16:6 – 10 where Paul looks like someone at the eye doctor trying on an assortment of frames — first this option, then another:

[1] Paul and his companions traveled throughout the region of Phrygia and Galatia, having been kept *by the Holy Spirit* from preaching the word in the province of Asia.

[2] When they came to the border of Mysia, they tried to enter Bithynia, but *the Spirit of Jesus* would not allow them to.

[3] During the night, Paul had a vision of a man of Macedonia standing and begging him, "Come over to Macedonia and help us." After Paul had seen the vision, they got ready at once to leave for Macedonia, concluding that God had called them to preach the gospel to the Macedonians.

We'd like to know about a dozen more facts, such as how in the world he knew it was the Spirit, but two things are clear: guidance in Paul's missionary work was shaped by the Spirit and by spiritual visions. In the first two paragraphs, Paul's good plan was blocked by the Spirit because the Spirit had other plans. The "man from Macedonia" appears to Paul in a spiritual vision to announce God has plans for him in other places. This is Spirit-led mission.

There are a few ways to respond to this apparently-hearing-God-speak kind of guidance. We can chalk it up to the bizarre and move on to rational, pragmatic approaches to decisions. (Charismatics get irritated when Christian guidance is taken from the latest research on decision-making.) Or we could assign Paul to the now-bygone era of the apostles when God was still whispering aloud to people. Or we could say this is how God always leads. Or we can do what we ought to do when it comes to the new freedom God has unleashed in the church: *let God guide this way if God wants to guide this way.*

Of course, the routine-oriented Anglican folks among us get nervous about Paul's seemingly disorderly approach, while the spontaneous sorts get electrified about how Spirit-led he was. But before we begin assigning this stuff to personality type, I want to ask you four questions that force us to ask if we really do believe God still speaks:

Is the Spirit still at work? Yes or No?
Are we listening to the Spirit? Yes or No?
What is the Spirit saying? Be honest.
Do you fear the Spirit's guidance? (I could have started here.)

Yes, there are some Christians today who are doubly nervous about someone who says God spoke to them — they are nervous about what that person hears and may do as a result, and they are nervous in part because God doesn't speak like that to them.

No one has been more forthright that God still speaks to us than Dallas Willard.[2] Here's where it all begins: God is, and God created us for himself. God has spoken to us in his Word, which means God is a speaking God. There's no way Bible readers can think God suddenly goes silent once Paul's wrapped up his mission. God also summons us to speak to him in prayer and meditation. So here's the question: Can we possibly believe God speaks to us and also that God asks us to respond in prayer and *then not think God speaks back?* Dallas Willard's term perfectly captures our relationship with God when he says we have an "interactive" relationship. Just in case you doubt that, read this hair-raising story.

GOD STILL SPEAKS

In Cairo, Egypt, a follower of Jesus named Hassan[3] was awakened "to a rough hand firmly clamped over his mouth" and a gun muzzle pressed against his temple. "Don't say a word … Get up, and come with me." The kidnapper, an imam, shoved him through the old streets of Cairo as Hassan began to think that "despite his best efforts to evangelize quietly, one convert at a time, Cairo's established religious authorities had found him out." He knew if anyone saw him being rounded up by an imam, they would think he deserved death. Soon the imam said to Hassan, "Up the stairs." Five stories later, the imam told him he would have to jump over to the roof of the building next to them. Hassan knew it was too far and protested. The imam said, "Get a running start." His death seemed inevitable; it was either a bullet or a fifty-foot fall. He jumped and made it to the roof. Immediately, next to him the imam landed as well.

The "assailant seized Hassan's right arm again and forced him toward a hatchway in the abandoned warehouse." Hassan gave himself to Jesus, knowing his end was imminent. Hassan stepped into a room lit by a candle. Ten Muslim men were waiting. The kidnapper then said, "We are imams, and we all studied at Al-Azhar University [a prestigious university for imams]." Then came the startling twist for Hassan. "During our time there," the imam said, "each of us had a dream about Jesus, and each of us has privately become a follower of Christ.... We each prayed to Jesus for His help.... Over time, He brought us together.... Now we meet here three times a week at night to pray for our families and for the people in our mosques to find Jesus too. We know you follow Christ. He led us to you."

Here were their next words: "Will you teach us the Bible?" (That's a spine-tingler for me.)

God still leads, and sometimes in the most amazing of ways: Hassan and Paul, imam men in Cairo and the man from Macedonia. Visions of Jesus like and unlike this are not uncommon among Muslim converts. Tom Doyle summarizes them this way: "Each one [having such a vision] recounted a powerful, gentle Person who overwhelmed him or her, not with unendurable shame as the Muslim leaders did, but with a pure love that reached deep inside." As I read this collection of dramatic stories, what struck me was how often the encounter with Jesus came with a mission, not unlike the experience of Paul with the man from Macedonia. Guidance for Paul was Spirit-led, even if it meant sudden changes in his plans.

CHURCHES NEED TO BE MISSION-LED

Yes, the Corinthians got irritated with Paul, but Paul would counter with the bold claim that the Spirit was leading him. Paul also countered with the claim that all his decisions were shaped by God's church-mission to expand the people of God into the Roman Empire. Scripture, God working through his Spirit, and the mission — these were Paul's guiding principles, and they need to top the list as churches make decisions.

Paul's guidance on the basis of mission gurgles out in 1 Corinthians 9:19 – 23, where the italicized words show that Paul's decisions were mission-led:

> Though I am free and belong to no one, I have made myself a slave to everyone, *to win as many as possible.*
> To the Jews I became like a Jew, *to win the Jews.*
> To those under the law I became like one under the law (though I myself am not under the law), *so as to win those under the law.*
> To those not having the law I became like one not having the law (though I am not free from God's law but am under Christ's law), *so as to win those not having the law.*
> To the weak I became weak, *to win the weak.*

Then he converts these details in a grand principle of stunning, freedom-shaped, new-creation guidance:

> I have become all things to all people so that by all possible means I might save some. I do all this for the sake of the gospel, that I may share in its blessings.

Some see here evidence that Paul was a chameleon. On the contrary, I say! Mission shaped everything Paul did. Now imagine you are Jewish; in fact, a messianic Jew who follows Torah. What would you think of Paul's words "to those not having the law I became like one not having the law"? Would you mutter to yourself, "Paul, don't tell me you are eating pork with Gentiles and eating kosher with Jews." (Don't tell me you wouldn't have thought that.) To which Paul would say, "Whatever I do is to win others to Christ." From the first to the last breath of each day, Paul breathed Scripture-shaped, Spirit-directed mission air. His mission was to get Gentiles in the church at table with Jewish believers in the grand experiment of a cross-cultural, multiracial, multi-status, and dual-gendered body of Christ. That's what mattered to Paul, and there's enough passion here to make the charismatics happy and enough constrained order to do the same for the Anglicans.

At dinner with a pastor and the staff on the evening before I was to speak at their church, the pastor began to talk about how mission guidance had created tension in the church. The older folks had built the church in the 1940s and 1950s, and they had been faithful and loving and supporting all along. No problems there, except time had changed the landscape. Downtown no longer housed their sorts, and those who were housed downtown were, as the pastor said it, "different." The challenge was either to close up shop, build a new church in the suburbs where many of the members lived, or do what Paul did and *let the mission guide the church*. They did the latter, a bundle of folks left, and ... well, time has shown that Paul's way of guidance is not just for apostles.

Yes, the church today is a fellowship of differents, including the dear lady on the front row and a couple who seemed dressed up for Halloween (but, no, that's their style). By the time I got in my car and drove to the airport, I thought I was back in one of Paul's house churches experiencing the challenges of a fellowship of differents. When mission guides, who knows who might show up to church on Sunday!

CHURCHES NEED TO BE ORDINARY-LED

One more element of guidance deserves our attention. Through all of this, though, we must observe that Paul made plans in ordinary ways. What we have seen is that his ordinary ways were interrupted because he listened to the Spirit of God as shaped by the mission. But he still made plans the way we make plans. Total spontaneity is rootlessness; total routine is over-rootedness. We must plant roots and then let God give growth where he wants. So let's remind ourselves of Paul's more ordinary plans lest we begin to think living on the edge of the mystical world is all we've got.

In Acts 15:2, Paul was part of a contingent commissioned by the church in Antioch to go to Jerusalem for the famous council that would decide if Gentile converts were to be circumcised. The whole of Paul's mission was at stake in the decision. This was rational, pragmatic, and ordinary planning. After the council said Gentiles should be Gentiles and Jews should be Jews, and once he was back on the mission field, Paul realized Timothy's status — Jew or Gentile? — was unclear because he was not circumcised even though his mother was Jewish. So, in an ordinary but clever move, Paul decided, "Let's get this guy's status regulated. Get a knife" (Acts 16:1 – 3). This made Timothy's presence with Paul a nonissue. Later Paul decided to change directions for his trip, heading from Greece north and overland rather than over sea toward Jerusalem. But he made this decision *to avoid persecution* (Acts 20:3). Also, many times Paul tells his readers that he "hoped" to visit them (Philippians 2:19, 23; 1 Timothy 3:14; Philemon 22). These are very ordinary plans and decisions.

So here's where we are. From Paul's life we learn a new kind of guidance, that we are to plan in light of God's Scripture-soaked mission, but we must be open to the Spirit's interruption. Here are four necessary words for that guidance: Scripture, Spirit, mission, and plans. Let me tell you the story of a man whose life illustrates each of them and shows how church-shaped his new life is.

TASS

The Palestinian Tass Saada was born in a tent on the Gaza Strip to poor parents.[4] When the 1967 Six-Day War displaced so many Palestinians, his family moved to Saudi Arabia, where his father became a successful businessman, and Tass (his name is Taysir Abad Saada) began a troubled life. Eventually this anger-filled young man joined Fatah, Yasser Arafat's military coalition in Jordan. He became a sniper who killed people in the name of Arafat, and his mission was "to destroy Israel." When he returned from his murderous life in Jordan to Qatar, where his family had moved, his father restrained him from returning to Arafat's forces, but his father did permit Tass to go to the U.S.

Through his story of finding a wife in order to get a green card in America, of working hard to put food on the table for his family, of adultery, and of being questioned by the FBI, Tass came to the end of his ropes. Then he encountered a Christian named Charlie and had a dream-filled, visionary, dramatic encounter and conversion that ended up transforming this once murderous man into a man seeking reconciliation of Jews and Arabs through the gospel of Jesus Christ. (Tass mirrors in some ways the mission of the apostle Paul.)

What struck me as I read Tass's story was what happened to him in his own kind of "Damascus road experience." On the morning after his dramatic encounter with Christ, while his wife, Karen, was in the kitchen, he slid to his knees to pray — but listen to God's mission that bubbled up miraculously in his prayer:

> And then I heard myself praying something totally out of character for me. "O God, bless your people Israel. O Lord, lead them back to their Promised Land. Let them see you as their God." What was this?!
>
> I clapped my hand over my mouth. I had never wished a single good thing for the Jews in my entire life. Why was I now praying for their interests? I had no explanation for the inner urge I felt to ask blessings upon them. It made no sense.

God speaks the grace of Yes over Jews and Arabs, and that grace prompts us to love whom God loves, which means we learn to love our enemies and pray for them and desire for them to join us at the table with Jesus in the church (or salad bowl).

Tass Saada's work in the restaurant business led him to a realtor whom he realized was Jewish. I love this man's honesty. Whereas prior to his conversion his thoughts would have been, "Sack him for lunch before he eats you for dinner," now he admitted, "I realized there was no more fight left in me. I had no desire to fleece him." Then the stunning realization that "the Jew, Jesus Christ, had drained me out of my long-standing hatred for all other Jews." Then it gets theological: "I began to see that the closer we all got to Jesus, the Messiah, the more reconciled we could become to one another." Tass experienced the church God has designed for his people.

Tass became an itinerant minister in the U.S., but eventually became involved in a ministry of relief, education, and gospel in the Gaza Strip; then a personal private meeting with Arafat in which he pressed the claims of Christ; and then onto the West Bank where one day he realized his new ministry location was in the exact spot his original hate for Jews was expressed in the famous battle at Al-Karameh, in March of 1968. "This was the place," he observed, "where so long ago I had come to fight and take life. Now, God was bringing me back to do good and give life."

Now go back and read Tass's story through the four words of guidance. It's all there, because God is still speaking.

17

A New Politics

Everything I have said up to this point leads to one grand synthesis: God's mission in this world is to create the church where God's will is lived out by *all* of God's people. God's new creation grace and love are experienced at the table of Christian fellowship and create a new people, a new community, and a new way of life marked by a holiness the Roman Empire either despised or had never seen embodied in a community. To use a word that jars some of us, God's mission in the church is God's kind of *politics*, but God's politics is not the world's politics, especially not Rome's. Enter Paul with nothing less than new creation, kingdom, or church politics.

Paul was a Roman, and Paul was a Jew. Because he was both, he answered to two rulers. At the top of the heap in Paul's world were the Roman emperors Claudius and Nero, as well as designated leaders in the Holy Land such as Herod Agrippa I and Felix and Festus, whom Bible readers meet in the book of Acts. Between these leaders and Paul were a host of lesser leaders who had the delegated power of the emperor. What did Paul think of them? Did he? Certainly! So what did he say about them? Paul was *very* political, and so *must* we be political — but we may need to consider afresh *how* Paul was political and *how* we are political.

No area is more important or more complex for us when it comes to a church-shaped Christian life than politics. We relate every day to the state, so we must discern how best to do this, always listening to the Spirit and keeping God's mission in the forefront of all decisions. Before I venture into this topic from the angle of what the New Testament teaches, I want to describe briefly a conversation I had with a Danish Christian in the summer of 2012 who reminded me of a reality that is grossly unrecognized in the U.S.

"Can I tell you what the difference is that I, as a political scientist, see between your president Obama and the candidate Romney?" said the young man to me over lunch.

"I'd like to hear your perspective," I encouraged him.

"None," he said. "They are so close in ideology and political theory that over here we think you can pick either and you will have the same president."

I'm sure my young Danish friend is accurate when it comes to political theory, but that doesn't seem to help Americans tone down their rhetoric or their emotions when it comes to election season (and we are seemingly in one all the time in the U.S.!) — Christians included. Before we take one more step, we need to remind ourselves of this ultimate Christian truth: the final rule will be a theocracy. God will rule through King Jesus over the whole world. With that important reminder baptizing every political controversy and voting season, we ask, *In the meantime, how do we live?* I begin with America's oldest attempt at answering this, because whether we like it or not, that attempt shaped our entire history.

AMERICA'S FOUNDERS

The Church of England in the late sixteenth and early seventeenth century struggled to find itself. Would it be Catholic? Would it be Protestant? The surges in one direction and then the other frustrated both Catholics and Anglicans. Arising in England was a group of devoted Christians whom we now call the Puritans. Many of us have grown up thinking of Puritans as a bunch of killjoys or hypocrites because many of us first learned of the Puritans in the face of one notorious hypocrite,

Arthur Dimmesdale, in the pages of *The Scarlet Letter*. A famous American writer, H. L. Mencken, once said what many now believe about them, that the Puritans were those who were "haunted by the fear that someone, somewhere, may be happy."[1]

No one says the Puritans were without their hypocrites and obsessions, but the stereotype is neither accurate nor fair. The Puritans created America, both religiously and politically, and as Americans they remain with us and a part of us to this day. What the Puritans of England wanted most was a godly Protestant country. So starting from the ground up, boatloads of Puritans came to the colonies, including one of America's forgotten founders, John Winthrop,[2] who was at the heart of the birth of Boston.

What we see in John Winthrop is a devoted (holy) Christian man, intent not only on a pure Anglican church, but also on a godly society and city. Winthrop referred to their new place as "a city on a hill," a phrase referring both to a pure church and city or, in his words, a "godly commonwealth." It's understandable. Christians want God's will, citizenship empowers all Americans, voting is a powerful political action, and voting for the most Christian option is natural. Winthrop's political vision was a vision of a Christian seeking to bring about God's will in a nation (as it is in heaven). Who can find fault with that?

But that Puritan experiment is America's *past*. At no time in American history has the Christian relationship to the state been more conflicted or painful for Christians than today. The church is divided by race, by gender, by economics, and now also by politics. Many would like the church to go away, and many of us are embarrassed by the church's witness in the last century. Maybe we need to revise our Bible verse to read, there is neither Jew nor Gentile, neither slave nor free, nor is there male and female, *and neither is there Republican nor Democrat*, for you are all one in Christ Jesus! For some, those italics may be the hardest item to chew in our fellowship of differents.

So let's go back to the Bible. What about Paul? How did he see the relation of the church and the state? Can he help us today? More than ever.

PAUL AND ROME'S POWERS

When the apostles, such as Peter and Paul, began to think about these things, they were experimenting on the basis of sound Christian convictions. Because they were already probing this issue of the church and the state in the first century, the New Testament gives us principles and beginning thoughts even if it does not provide complete theories. Because they were only probing our questions, Christians today, in radically different conditions than what Paul and Peter experienced, will have to work out a method of relating to the state that goes way beyond anything the apostles ever imagined. They didn't, for instance, vote for an emperor. Emperors seized power by killing others and asserting power.

In that context, Paul was called by God into a ministry of getting Roman Gentiles saved and working hard at getting saved Gentiles to live in fellowship and peace with saved Jews. Paul had a plan, a plan that countered Rome at each and every step. Every element in Paul's plan raised the hopes and created worrying wonders in each of Paul's house churches. God's kind of politics begins with these elements:

1. There is one God (going against Rome's gods).

2. God is Israel's God made known in his Son, King Jesus, the Lord who saves both Jews and Gentiles (this blasphemed the emperor's self-image and exalted status).

3. The true people of God, or *ecclesia* (church), is comprised of those who believe in Jesus and who live under his rule (this denied Rome's sense of privilege).

4. The way to live is to follow the Bible's teachings, from Torah to Jesus to the apostles' teachings (and this cut into the fabric of the Roman system of laws and culture).

Paul could have believed that the way to relate to Rome was for Israel, now headed by King Jesus, Lord of both Jews and Gentiles, to go to battle with Rome. But Paul had surrendered the way of coercion for the way of crucifixion because his "political theory" was the gospel. That grace-expanding gospel created an alternative way of life for God's radical social experiment, the church, and that gospel also turned the church into a kingdom base of operations in the Roman world. What was the inner dynamic? I suggest we learn four principles from Paul:

Be Good Christian People in the Empire

Paul was a Roman citizen who appealed to his status when under trial before Festus (Acts 25:11). When Paul speaks of Rome, he does so respectfully, and at some level he believed God's hand controlled even Rome (Romans 13:1 – 7). Paul's message clearly challenged the exalted claims of the powers of Rome, but he believed his followers were to constrain their freedoms (1 Corinthians 7:17 – 24) and pray for their rulers (1 Timothy 2:1 – 4). Perhaps we need a reminder that the ruler on the throne when Paul said this was none other than Nero, an egomaniac, murderous despot who murdered his own wife, Octavia, so he could marry Poppaea (who was evidently a convert to Judaism). By the way, Nero was as debauched sexually as any person in human history. As if these aren't bad enough, there are reasons to think he was the one who killed both Peter and Paul. So Paul is praying then for his future murderer!

Whatever we think of politics today, we too are called to pray for our leaders. I was once speaking at a church during election season, and I spoke about this very theme. After the service, a man confronted me, saying that he would never pray for President Bill Clinton. I countered that Peter said in 1 Peter 2:17 that all Christians were to "honor the emperor." To which he said, "Never!" So I reminded him that Peter was talking about Nero. I was doing my best, and not at all successfully, to calm him down and consider praying for our leaders, and he got steamed even more. I tried a new tack by quoting a well-known pastor's recent prayer for the president and for our country, and the man shot back against that pastor with, "He's an idiot!" (I decided the wisdom of never talking at family gatherings or churches about politics might be the wiser course.) I cannot see how that man's red-faced, saliva-spitting anger was what Paul had in mind. Even more so when we consider what's next.

One of the most potent revelations of how the churches of Paul were to relate to the state can be seen in 1 Thessalonians 4:10 – 12:

> And in fact, you do love all of God's family throughout Macedonia. Yet we urge you, brothers and sisters, to do so more and more, and *to make it your ambition to lead a quiet life: You should mind your own business and work with your hands, just as we told you, so that your daily life may win the respect of outsiders and so that you will not be dependent on anybody.*

But for that first generation of Christians who sometimes experienced the rough side of the power's tongue and the sharp side of their swords, being a good citizen never meant doing whatever Caesar asked. Good citizenship is a posture of the one whose primary citizenship is under King Jesus. It is the posture of *engagement* for the sake of the kingdom, but it is never the posture of total obedience or subservience to Caesar.

Recognize the State as a Temporary Good

It was back at the beginnings of the Christian church that Paul began to think about how to relate to the state. In Romans 13:1 – 7, Paul affirms that God's providence includes rulers and states. In 2 Thessalonians 2:5 – 11, Paul speaks of God as the "restrainer" in the world. These two sections in Paul's letters lead to the conclusion that all state powers are temporary. Government, then, is at best designed as a temporary good. The state is a good but temporary arrangement designed by God.

But most of us know that this is just the starting point. What happens when we encounter the Taliban in Afghanistan or an Idi Amin or a Robert Mugabe or Pol Pot? At that point Paul's "good government" would no doubt be turned inside out to witness to the evil "principalities and powers" that corrupt God's designs. So our relationship to the state must be nothing less than "ambivalent." Yes, it's within God's design, but when it oppresses, the Christian cannot support the state.

So we have to conclude that the radical importance of the church is not to serve the state, which many Americans think is going on far too often today. Instead, the state is designed by God for the church! Yes, this turns things upside down, which is Paul's habit. God's grand experiment of a new kind of community in the church is God's central plan for the world, and the state is good so far as it supports what God is doing in this world.

Challenge the State with the Gospel, Even If It Means Resistance

The Christian may be a good citizen, but citizenship and patriotism or nationalism have limits. The Christian may see the state as a good, but it is a temporary and not eternal good. Our politics are the "politics of Jesus," or the politics of God. Ultimately, God rules through King Jesus, and King Jesus' citizens live under him. The gospel message subverts any other message that lays claim to a person deeper than the claim of Jesus. To the degree that the state's claims are consistent with King Jesus' claims, the Christian is a good citizen. The moment the state lays claim beyond what Jesus claims, the Christian citizen is called to follow Jesus, regardless of what that means for one's life.

Paul may have been under the jurisdiction of Caesar and Felix or Festus, and he may have had some rights and protections because of his citizenship. But when Paul entered Rome and was imprisoned, Paul made it clear that the Spirit and his gospel mission — not the emperor and his mission — laid claim to his life. Speaking of Paul's imprisonment, the writer Luke pens these ironic words, which are nothing less than a form of revolutionary, peaceful insubordination:

> For two whole years Paul stayed there in his own rented house and welcomed all who came to see him. He proclaimed the kingdom of God and taught about the Lord Jesus Christ — with all boldness and without hindrance! (Acts 28:30 – 31)

For Paul, Caesar was a temporary good, but the moment he crossed the line, out came the rule of King Jesus.

A Glowing Example

Karl Barth was the twentieth-century's most significant theologian.[3] With the rise of Hitler and his rhetoric about a pure race state, Barth saw trouble looming on the horizon. Many sat by, hoping the looming potential would not run its feared course, or trusting that things would alter their course — or simply joining in to one degree or another. Barth did not. As he said, "I myself could not very well keep quiet, but had to undertake to issue the necessary warnings to the church about the danger it was in." Most importantly, Barth saw National Socialism as a diabolical renunciation of the first commandment. So, contrary to the order from the Third Reich, Professor Karl Barth refused to begin class with *Heil Hitler!* and on November 7, 1934, he resisted the oath of loyalty. "I did not refuse to give the official oath," he said, "but I stipulated an addition to the effect that I could be loyal to the *Führer only within my responsibilities as an Evangelical Christian."*

Knowing what may come, on November 26 Barth's class sung a hymn to God's good guidance, and the next day he was dismissed. When on trial, Barth announced that the Third Reich was "making Hitler a god incarnate and offending most seriously against the first commandment." On March 1, 1935, Barth was served with a total ban on speaking in public and soon was teaching in Switzerland, where his career as a theologian grew to colossal proportions. Barth's forthright resistance to National Socialism was more than the reflex of a contrarian. This was a man who saw idolatries defacing the glory of God. Barth illustrates that the state is a temporary good at best and other times an evil to be resisted, and his posture toward the Third Reich grew out of the apostle Paul's own teachings.

Let's be clear here: this isn't just Hitler stuff — this is Paul stuff. In AD 14, the Romans created an inscription in a city called Messene (in Greece) that put into stone what Romans thought of the death of Caesar Augustus and the transition of unlimited power to Tiberius.[4] We read these words: "To God Augustus Caesar and Tiberius Caesar." Augustus' wife, Livia, is called a "goddess." Paul could not participate in such language, for he recognized one God and one Lord, and Caesar's claim was nothing less than idolatrous and blasphemous. It must be resisted.

The Best Way to Be Political Is to Be the Church

Jesus talks about the *kingdom* all the time, and *kingdom* is a 100 percent political word. To use the word *kingdom* in Jesus' world was to speak of a king governing citizens, land, and law.[5] Jesus came to establish his kingdom, and that means God's new work in which he rules, rescues, ransoms, and redeems a new creation people who are to live under him as King.

It is no accident, then, that Paul called the kingdom fellowship of those under King Jesus a "church." The word *church* translates from the Greek word *ekklesia*, which means a *political* gathering of citizens, and these political gatherings concerned the elites of the Roman cities who distributed the power of the emperor and exercised authority in the cities. When Paul decided to focus on his fellowships with the word *church*, he chose a term that meant what kingdom meant for Jesus: God's new society.

This new creation fellowship, the church, is a profoundly political way of life, but it is a new kind of politics. We must be *political* — but we must do it by being profoundly *church*. The best Christian churches subvert the politics of the day, not just by opposing the heinous assault of death in abortions, but by creating a culture that brings the life of God for all. This salad bowl church, this fellowship of differents, is nothing less than a new way of being political.

This all draws to one point, and that is that the primary relation of the Christian to the state is to live under King Jesus in the church, the body of Christ, in such a way that we embody Christlikeness in a way that witnesses to the world. That way of life is God's way, the way of Jesus, the way of the Spirit — in a redeemed people that transcends old divisions. In the new creation society, we find Romans getting along with Greeks, and Jews getting along with Gentiles, men getting along with women, and slaves getting along with the free and powerful, and, yes, Democrats getting along with Republicans. Paul's political theory, in fact — God's kind of politics — is the church. The new creation way to be political is to be the church! Nothing, irony of ironies, is more political than life in the salad bowl.

This is both God's grand experiment in the world and our greatest challenge. I hope you agree with me that the hope for the world is the local church, and that the heart of God's plan is found in creating a whole new society in a local church. If we do this, we will flourish — a theme vital to understanding a church-shaped Christian life.

PART 6

FLOURISHING

18

We Have Landed, but We Want the Land

All we need to flourish in God's grand experiment, the church, is the Spirit of God. All we need is God's power for what God wants to accomplish, so I want to quote Jimmy Dunn's tongue twister one more time:

> The Spirit of God transcends human ability and transforms human inability.[1]

Our ability, our hopes, our efforts, and our strategies are insufficient to bring us all into one body. Believing in the power of "our-ness" is why some gravitate to separate-but-equal churches and why others resort to uniformity-by-conformity churches. In one, there is no challenge to cross ethnic, cultural, and gender lines, while in the other you either agree or go home. Either way, we get "our" wishes. Twenty centuries of dismal disunity and the witness of a fractured church ought to convince us of our raw inability to be the church God wants us to be. The hope of this book is that that history will be reversed by a renewed commitment to be the church God designed, a church that flourishes in a salad bowl fellowship of differents.

But there is gospel — resurrection and new creation — news here: the Spirit can take our abilities and *transcend* them, then take our inabilities and *transform* them into the gracious power of unity. To flourish, then, we need to be Holy Spirit people. The only way the church can be God's kind of church is through the power of the Spirit. Only the Spirit empowers us to transcend differences and to transform our preferences into love for others. There are many teachings about the Holy Spirit in Paul's letters, so I will reduce them to six.

IF JESUS AND THE APOSTLES NEEDED THE SPIRIT, SO DO WE

Some of us think so rarely about the Spirit that when we encounter verses about the Spirit, we can be surprised — especially when it comes to Jesus. Did he *need* the Spirit? Yes. Why? Because he was fully human. When Peter explained Jesus to a Roman military leader, a Gentile named Cornelius who understood power, he described him as the über-powered human:

> You know what has happened throughout province of Judea, beginning in Galilee after the baptism that John preached — how God anointed Jesus of Nazareth *with the Holy Spirit and power,* and how he went around doing good and healing all who were under the power of the devil, *because God [in the Holy Spirit] was with him.* (Acts 10:37 – 38)

Not once, but twice in these verses, Peter declares that Jesus accomplished his ministry through the power of God's Spirit. Consider what this implies about Jesus' ministry:

+ When Jesus healed a leper, it was because the Spirit of God was on him.

+ When Jesus converted Peter, it was because the Spirit of God was on him.

+ When Jesus broke boundaries by inviting prostitutes and tax collectors to the table for fellowship, it was because the Spirit of God was on him.

+ When Jesus exorcised demons and evil spirits from others, it was because the Spirit of God was on him.

He didn't do these things simply *because he was the Messiah*, but because as the Messiah God's Spirit was alive and at work in and through him. As Gerald Hawthorne, one of Wheaton College's all-time great professors, puts it:

> The Holy Spirit was the divine power by which Jesus overcame his human limitations, rose above his human weakness, and won out over his human mortality.[2]

So we can't be surprised to see that same Spirit at work on the even more "human" Peter and Paul and everyone else in the earliest churches. Acts tells that Peter was "filled with the Holy Spirit" (Acts 4:8). Later, after Peter had preached to the Gentiles, "the circumcised believers [messianic Jews] ... were astonished that the gift of the Holy Spirit had been poured out even on Gentiles" (10:45).

We need to drink this in big gulps: Jesus, Peter, Paul, and each of us need the Spirit. The same Spirit at work in and through Jesus is the same Spirit at work in Peter, Paul, the early Christians, and you and me. If you believe that, and if you believe that God's Spirit can transcend your abilities and transform your inabilities, then we can all flourish enough to reveal in our church a glimpse of God's kingdom vision for us. But this can only happen by the Spirit.

The Spirit is the key. When I was in high school, a basketball player friend, Mike, one class ahead of me, secretly told me he had a key to the high school that would get us into the building, the locker room, and the gym. This was of course not legal, but we weren't up to any mischief or concerned about what was legal or not — we simply wanted a place to play. Some teachers knew and didn't care. Those were the days, my friend. Mike said he'd give it to me to make a copy, but I had one hour. So off I went to the local store to get a copy of the magical key, and I returned within an hour with the original for him. I carried that key with me for three years.

On Saturday or Sunday afternoons it was not uncommon for a group of us to meet in the gym to play hoops. We were well behaved; we never broke any windows. We sometimes turned on the Harlem Globetrotter music to warm up and show off our skills. One time someone left out the scoreboard box, so we took turns keeping track of the score. We just wanted to improve our basketball skills, and anyone who wanted to join us was welcome. Having that key made a number of us much better basketball players than we would have been. We played hard and we practiced our skills; we challenged one another as if the coaches were watching. So a number of us who played on the team knew the key to our skills was the key in the pocket. When I graduated, I gave my key to my father, a teacher and a coach (and probably a slightly relieved teacher and coach).

That key was our key to improvement. The Holy Spirit — in us and for us — is the key. We need this reminder as we move now to a second theme about the Spirit in Paul's wisdom.

WHAT THE SPIRIT OCCUPIES, THE SPIRIT TRANSFORMS

The Spirit has come to occupy the church, and when he does, everything becomes new. To recall Paul's famous words to the Corinthians, "If anyone is in Christ, the new creation has come: The old has gone, the new is here!" (5:17). The Spirit has come to transform us, so let's pause to observe what is going on when we say the Spirit makes all things new.

God's gracious love for us is about his being with and for us so that we can enter into the great "unto" of the kingdom. God is *supremely and personally* "with us" in the Spirit, and this is proof that God is "for" us. Now the inevitable: *when God is present in us in the Spirit, transformation must occur.* Why? Because the more God is present, the more godly (or god-like) we become. God's presence is a transforming presence.

EACH OF US HAS THE SPIRIT AND GIFTS, INCLUDING YOU

The Spirit was not given just to the apostles or prophets. The Spirit was not given just to super saints or to elite Christians. Being Christian and having the Spirit are one and the same reality. Each of us has the Spirit and each of has gifts for the sake of the church. (We will look at spiritual gifts in the next chapter, where we focus on the Spirit and the local church.)

The early apostles were conduits of the Spirit, and empowered by the Spirit at Pentecost they began dispensing the Spirit to all. When Peter and John laid their hands on brand new converts in Samaria, they received the Holy Spirit (Acts 8:17). Following Saul's encounter with the risen King Jesus, Ananias, a disciple of Jesus in Damascus who had heard stories about Saul's ferocity, laid his hands on Paul, and he received the Spirit (9:17 – 19). Many might be tempted to say, "Yes, but that's the apostle Paul, and God had special plans for him, so God gave him a special anointing." Peter would not agree, however, because when an ordinary Gentile and his friends and family heard Peter's gospel sermon, they too all received the Spirit.

> While Peter was still speaking these words, the Holy Spirit came on all who heard the message. The circumcised believers who had come with Peter were astonished that the gift of the Holy Spirit had been poured out *even on Gentiles*. For they heard them speaking in tongues and praising God.
>
> Then Peter said, "Surely no one can stand in the way of their being baptized with water. They have received the Holy Spirit just as we have." So he ordered that they be baptized in the name of Jesus Christ. Then they asked Peter to stay with them for a few days. (Acts 10:44 – 48)

> "As I began to speak, the Holy Spirit came on them as he had come on us at the beginning. Then I remembered what the Lord had said: 'John baptized with water, but you will be baptized with the Holy Spirit.'" (11:15 – 16)

I chuckle every time I read "even on the Gentiles" (in italics above). It's almost condescending or patronizing, as if this is the greatest miracle of all, that God would dwell with Gentiles. It sounds a bit like a Chicago Bears fan saying, "Even Green Bay Packer fans understand this!"

When the Spirit comes, Jewish believers and Gentile believers both get the Spirit; when men and women become believers, both get the Spirit; and when slave or free turn to Jesus, both get the Spirit. The Spirit comes on each of us.

We've got the key, and what we've got is the Spirit, and what that means is that all things are new because the Spirit is *God's personal presence* that empowers us to flourish in the church. Let's remind ourselves of what we have just seen: Jesus, Peter, the Pentecost Christians, Paul, and all the converts — Jews and Gentiles — received the Spirit. They didn't have to beg for it. To get the Spirit one must simply believe and receive. God sends the Spirit to all who ask.

WE CAN BE FULL OF THE SPIRIT

Everyone can be *full of the Spirit*. Some of us know the experience of intoxication from alcohol or pot or some drug. Some of us know the experience of being drugged by a doctor enough to enter the other side. I've had a couple surgeries and experienced the power of sedatives. Paul uses the image of intoxication for *what is possible for every Christian* — only Paul's desire is not the inebriation of wine but the inebriation and intoxication of the Spirit. Here are Paul's own words:

> Do not get drunk on wine, which leads to debauchery. Instead, be filled with the Spirit. (Ephesians 5:18)

Paul contrasts being filled with wine with being filled with the Spirit. Alcohol leads to being "wasted" (another translation for "debauchery"), but Spirit-filling, Paul goes on in 5:19 – 20, leads to the fully conscious and highest forms of human communication, "speaking to one another in psalms, hymns, and songs from the Spirit," as well as "giving thanks." Paul knows from all his missionary journeys how drunks get to singing and carousing in their stupor, and he also knows that when the Spirit descends, it transforms people from singing vile songs to glorious, God-drenched praises.

Again, this is not only for super saints such as Paul and Peter. This is for everyone. Paul tells ordinary Christians in Ephesus that they are to get loaded with the Spirit. And when that happens, they will transcend all differences and diversities in a spiritual unity celebrated in Spirit-inspired songs.

THE SPIRIT BATTLES THE FORCES OF EVIL THROUGH US

Christians need the Spirit because even though the new day has come, even though transformation is happening, and even though new creation is thawing Satan's deep freeze of death in the cosmos, the battle is still on. The Spirit-filled apostle Paul went nose-to-nose with the gods and goddesses and spirits of Ephesus and performed miracles of liberation (Acts 19:11 – 12). Some charlatans aped Paul's Spirit-empowered works, but that backfired when the power of Jesus was so great that it led to a praise fest and "the name of the Lord Jesus was held in high honor" (19:17). Remarkably, Paul's Spirit-filled ministry in Ephesus led to a revival:

> Many of those who believed now came and openly confessed what they had done. A number who had practiced sorcery brought their scrolls together and burned them publicly. When they calculated the value of the scrolls, the total came to fifty thousand drachmas. (Acts 19:18 – 19)

We don't often act as if we believe there are sinister forces at work in our world, so some ignore passages like this. Others allegorize the demons and principalities and powers into nothing more than systemic injustices. But this is just another way of taming our consciences to deny spiritual powers; reality's stories lead me to contend that Paul's battle is our battle. The prince of this world wants to rule as long as possible, but God's powerful Spirit is at work to defeat the powers of darkness.

Now on to the last theme in Paul's letters about the Spirit, a most interesting one.

WE HAVE LANDED, BUT WE WANT THE LAND

One of my all-time favorite experiences was visiting the Holy Land. Roger Green, a wonderful professor at Gordon College, was our tour leader. Our group all met at the airport in Boston and flew to Amsterdam, where we sought to relieve the stupor of hours in a plane with nothing but snatches of sleep. Then we all boarded another plane and headed to Tel Aviv. We landed in deeper stupor, but our stupor was now complicated by the excitement of being in the Holy Land. We found our hotel — whoops, they changed our hotel — so we drove to the next one, grabbed our bags in the late evening sun, carted our luggage to our room, met in the restaurant area, and had our first dinner in the Land.

We did our best to sleep under the goofy stupor of too many time zone changes, but I awoke early, opened the patio window, left the room, and took in my first morning sun in the Holy Land. The first thing I saw were parrots dipping and bobbing with their glorious flight patterns. But we didn't come to the Holy Land to hang out at a modern hotel watching parrots. We came to see where Jesus walked in Galilee and where Peter lived in Capernaum. We came to see Qumran and Masada and the center of it all, Jerusalem, and the Temple Mount. We had landed in Tel Aviv, and we could smell the air, see the sky, and feel the warmth of its sun — but we wanted more. We had landed, but we wanted to scout out the Land.

The Holy Spirit in us is God's promise that we have landed, that though we experience earthly and broken realities, the kingdom land of full redemption is around the corner. And Paul uses some remarkable language about the Spirit, telling us three different times that with the Spirit we have landed:

> Now it is God who makes both us and you stand firm in Christ. He anointed us, set his seal of ownership on us, and put his Spirit in our hearts *as a deposit, guaranteeing what is to come.* (2 Corinthians 1:21 – 22)

Paul uses another image for this same concept when he writes to the Romans not long after his letter to the Corinthians:

Not only so, but we ourselves, who have the *firstfruits* of the Spirit, groan inwardly as we wait eagerly for our adoption to sonship, the redemption of our bodies. (Romans 8:23)

We detect only a slight difference when much later Paul writes to the Ephesians in these words about the Spirit:

… who is a *deposit* guaranteeing our inheritance until the redemption of those who are God's possession. (Ephesians 1:14)

And do not grieve the Holy Spirit of God, with whom you were *sealed* for the day of redemption. (4:30)

Here's what Paul is saying: We've got the Spirit, and the Spirit in us is a "seal of ownership" and a down payment that guarantees our participation in the kingdom. This is a way of saying once again that salvation, as we saw a few chapters back, is a lifelong (and longer) process.

SPIRIT FLOURISHING

In your local church, God — you gotta believe this — is cooking up his future kingdom. When we look around, we don't see that glorious kingdom so much as broken, wounded, and messed-up fellow Christians on a journey. In fact, we see tensions, divisions, and hassles with one another. That is why God has sent the Spirit into us — to transcend our natural abilities to love one another and to transform our inabilities to dwell with one another in a way that witnesses to God's grand experiment, the church.

19

The Exposure Challenge

Be careful what you read or watch intensively. If you read the *New York Times*, you begin to lean left like the *New York Times*. If you read *The National Review*, you begin to tilt right like *The National Review*. If you absorb *The Simpsons*, you may well become a smart aleck. If you watch Colbert or Jon Stewart or David Letterman, you get cynical. Some connect everything in a conversation to musical lines because they listen to music all the time, while others find a way to mention Seth Godin because they read him, and still others quote their pastor as if he or she were the Bible. I've been around scholars of Greek classics who quoted Homer, Plato, or Aristotle about everything. One of my friends' regular quotations of Flannery O'Connor prompted me to read her, and what a discovery she has been in my life. I have other Jewish friends who are into the rabbis, and they can quote the rabbis like they eat them for breakfast, lunch, and dinner. I've met some who seem to know the characters in the Harry Potter books personally.

One of my friends had never read much of Dietrich Bonhoeffer until he read Eric Metaxas's book *Pastor, Martyr, Prophet, Spy*. Then he read some of Bonhoeffer's own books, and he said to me one day in my office,

"Scot, I had no idea how much influence Bonhoeffer has had on your thinking until I read Bonhoeffer."

I countered with a big "Jawohl!" (Google it.)

A colleague of mine the other day said he was looking for a quotation from Bonhoeffer.

"You mean the famous one? 'When Christ bids a man come, he bids him come and die.' That one?"

"Yes," he said.

"That's R. H. Fuller's famous translation," I said, "and it's more poetic than Bonhoeffer's German." So I quoted the German: "Jeder Ruf Christ führt in den Tod." Then I translated it for David Fitch: "'Every summons of Christ leads to death.' Not as poetic as the famous English translation!"[1] That conversation made me realize how much I have been exposed to Bonhoeffer.

SOWING AS EXPOSURE

Exposure to a single influence begins to transform us into its image. What if our single-most influence was the Spirit of God? What would happen to us if we turned our face constantly into the light of the Spirit? What kind of flourishing would we experience in the Spirit?

Paul says there are two kinds of people — those who are exposed constantly to the *flesh* and those who are exposed constantly to the *Spirit*. In Galatians 6:8 he says, "Whoever sows to please their flesh, from the flesh will reap destruction; whoever sows to please the Spirit, from the Spirit will reap eternal life."

As I type this, I have just read that Dallas Willard, a man who has helped so many with his writings and pastoral wisdom, has gone to be with the Lord. When I think of Dallas, I won't think of "RIP," but rather of "VIM," — his *vision* to be Christlike, with the *intent* to make it happen, through the *means* of turning to the face of God through the spiritual disciplines. Dallas Willard's focus in life was "sowing to the Spirit." To "sow" is to commune with God, to speak with God in prayer, to trust in

God, to request of God, to rely on God, to read God's Word, to practice spiritual disciplines before God, to fellowship with God's people, to celebrate Christ in the Eucharist, and to worship and devote oneself to love, obedience, and service. In other words, sowing is about exposure — constant exposure to the God whose grace transforms. And exposure to the Spirit yields Spirit-formed lives and people who live well with others in the salad bowl.

HEY, LOOK AT YOU GUYS!

It all began when the college tuition bills were coming to an end and our two adult children were leaving and then were gone, employed, and married. Kris and I were able to save a little more and think about some house projects. We began with the carpeting. We knew under that old carpeting was a wooden floor, so we had the floors done professionally, though we didn't realize the house would be a dusty, smelly mess for two weeks, and that our entire house's furniture would be on the back porch under plastic wrap. The wooden floors changed the interior of the house, so we decided to do some outdoor landscaping, including a brick walkway. Then we got a garage. Next we saved for a couple years and had some old windows replaced and installed new siding on the house. Then we saved some more and asked a wonderful friend and contractor, T. K., to redo our kitchen and to convert our screen porch into a four-seasons room. The next summer our bathroom was updated.

While T. K. was doing all this, we got more serious about plants and decorative grasses for our yard, and they've become our hobby. Then T. K. replaced all the original interior doors from the 1950s in the house, and we redid the upstairs bathroom. T. K. is extraordinarily talented with his woodworking skills, so he made us a living room table and a small table for our four-seasons room. T. K. finished up our remodeling by building a patio and pergola where we now cook on the grill and eat most of our dinners (until winter comes).

We have the same house, but it is no longer the same house. It is a new creation of the old — with the same foundation, same walls, same structure, but with entirely new inner and outer realities. One could say it is an old home made new over a decade. After one of the more recent new creations by T. K., our daughter, Laura, came into the house, looked around, and announced, "Hey, look at you guys!" Which is exactly what the apostle Paul might have said to some of the Christians in the house churches in Rome, Corinth, or Ephesus. He would have said, *Hey, look at you exposed-to-the-Spirit Romans!*

What happens when we are exposed to the Spirit? What does it look like? I suggest the Spirit will make us better, bigger, bolder, and brighter. So let's take the Exposure Challenge to see if the Spirit is doing what the Spirit alone can do.

EXPOSURE TO THE SPIRIT MAKES US BETTER

A person exposed to the Spirit is filled with the Spirit and manifests the fruit of the Spirit. Here they are, and I will turn them into a list to slow us down enough to read them more closely (please don't skip over them):

> But the fruit of the Spirit is
> love,
> joy,
> peace,
> forbearance,
> kindness,
> goodness,
> faithfulness,
> gentleness and
> self-control.

When the Spirit takes root in our life, the Spirit brings forth fruit. That is to say, the Spirit makes us morally better. The big idea for Paul is that the Spirit is in us to make us more Christlike, more godly, more loving, and wiser. Furthermore, the first fruit — love — is first because for

Paul love is the heart of the Torah, the central Christian virtue, and the singular bond that brings peace in the church. Jews and Gentiles, slaves and free, males and females are one in Christ, and that oneness is sustained when they love one another through the Spirit.

What can we do about this? Perhaps we could take the words and practice of John Stott.[2] "Every day," Stott tells us in *The Contemporary Christian*, "for perhaps twenty years I have quoted [this list of the fruit of the Spirit] to myself in my morning devotions, and prayed for its fulfillment in my life. When I am asked what my favourite text is, I usually give this one." But there's even more in the fruit of the Spirit we need to see. The Spirit's task is to transform us into Christlikeness. So one more observation from John Stott's reflections on daily need for the fruit of the Spirit:

> I am sometimes asked ... whether at my age I have any ambitions left. I always reply: "Yes, my overriding ambition is (and, I trust, will be until I die) that I may become a little bit more like Christ."[3]

A person who is flourishing with the fruit of the Spirit looks like Christ, which is a way of saying that they become better.

EXPOSURE TO THE SPIRIT MAKES US BIGGER

How does the Spirit make us bigger? By assigning us a gift in the big, cosmic mission of God. Through the Spirit's gifts, we become participants, actors on the divine stage, people gifted by God with an assignment and responsibility in the church of God. We must also see the paradox here that God's gifts make us bigger by making us needier! How so? What we learn from the gifts is that God gives to us a gift, but he gives everyone else a gift too, so that we need one another if the body of Christ is to function well.[4]

There are four lists of gifts in the New Testament, the most complete one being in 1 Corinthians 12:8 – 10, 27 – 28,[5] which I've arranged here into a list:

To one there is given through the *Spirit* a message of wisdom,
>   to another a message of knowledge by means of the same *Spirit*,
>   to another faith by the same *Spirit*,
>   to another gifts of healing by that one *Spirit*,
>   to another miraculous powers,
>   to another prophecy,
>   to another distinguishing between spirits,
>   to another speaking in different kinds of tongues,
>   and to still another the interpretation of tongues....
Now you are the body of Christ, and each one of you is a part of it. And
God has placed in the church
>   first of all apostles,
>   second prophets,
>   third teachers,
>   then miracles,
>   then gifts of healing,
>   of helping,
>   of guidance,
>   and of different kinds of tongues.

When the Spirit comes, the Spirit assigns everyone a responsibility in the church, and in so doing the Spirit takes us away from our selfishness and individual life and makes us bigger. We flourish in the big work of God in this world.

The four lists of the spiritual gifts differ, leading me to the observation that *these are representative examples of the Spirit's assignments.* I respect those who have compared the lists and tallied them and come up with *the* list of about twenty spiritual gifts. I further respect that such folks are trying to get people to think which of the gifts they "have" in the church, for all Christians need to ponder God's assignment. But I'm afraid being preoccupied with this list sometimes gets things backwards. Instead of looking at the list and wondering which one is me, a better approach is to ask, "What is the Spirit gifting me to *do* in the fellowship?" The answer to that question is your "gift."

You and I are given an assignment that locates us in what our big

God is doing in this world. If that doesn't make us bigger, I don't know what does! Becoming "bigger" in this way also takes on direction, because our gifts are *for [unto] the good and unity of the body of Christ*. In one of Paul's last letters, he said this with utter clarity, so I will quote Ephesians 4:12 – 13, and break it up to make it easier to see why God gives us the gifts. First, they are given to God's people as an assignment:

> To [unto] equip his people for works of service ...

Why? Notice how oriented toward the "we" of the church this is:

> ... so that the body of Christ [not just "I"] may be built up ...

And now the final end of the gifts:

> ... until we all reach unity in the faith and in the knowledge of the Son of God and become mature, attaining to the whole measure of the fullness of Christ.

This is the big plan of God, and the gifts make us bigger by plugging us into that plan.

EXPOSURE TO THE SPIRIT MAKES US BOLDER

When the Spirit is unleashed in us, our inabilities are transcended and our abilities are transformed. Whether we are timid or courageous, the Spirit can take our works and make them bold, or take the overly bold and temper them with graceful boldness.

The boldness of the apostles jumps out from the pages of the book of Acts. Pardon a list of Bible references, but this idea of boldness is too often ignored by Bible readers, so I want to make it clear by giving five examples of Spirit boldness:

1. At Pentecost Peter announced, "I can tell you *confidently* [or boldly] that the patriarch David died and was buried" (Acts 2:29).
2. Next, "When they [the Jerusalem's leaders] saw the *courage* [boldness] of Peter and John and realized that they were unschooled,

ordinary men, they were astonished and they took note that these men had been with Jesus" (4:13).

3. Peter prays, "Now, Lord, consider their threats and enable your servants to speak your word with great *boldness*" (4:29).

4. Peter's boldness was catalytic, for "after they prayed, the place where they were meeting was shaken. And they were *all* filled with the Holy Spirit and spoke the word of God *boldly*" (4:31).

5. Note finally Paul's preaching while held in custody and awaiting trial in Rome: "He proclaimed the kingdom of God and taught about the Lord Jesus Christ *with all boldness* and without hindrance." (28:31).

Spirit exposure lifts someone from being timid to having Spirit-inspired courage. Nikki A. Toyama,[6] an Asian American, was asked by a friend one day, "When did you realize you are a voice?" At least two complications had arisen for Nikki. First, as an Asian American female, she grew up with a standard set of *Asian cultural* expectations, for Asian women are to be demure and silent, and to develop a voice through actions such as hospitality. Second, Nikki is part of a *Christian culture* where the quiet female often fits more suitably than a woman with a voice. That context fueled her consternation when she was asked if she was a voice. Being a voice found a new orientation for Nikki, for "voice is not a Western concept only," she said. "Perhaps by looking at voice as *influence*, we may begin to discover what Asian voice, specifically Asian women's voice, sounds like."

Where did she find help? In the stories of women in the Bible. "These women," she realizes, "represented godly voice: they used their presence, influence, or authority to advance God's kingdom." The woman she most identified with was the immigrant woman Esther, whose voice saved Israel's voice! So Nikki confesses, "I found my voice, reflected to me, in the revolutionary literature of the Old and New Testaments." She wasn't comfortable with the extroverted American voice on street corners, but she grew accustomed to her Asian "gracious way of bringing up hard topics" from "an unimposing reputation." She continues that Asian women "can also say hard things to people — our small size or 'cuteness' softens our message.... I've discovered that I have a voice."

In other words, the bold gospeling of the apostles doesn't mean loud, argumentative polemics like fired-up TV preachers. Spirit-generated boldness can be cool and rational, emerge from small frames, and flourish abundantly.

EXPOSURE TO THE SPIRIT MAKES US BRIGHTER

Having just spoken of the rational boldness of the Spirit, let us not forget that one of the most common themes of what happens with long exposure to the Spirit is that we become *theologically wiser and brighter*. In fact, our Bible informs us that the Spirit grants wisdom, knowledge, and guidance — and that the Spirit speaks through us prophetically so that we will know the "things of the Spirit." Because I aim to anchor the important ideas in this book in the Bible, I want to quote more verses than usual, this time from the book of Acts. These verses show the early Christians gaining wisdom and insight into God's plans because God's Spirit enlightened them.

The Spirit reveals divine plans at times: "The Spirit told Philip, 'Go to that chariot and stay near it'" (Acts 8:29). To Peter, "the Spirit said to him, 'Simon, three men are looking for you'" (10:19). The Spirit inspired Agabus to prophesy (11:28). The Spirit told the fellowship at Antioch — and this is how Paul got his salad bowl missionary work started — "Set apart for me Barnabas and Saul for the work to which I have called them" (13:2). We see Spirit-directed decisions: "It seemed good to the Holy Spirit and to us not to burden you with anything beyond the following requirements..." (15:28). One more, this one from Paul: "And now, compelled by the Spirit, I am going to Jerusalem" (20:22). People who routinely expose themselves to the Spirit recognize the Spirit's promptings, and if you want to see this on display read 1 Corinthians 2:6 – 16.

These are some serious claims by the apostle Paul and by the earliest Christians, but what they set their claim on was that *exposure to the Spirit makes a person flourish and become spiritually brighter.* The Spirit-saturated person has Spiritual Intelligence. By the Spirit, that person comprehends the incomprehensible; by the Spirit, that person embraces what was previously unembraceable; by the Spirit, that person sees into her or his heart to a depth previously obstructed. And sometimes the Spirit prompts us or nudges us, and we act on that guidance, only knowing afterwards that it was God's providence at work. Sometimes the Spirit prompts us to speak things we wouldn't have said otherwise, and because we do, someone else hears from God.

When I think of someone today who exhibits this Pauline Spirit-brightness, I think of Tim Keller, whose approach is pastoral, sensitive, intelligent, culturally alert, but gracefully bold. His sermons and books reveal what I am calling Spiritual Intelligence. As a Manhattan pastor to postmodern, politically influential, and financially clever cultural leaders, Keller explains how he does it:

> The young secularists of New York City are extremely sensitive to anything that smacks of artifice to them. Anything that is too polished, too controlled, too canned will seem like salesmanship. They will be turned off if they hear a preacher use noninclusive gender language, make cynical remarks about other religions, adopt a tone of voice they consider forced or inauthentic, or use insider evangelical tribal jargon. In particular, they will feel "beaten up" if a pastor yells at them. The kind of preaching that sounds passionate in the heartland may sound like a dangerous rant in certain subcultures in the city.[7]

That collection of sentences is why pastor after pastor throughout the world today drinks from the flourishing wells of Tim Keller. He is an example of a man who has been exposed to God's Spirit and who has wisdom for our age.

We are left with one question: *How exposed are you to the Spirit?* Turn your heart, turn your face, turn your mind to the Spirit.

20

Pete the Mechanic

Think about your church's leaders. You may have preaching and senior and executive pastors, choir directors, youth ministers, senior citizen ministers, young adult ministers, compassion ministers, education pastors, missions directors, and one I saw recently — a Pastor of the Table — someone whose ministry is to help Christians eat healthier and to dine with other Christians more often.

Now think about the pew-sitters and what they do each day. Some teach school, some landscape, some sell clothing at a retail store, some are working their way up in a Fortune 500 business, some are homeschooling moms and dads, some sell insurance, some sell stocks, and some travel weekly while others haven't left the village in years.

Paul's life was not like your pastor's or any of the above because Paul, as I sketched earlier, was not employed by a church. Paul was what we now call a *tentmaker*. In fact, our English word *tentmaker* comes straight from Paul's life, a life of ministering while also toiling away in the shop. In other words, he lived like many of our pew-sitters while he did the ministry of a pastor.

Unlike pastors today, Paul's life was more like Pete the Mechanic, who has been working on our cars — and now my son's family's cars — for two decades. We trust him because he's honest and reliable, but even more important, he's devoted to serving others in maintaining cars as well as an active, devout, and mission-oriented Christian. Like Paul, his days are for the workshop and, again like Paul, God's mission permeates his shop. I can't go into his workshop without Pete caring for my car, as well as Christ and church and faith entering our discussion. The last time I was there, Pete told me he was planning on retiring in a few years so he could devote all of his time to Christ's work in his local church.

Paul gospeled from Jerusalem to Rome and perhaps beyond, and he wrote brilliant letters to his churches, and he stopped to pray throughout the day, and ... and ... and all this *occurred in an otherwise ordinary, physically demanding, and harried life of labor.* No doubt during his workday, when the time was opportune, he told others about Jesus and discipled those who were already believers. But for much of his day the apostle purchased fabric or leather;[1] then at the workbench he cut and sewed the material together and sold what he made in the marketplace as tents and awnings and other works of leather.

Paul did not spend his day in the famous libraries of the Roman Empire, such as the one in Ephesus, nor did he spend the day alone on a hillside in prayer and meditation with others there to provide his meals, as if he were at a monastery or on a retreat. Nor did he spend the day reading and preparing for sermons. *Paul spent his day making tents and his lengthy siesta and evenings struggling for holiness and love among the bewildering mix of Jewish and Gentile believers in his house churches.* He was a full-time laborer both in his tentmaking and in exercising his spiritual gift. (If you're wondering about it, it is likely that Paul was not married.)

We are tempted, at least I know I am, to think we could do far more for God if we could just get released from our vocational work to focus all our time developing our gifts and ministering. We are tempted, in other words, to do precisely what did not happen with either Jesus or Paul or Peter. To be sure, the last three or so years of Jesus' life seemed to have been "full-time" ministry, though he spent the first thirty or so years as an artisan of some sort, one option being a carpenter. But, as we've seen, Paul routinely emphasized that he supported himself. My aim here is not to convince ministers to get a "real job," but instead for those with "real jobs" to comprehend that we are called to flourish in our gifts through that job.

We are designed to flourish in a local church while accomplishing the vocation God has given to each of us.

PAUL AT WORK

It will take a bit to flesh out Paul's philosophy of work, but we need to sketch it because everything makes sense once we get this in mind. In the Jewish world, rabbis expected fellow rabbis to work a trade,[2] but in the Roman world, manual labor was ranked below the dignity of a teacher. As a teacher in the Roman world, Paul's first option is that he could have charged fees for his teaching and preaching. Had he done this, the house churches as a social association would have been elevated within the Roman culture, because the Romans valued those who could afford to hire their own teachers. Second, Paul could have entered into the household and employment of someone famous and wealthy. Third, he could become like one well-known Roman group of teachers called the Cynics, who begged on street corners for their resources. Or finally, which is what Paul chose, he could work at a side job, the lowest status in the Roman world for teachers.

The Corinthians were irked that Paul chose, purposefully it seems, this low-status option of a manual laborer and teacher. They had the opportunity to establish their house churches as a reputable association if Paul were financed by them (and dependent on them).[3] But Paul chose not only *not* to be dependent; he chose manual labor: "Stigmatized as slavish, uneducated, and often useless ... [the artisans] were frequently reviled or abused, often victimized, seldom if ever invited to dinner, never accorded status, and even excluded from one Stoic utopia."[4] The Corinthians preferred a nobler status for their apostle, but Paul saw the work of an artisan as embodying the gospel. In fact, he intentionally chose to be an artisan as a way of embracing the foolishness of the cross.

Yes, as an apostle he knew others would provide if he were to ask. But he chose to work although he knew he had the "right," as a gospel minister, to have the necessities of life provided for him so he could concentrate on the gospel. One of Paul's best examples of almost flashy rhetoric can be found in 1 Corinthians 9, where he first makes a powerful argument for financial support:

+ that he is an apostle and that God used him to found the church in Corinth
+ that he therefore has the right to "food and drink" and to be accompanied by a wife
+ that other vocations teach the same
+ that the Torah itself reveals provision for the worker
+ that spiritual ministry deserves material provision
+ and that other Christian ministers claim this right

After eleven verses like this, Paul utters this incredible statement: "But we did not use this right. On the contrary, we put up with anything rather than hinder the gospel of Christ" (1 Corinthians 9:12). Then he adds more to the swollen list of arguments already made when he points out that temple servants get paid and that Jesus "has commanded that those who preach the gospel should receive their living from the gospel" (9:14). But he returns to his decision that "I have not used any of these rights" (9:15). Instead of claiming what was his right, he chose to work, and by choosing *not* to claim his rights, he set a premier example of one way to live out the gospel in a world so intent on status, prestige, and glamor. Our world says, "Do something significant!" and Paul answers back, "Do something insignificant for the love of God!"

FLOURISHING THROUGH OUR VOCATIONS

So unlike our view of professional ministries today, Paul "apostled" while a tentmaker. Paul worked — he worked hard — and he chose to work hard instead of living off the support of others, *and he still flourished.* In the cracks of his day, in the evening and late into the night, on weekends, and in his travels, Paul used the opportunities he had to create and sustain house churches of Christians from all walks of life. He didn't neglect his labor, for he tells us he profited enough from his tentmaking that he paid for his companions. While working, Paul used his shop as a front porch for conversations about the gospel: "So he reasoned in the synagogue with *both Jews and God-fearing Greeks,* as well as in the marketplace [where he made tents] day by day with those who happened to be there" (Acts 17:17). In other words, he turned the workshop into double duty. As he labored, he gospeled and exercised his gifts.

We learn one of the great lessons by watching Paul — that we need not be "full time" to fulfill God's Spirit-directed assignment in our local fellowship. We may have a full-time job, and it may be the kind that demands 100 percent of our time and attention to do well. We can perhaps squeeze in a breakfast prayer group or a lunch Bible study along with fellowship and worship on Sundays, but I suspect that most of us are like Paul — cramped for time. Because his schedule was not open, Paul's ministry permeated his life, whether he was making tents or meeting in the evening with believers. To repeat, *we are called to flourish in the life we're given, not in the life we're not given.* So what can we do in order to flourish as we seek to live out God's grand social experiment?

People Who Flourish Know Themselves

Many of us try to do more than our time permits, or spend too much time feeling guilty, or become angry or bitter about those who are afforded the opportunity to devote all their energies to their gifts. So let me begin with this: *you have to know yourself, what you are called to do, and to do that within the time limits you have.*

My wife, Kris, is a psychologist who works at the Meier Clinic in Wheaton, Illinois. She carries out full days. But Kris is also an introvert, so when she arrives home after her day's work, she needs time to relax and replenish a system taxed by lots of contact with people. She also needs weekends to replenish. We might pause here to remind ourselves — or learn if we've not heard this — that introverts are worn down by social engagement while extroverts (her husband) are energized by social contact. I get so energized by teaching that if I teach in the evenings, I struggle to fall asleep and often sleep only fitfully. So Kris guards me from accepting too many evening engagements.

Many churches, if you haven't thought about this, are shaped by and for extroverts, and for some introverts a church service is overwhelmingly demanding emotionally, as they'd prefer more quiet, more reflection, softer music, and gentler-toned messages.[5] So we have to come to terms with who we are, what our gifts are, what our capacities are, and if the desires for ministry we have are sustainable in the vocation we have. Wise people exercise their gifts within their capacities.

Some have energy their whole life through, working all day long and spending evenings with friends, at soup kitchens, or in Bible studies. Some don't have energy for all of that, so they limit evening and weekend engagements and might want to watch a movie alone. Others, however, see energies surge and then slow down some. Aging (better yet, maturing) often means changes in knowing ourselves and in the sorts of ministries we can carry out. When we are young, we might have more time and energy for various ministries, but that will often give way more and more to family and demands from them, and we may need to cut back on some of our engagements and ministries. We have friends with small children for whom getting to church on a Sunday morning, because of naps and sicknesses and all the little things that turn life more hectic, is a major challenge. Because of sleep schedules, an evening group Bible study is more than difficult to manage. But our kids grow up, and we may find more energy and time for ministries. Then we may discover as we age that we don't have the same energy we once did. Wise churches recognize life's patterns for the fellowship.

It is far too easy to think Paul did nothing but work like a dog all day long and then minister far into the night every night and every day and every week and every month for years and years — when the New Testament doesn't say this and the evidence is far from clear on how much leisure Paul had or needed. In other words, let's not import a workaholic personality type on Paul. Instead of trying to live up to an imagined life in Paul, let's know ourselves and exercise our gifts within our own capacities. God doesn't ask us to be Paul; God asks you to be you, and being you is good enough. Not only is it good enough — it's right.

People Who Flourish Do So Where They Are

We are constantly tempted to think "real ministry" occurs by those who are "full time," while those who have a "real job" can only offer support to those who do the "real ministry." Part of our problem lies in our preaching and teaching and story-telling. We hold up as examples of the Christian life those who are (usually male) heroic ministers of the gospel — the Augustines and Calvins and Luthers and Edwardses and Billy Grahams and the missionaries and the social activists. While we may not intend to diminish the importance of the vocational life of ordinary men and women, we do so by rarely illustrating the Christian life through the example of the local barber or the local teacher or the local merchant.

I maintain that Paul flourished in his gift of being an apostle *as a tentmaker.* We don't hear a lot about his tentmaking, but we have enough glimpses to know the local Christians knew Paul's tents as well as they knew his sermons. So let's remind ourselves often that we are designed by God to flourish in whatever calling we have — like Pete the mechanic or like Niggle, the leaf painter.

Someday Your "Leaf" Will Become Its Tree

My favorite short story of all time is by J. R. R. Tolkien's almost-autobiographical "Leaf by Niggle."[6] Niggle was single, and his vocation was painting leaves. He lived next to Parish's family in an out-of-the-way place, and the lame Parish and his needy wife were demanding and ungrateful neighbors. Niggle's passion in life was to paint leaves, but his kindhearted nature made him a likely person on whom others relied. He wasn't always happy about his willingness to help Parish and others — by patching roofs and running errands — but he helped anyway, sometimes with a curse under his breath. Most important for Niggle, these interruptions kept him from getting his leaves painted.

Tolkien's sketch of Niggle's daily passion, his painting, opens up for us a powerful image of how to see our work. Niggle, he observes, "was the sort of painter who can paint leaves better than trees. He used to spend a long time on a single leaf." One of Niggle's paintings began with a leaf caught in the wind, and then it became a tree with "fantastic roots," and then a country began to develop behind it, and there was a forest and mountains with snow.

Tolkien depicts Niggle's impending death as a journey, and Niggle's Driver for that journey arrived. After his death, and because Tolkien was a traditional Roman Catholic, Niggle spent some time working in an intermediary place (purgatory) until a Porter took him to heaven itself.

It is here that the genius of Tolkien's theory of work — and I would like to say a *genuinely Christian* theory of work — comes to life. Niggle receives a bicycle, and he goes "bowling downhill in the sunshine" until he realizes the turf under him reminds him of another "sweep of grass." Then he sees the "Tree, his Tree, finished." It is the Tree he "had so often felt or guessed, and had so often failed to catch." He sees it all as a gift. Ah, the leaves — they were all there as he had imagined them, but never been able to paint quite right. Some were there that had only budded in his mind. The Forest, too, as well as the Mountains — they were all there. (And Tolkien's use of capital letters shows just how important and serious his earlier labors were, but now they stood there in reality, utterly perfect.) Niggle learns that this little piece of heaven is called "Niggle's Picture," and Parish will be with him, and Parish will live in "Parish's Garden."

Perhaps the most magnificent dimension of Tolkien's vision is its theology of work: *what we do now is a glimpse of what we will do then.* What we do now also prepares us to do what we will do then. What we do now will become the raw materials of what we will do then. What we do now, however incomplete and however below even our own standards, will one day be swallowed up into God's redemptive perfection, and our work will radiate with God's own glory. A rich component of our work, whatever it is, is that in it we are leaning into the perfect vocation God has in mind for us in the New Heavens and the New Earth.

So lean into your vocation toward your local church — and, therefore, toward the kingdom of God.

21

Teacher with the Big Fancy Hat

To an ordinary first-century (non-Christian) Roman, the Christians gathering into what they called "churches" must have seemed quirky, eccentric, weird, even mysterious. These Christians called a crucified man "King," claimed serving was ruling, and gloried in sacrificial love when everyone knew Roman glory resulted from conquering others. They opposed what the Romans called wisdom, opting instead for "foolishness." And then, right in the middle of this weird deck of cards called the church, they somehow connected suffering to flourishing.

Life in the first-century Roman church brought suffering to the front of the discussion. Today, however, we have done our best to push it back into the corners, out the vestibule, out the door, and, we hope, gone for good. But the reality is that flourishing and suffering are one of the most important connections Christians have ever made.

Have you ever wondered what the apostle Paul looked like? Was he tall and handsome? Was he short? Or was he stooped and bow-legged — as someone claimed in the early church? Here's what that source, called *The Acts of Paul and Thecla*, said of Paul: "And he [Titus] saw Paul coming, a man small in size, bald-headed, bandy-legged, of noble [manner], with eyebrows meeting, rather hook-nosed, full of grace." When I read that text aloud in class, one of my students barked out, "Dude was a uni-brow!" We don't know for sure, but I suspect this image is more accurate than not. But there's something far more noteworthy about Paul's appearance.

What do you think he looked like after a life of physical abuse? Luke tells us that right after his conversion, after he had returned to Jerusalem for a brief but quite eventful visit, the "Hellenistic Jews" were upset enough with him that "they tried to kill him" (Acts 9:29; 20:3; 21:31 – 32; 23:12 – 15). Some of these attempts would have showed up on his body like tattoos. In Philippi, Paul was stripped and then beaten with rods — "severely flogged," Scripture puts it — and then they put this severely flogged man into prison stocks. And if we think they washed him down, we are misled (16:22 – 24). So surely he had deep wounds, cuts, bruises, infections, and scars from head to foot. This one set of lines from 2 Corinthians gives us all we need:

> I have worked much harder, been in prison more frequently, been flogged more severely, and been exposed to death again and again. Five times I received from the Jews the forty lashes minus one. Three times I was beaten with rods, once I was pelted with stones. (2 Corinthians 11:23 – 25)

Paul's specifics can be tallied alongside my own list of what he suffered, which includes routine verbal opposition and abuse (Acts 13:45; 14:2; 17:13; 18:6; 19:9); trumped-up false accusations (21:27 – 29), legal or not (18:12); physical expulsion from cities (13:50); attempts on his life (14:5 – 6); beatings (21:32); and betrayal by fellow Christians (2 Timothy 1:15; 4:16).

When I had hair, I used to get my hair cut at Libertyville Barber, and that barbershop was and still remains a culture unto itself. (If you happen by, step in and you'll see what I mean. Ask for Brad.) On the wall at that time was a picture of a lost dog with a caption that said something like this: *Missing, three-legged dog, blind in the left eye, missing his right ear, suffers from hemorrhoids. Answers to the name Lucky.* I think that's how Paul saw his own life and body! But instead of "Lucky," Paul would have used the name "Blessed."

Alongside what we have said about Paul's beaten body, listen to these words of Rodney Reeves about Paul's experiences:

> Paul was a poor speaker. He worked with his hands to make a living. Bad things happened to him all the time. The churches he started were filled with problems. He was run out of nearly every town he visited. The Romans despised him. His own people abused him. Other missionaries mocked him. Give these circumstances, only a fool would say he was blessed by God.[1]

After listing Paul's own cross-shaped life as the true kind of life, Rodney Reeves then puts down his book, takes a sip from his coffee, looks us in the eye, clears his throat, and observes with firm clarity:

> The problem today is we don't think Paul was right about that. In fact, in most of our churches we believe just the opposite: only the best and brightest are put on the stage to teach the rest of us how to overcome our weaknesses.... The message is undeniable: only the healthy, wealthy and wise have anything to say. The sick, poor and foolish should keep their mouths shut.[2]

Paul was a sick man, a poor man, and a foolish man. Back to our question: What did Paul look like? By the time he died, that body of his must have been scarred all over. There is something morbidly fascinating about this beaten, bruised, broken-boned, and bloody man — and that he pondered suffering puts each of us in his debt.

Paul, paradoxically, connected suffering to flourishing. I suspect our great apostle looked at his bumps and broken bones and saw them as signs of grace, signs of the gospel, signs of his faithfulness to his Lord, signs of what he endured so Gentiles and Jews would come together in the salad bowl, and signs of the kingdom of God. Why? Because a flourishing Christian experiences suffering through the eyes of faith. Instead of looking at how Paul explained suffering as "lessons about suffering," I suggest we see his explanations as *expressions of a flourishing Christian in the midst of suffering.*

SUFFERING: PAUL'S AND OURS

Do you think the suffering from persecution — that is, something directly resulting from one's faith — should sit down next to other kinds of suffering? Like the injustice of poverty, a life of sickness, cancers too early in life, having a spouse die before her or his time, sexual abuse, ethnic prejudice, age discrimination, job cuts? Are these comparable to persecution?

Yes and No. First the No. No, because some of our own sufferings are not attributable to our life of following Jesus. Some of our sufferings are the random experiences of human existence. But Yes in the sense that physical suffering of any sort puts us face to face with pain and with the questions of how to endure, how to engage, and how to live through the suffering. In that sense, then, all suffering challenges us to believe in God, to hope for justice and the kingdom of God, and to trust the gospel as each of us faces suffering.

Margaret Kim Peterson, a professor at Eastern University and an author of a number of books, married Hyung Goo Kim, who in an earlier time in his life had contracted AIDS. She wrote beautifully about their life together and about his death in her book *Sing Me to Heaven.* She then married Dwight Peterson, a man who at eighteen contracted transverse myelitis and has been in a wheelchair ever since. The Petersons have a son. Dwight is now (as I write this) in hospice care dying of infections from a "pressure ulcer." Margaret, who encounters these ravaging powers of death in a rational, pondering, faithful, steely, and hopeful disposition, has suffered, is suffering, and will suffer. When Dwight was asked to give the convocation address at Eastern University, he chose as his topic *weakness,* the very term Paul uses of his own sufferings.

What strikes me about Dwight's address[3] is that his approach is the same approach the apostle Paul gives for his own persecution. With some wit and no romanticizing of pain and suffering, Dwight asked the big question: *What if we choose weakness as the approach to life?* He answers that "we might turn out to be a bit more like Jesus." But Dwight drills down to deeper reality:

> If you think being a Christian is largely about winning, dominion, wealth, influence, political power, and even empire, you're not following the gospel of Jesus Christ. Because the God we see in Jesus Christ lived out his life in weakness.

Dwight continues to observe that if we choose the way of Jesus and Paul — the way of weakness as they define it — we would be able to receive more gracefully and more faithfully. Learning to see suffering, as Paul did, through the word *weakness* reshapes suffering into a life of flourishing.

IN SUFFERING WE PARTICIPATE IN JESUS' OWN SUFFERINGS

When I read Dwight's address, I saw Jesus and the cross — and on that cross the very heart of God. The gospel, according to Paul, can be summarized in three statements: "Remember Jesus Christ, raised from the dead, descended from David" (2 Timothy 2:8). Paul says, "This is my gospel," but then Paul makes a dramatic move because he ties our endurance of suffering to Jesus' own sufferings:

> If we died with him,
> we will also live with him;
> if we endure,
> we will also reign with him. (2 Timothy 2:11 – 12)

Everything from social exclusion and verbal abuse to physical abuse and martyrdom is what Paul means by endurance. Not that I'm suggesting even for a moment that we need to endure abuse in order to take up our cross — far from it. (Leave that situation immediately and seek help.) In every form of suffering, however, we directly experience the gospel, because the gospel is about suffering giving way to death and beyond death to the victory of resurrection. And God lovingly draws us into his experience in every experience of suffering.

Connecting suffering to Jesus transforms suffering from something to avoid into something we share with our Lord. This is why Paul told the Christians of Asia Minor that "we must go through many hardships to enter the kingdom of God" (Acts 14:22). He's not saying we ought to create social conditions so we can generate some persecution, but instead that a faithful and flourishing life will lead to experiencing suffering. One is reminded of the famous words of George Macdonald, who said that Jesus "suffered unto the death, not that [we] might not suffer, but that [our] suffering might be like his."[4]

IN SUFFERING OUR CHARACTER IS FORMED

A flourishing follower of Jesus sees what happens to her or to him through suffering, and I want to make this clearer by separating Paul's famous lines:

> Not only so, but we also glory in our sufferings, because we know that:
> suffering produces perseverance;
> perseverance, character;
> and character, hope. (Romans 5:3–4)

The Christian who endures becomes a more mature Christian because of the endurance. Suffering, in other words, becomes a means to flourish. The next story illustrates the point.

LADY WITH THE BIG FANCY HAT

Behind some of America's most influential evangelicals is a woman, and I'm not talking about mothers and wives and sisters behind a man. Behind much of the Sunday School teaching curriculum now used in churches around the globe is a woman most Christian leaders have never heard of: Henrietta Mears.[5] She was a public school teacher in Minnesota when Dr.

Stewart MacLennan was the guest preacher in her home church. MacLennan was pastor at Hollywood Presbyterian Church who saw potential in Henrietta and her sister. So he invited them for a "visit" that became a life (along with better weather). Henrietta, dressed always in her famous big fancy hats, took a small Sunday school program of four hundred and it grew to six thousand! Her Sunday school, in fact, became a worldwide ministry, beginning with curriculum and a publishing house, as well as a book called *What the Bible Is All About*. For years that book, "nothing" more than her Sunday school notes, was a gift given by the Billy Graham Evangelistic Association to anyone who came forward to profess faith in Christ. The estimation is that more than four million of those books have been printed. Henrietta was called "The Teacher" by all who knew her, but Billy Graham's words about her are perhaps best known:

> Dr. Henrietta C. Mears is one of the greatest Christians I have ever known! I doubt that any other woman outside my wife and mother has had such a marked influence on my life. Her gracious spirit, her devotional life, her steadfastness for the simple Gospel, and her knowledge of the Bible have been a continual inspiration and amazement to me.

Why tell this? Because her character was formed in suffering. The lives of many Christians are wrapped in undocumented misery or, at least, unknown but to a few. I think of a decade or more of dysfunction surrounding C. S. Lewis in his most influential years. His brother, Warnie, suffering from alcoholism, and Mrs. Moore, a woman whom Lewis cared for and about, suffering dementia. These sufferings led to his own. His more-than-peculiar marriage to Joy Davidman was quickly followed by her cancer, Lewis's own absorption of her pain, her death, and his emotional and originally pseudonymous *A Grief Observed*. Few knew the suffering of Lewis.

The same was true of Henrietta Mears. Marcus Brotherton, one of her biographers, sums up her early years well:

> Sometimes deep spiritual comprehension comes through times of loss or the death of a loved one. That dark night in her dorm room [where she learned of her mother's death] seemed to conclude Henrietta's childhood

and launch her into adult life and ministry with newfound strength and vitality. Already her life had been marked by joy and sorrow, luxury and pain. By the time she was 20, she had lost two siblings and her mother — her father would soon follow. One of her brothers was deaf. She had been sick for two years, and then healed. Her eyesight was a constant liability.

Indeed, a woman with bad eyesight wrote a book that influenced the entire world of evangelical Christianity. Henrietta never married, but her sister Margaret was her constant companion — in fact, she managed Henrietta's life and home. When Margaret died, it was a serious blow to Henrietta, one that tested her capacity to press on. The Wednesday after her sister's passing at a college prayer meeting Henrietta opened with Paul-like words that revealed what suffering had accomplished in her:

> I had thought that I would not come tonight. Then I realized what an opportunity I would be passing up if I did not come. I have been teaching you collegians for the last 25 years that God is able and that He does sustain us in any situation. I am here tonight to tell you that my God is able, and that He is my sufficiency at this very moment.

No doubt, Henrietta's character was formed through all her suffering and joy.

IN SUFFERING WE CREATE OPPORTUNITIES TO SHOW OUR LOVE

Suffering is present in the local church in a variety of ways, but one element that deserves our attention here is that when someone in this fellowship of differents begins to suffer, we are given the opportunity to suffer with them. We can see this theologically: as Christ died *with us*, so we are to die *with Christ*. But there's more, for when others suffer, we enter into their suffering sympathetically as an act of love, and sometimes our act of sympathy works redemptively to relieve those who suffer. I think this is in part what Paul meant in that most difficult of verses in Colossians 1:24: "Now I rejoice in what I am suffering for you, and I fill up in my flesh what is still lacking in regard to Christ's afflictions, for the sake of the body, which is the church." Allow me to say that Paul is suffering sympathetically and for the good of others.

We too can enter into the suffering of others, and we do this in a common experience in our fellowships. My wife has a good friend who recently discovered she has cancer. Beside the numbing realization that having cancer does to our deepest being, and beside the worrying and Googling and asking around that the dreaded disease does to us, her friend has told Kris her story. Kris has spent time on the phone, jotted one short email after another, reminded her of her prayers, and has expressed loving sympathy through their embraces and tears. I can say, by watching Kris, that she has taken on her friend's pain and suffering, and from what I have heard in conversations, her friend has found some sympathetic relief in Kris's love.

IN SUFFERING WE FACE A CHOICE: SELF OR OTHERS

Suffering has a way of making us think about ourselves. Whether we have a small ache or more serious sickness leading us to wonder if we have a dreaded disease, our tendency is to think about ourselves, to dig inside, and to brood over life and death and eternity. Perhaps even to feel sorry for ourselves. I'm sure Paul did the same, because after all he'd been through, he could easily provide a listing of all his sufferings! But there's something quite notable about this flourishing apostle's thoughts on suffering — another help he provides us with facing suffering. It is one of my favorite set of lines by Paul about suffering, and I have italicized the major expression, which reveals Paul has turned the temptation to self-absorption into an opportunity to serve his house churches:

> Remember Jesus Christ, raised from the dead, descended from David. This is my gospel, for which I am suffering even to the point of being chained like a criminal. But God's word is not chained. *Therefore I endure everything for the sake of the elect, that they too may obtain the salvation that is in Christ Jesus, with eternal glory.* (2 Timothy 2:8 – 10)

Paul has a "missional" orientation even to his suffering. Sitting in the middle of the church with all these new Gentile followers of Jesus, Paul is suffering — but he thinks of others. Paul also challenges his own suffering in order to lead others into Christlikeness, holiness, love, and peace.

There's more. Paul knows that his suffering, shaped as it is by gospel and the development of character, encourages others to endure. Notice what the bruised-up Paul says in the midst of suffering in prison:

> And because of my chains, most of the brothers and sisters have become confident in the Lord and dare all the more to proclaim the gospel without fear. (Philippians 1:14)

Suffering, for the flourishing follower of Jesus, accomplishes what the eye does not see but the heart knows — that God is at work, and that he will turn the crosses of suffering into the resurrections of new creation.

Here we find ourselves plopped down in the salad bowl of all sorts of ingredients. There are, in fact, perhaps too many for us to take in at once. That is, when the church is what God designed it to be, it is a fellowship of differents: Asian and African Americans, Latins and European, men and women, young and old, manual laborers and the aristocratic wealthy, intellectual types and pragmatic types — pull out your Myers Briggs scales and scan them — and we are all together. That is what the church is supposed to be.

But doing so is a challenge, and I want to suggest that working for this kind of fellowship entails suffering, some of it emotional and some of it physical. That, too, is what the church is about. Flourishing in this new community is what God wants for us, and when we let that work of God shape us, we will discover something that transcends what anyone could expect.

22

On a Walk with Kris

On a walk with Kris in the crisp air that a Midwest autumn provides — the trees turning shades of yellows and reds, the sky piercing blue — in the quiet moments of that walk, I asked myself what one word best summarizes Paul's vision of the flourishing Christian life. And the one and only word that came to mind was the word *joy*.

Paul says flourishing is being filled with joy. "May the God of hope," he prays for the Roman Christians, "fill you with all *joy* and peace as you trust in him, so that you may overflow with hope by the power of the Holy Spirit" (Romans 15:13). That's about as good a verse as you can find for what Paul believed about the Christian life — churches flourishing in joy and hope through the Spirit. Right there, in the midst of all his suffering, in the midst of the hassles with the Corinthians, in the midst of house churches composed of folks who had never once enjoyed any kind of social fellowship, Paul swallows all the negatives up with this word *joy*. He wants the whole fellowship to be intoxicated with a God-shaped joy.

Joy is easily connected in our culture with the word *happiness*. So we wonder how it is that Denmark is the happiest country in the world in spite of widespread disbelief in God. Maybe it's basic income levels or educational opportunities, or personal rights or houses and land and internet for everyone. But we're missing the point. These cultural studies might be inklings of what makes a person "happy," but the word *happy* and the word *joy* are not at all the same. So first, a bit of a romp into happiness studies so we can learn to transcend "happiness" with the Christian idea of "joy."[1]

HAPPINESS

I typed in "happiness" at Amazon.com and in an instant discovered there were 263,716 titles connected to that keyword. Titles connected to Jesus rival happiness at 259,497. Happiness, apparently, is an industry and something we can achieve, so we get titles such as these:

> *The How of Happiness: A Scientific Approach to Getting the Life You Want*
> *Happier: Learn the Secrets to Daily Joy and Lasting Fulfillment*
> *Authentic Happiness: Using the New Positive Psychology to Realize Your Potential for Lasting Fulfillment.*

What is happiness? No one less than Richard Layard, one of Britain's best-known economists and a world expert on inequality, reveals an answer that just about everyone already knew: "Happiness is feeling good, and misery is feeling bad." The philosopher Jennifer Michael Hecht also says "happiness is feeling good."[2] Happiness studies seek to find who is feeling good, and feeling good is connected to good things in our life, such as income, houses, clothing, cars, good-looking spouses, and bright little children who win all their soccer games and who go on exotic vacations for Spring Break and who come back with happy faces and tanned skin.

But Layard reminds us that "as Western societies have got richer, their people have become no happier." In spite of all of our economic growth, we are not getting happier and here's why: happiness works by comparing ourselves to others. As long as we (Westerners) have more than our neighbor, we are happy. The move from poverty to a more comfortable life, to be sure, does increase a person's happiness, but beyond basic possessions those increases don't make us happier. Why? It's called the "hedonic treadmill." In brief, the more we have, the more we want, and the more we want, the less we can get and the less we are happy. The treadmill keeps running, and it wears us down. A study of two million people concluded that we live in a pattern of happiness: under forty we are not so happy, forty-somethings are happy, and older folks are not as happy — at age forty-four we reach our peak of happiness. Yikes, I'm more than fifteen years past my happiness prime!

But what would these happiness experts say about Paul's happiness rating? He'd be at the bottom of their studies. There really is no need to ask, however, because Paul was into "joy," not "happiness," and the difference between the two is dramatic. So here are two golden points about joy from Paul's life:

Joy is an experience *only* for the flourishing follower in fellowship.
Joy occurs regardless of life's circumstances.

We might add a third point.

Forget happiness and go for joy.

We fasten this chapter on joy to the previous chapter on suffering. There we saw that in the midst of suffering, the flourishing Christian experienced the gospel, character development, and the heart to serve others. What Paul means by "joy" flows directly from the gospel — the story about Jesus who suffered on the cross, who was buried, who was raised, and who is now ruling as the exalted one. So suffering and joy are not incompatible. Getting rid of suffering is what happiness studies are all about, but the Christian sense of joy counters all that. For Paul, those who experience suffering in a gospel-shaped way are those who know the meaning of joy. From the previous chapter on suffering, then, we can claim that the apostle Paul, Margaret and Dwight Peterson, and Henrietta Mears knew joy. It does not matter if they were or are "happy" as defined today. I'm quite confident that Paul might turn up "miserable" in modern happiness studies, and he'd do so full of joy! (And be quite happy about it.)

PAUL'S JOY ON DISPLAY

Paul is in a major Roman colony called Philippi, along the northern coast of Greece. He looks for a synagogue, thinking one close to a river (for purity immersions) is likely, and meets up with Lydia who gives her life and home to Jesus (and Paul). Once on his way to the synagogue, often called a "house of prayer," he encounters a demon-possessed woman and exorcises the demon. Her liberation threatens the profits from her prophecies, and for upsetting the economic and religious balance in Philippi, Paul and Silas are dragged before the authorities, stripped and beaten with rods, and tossed into prison where their feet were placed in locks. Now comes the joy part:

> About midnight Paul and Silas were praying and singing hymns to God, and the other prisoners were listening to them. (Acts 16:25)

Here Paul's "theory of joy" (if he had one) is on display. Because of his mission, he starts in the synagogue and expands its reach to include Gentiles. Then comes persecution, and in the midst of his imprisonment in Philippi for declaring an include-the-Gentiles-and-Jews gospel, he and Silas are praising God. Not because they are unfeeling. Not because they are doing this as a kind of nonviolent protest. No, they are filled with joy because they know their experience of suffering (as we discovered in the previous chapter) is participation in the gospel.

It doesn't end there. An earthquake jolts the place, freeing them, and the jailor knows his life is in jeopardy if the prisoners escape. Paul calms him down, and the man begs Paul to tell him how to be saved. He must have learned the gospel message about salvation from their joyful praises, and Paul "gospels" him by pointing him to Jesus, when he says, "Believe in the Lord Jesus and you will be saved — you and your household" (Acts 16:31). The converted jailor then washes their wounds, takes them to his house, and feeds them. We then read that the jailor "was filled with joy because he had come to believe in God" (16:34).

Paul's theory of joy is exercising the gift God has given you, experiencing the gospel in suffering if such occurs, knowing that God is still at work, and sharing that joy with others in the fellowship of the church.

What is joy? Joy is the inner satisfaction that comes from understanding our location in life in light of who God is and where God will eventually bring us — his kingdom.

AIM AT JOY

Joy is not something we purchase or create. Joy is one of the fruits of the Spirit, which is to say joy emerges in the flourishing follower because of the inner work of the Spirit (Galatians 5:22). But joy is not an accident for the apostle. The following lines from the span of Paul's career show the importance of joy:

> *Rejoice* always. (1 Thessalonians 5:16)
> Finally, brothers and sisters, *rejoice*! (2 Corinthians 13:11)
> *Rejoice* in the Lord always. I will say it again: *Rejoice*! (Philippians 4:4)

Very few get through reading this list of verses without asking why Paul thinks he can *command* people to be joyful. But commanding us to rejoice suggests that joy is within our capacity to choose. Joy, then, is a desired aim of the flourishing Christian, and one of Paul's ministry aims was for his churches to be full of joy:

> For what is our hope, our *joy*, or the crown in which we will glory in the presence of our Lord Jesus when he comes? Is it not you? Indeed, you are our glory and *joy*. (1 Thessalonians 2:19 – 20)

> Convinced of this, I know that I will remain, and I will continue with all of you for your progress and *joy* in the faith. (Philippians 1:25)

We might be a bit taken back by how significant joy is to Paul, so perhaps we need to back up and think this through. Paul's mission was for other people — like the Thessalonians, the Corinthians, and the

Philippians — to grow into Christlikeness. And their growth in that direction *brought joy to Paul.*

SHARE YOUR JOY

Lynn Cohick, countering nearly everything we read about in happiness studies, says, "Joy comes from people, not things. Joy comes from relationships, not from circumstances or experiences."[3] The Christian life is not lived alone because God designed it as a fellowship for each of the ingredients — each of the differents — in the salad bowl. Fellowship is about sharing life. We can share one another's joy, as Paul notes when he writes, "I had confidence in all of you, that you would all share my joy" (2 Corinthians 2:3). He makes this even clearer in Romans 12:15 when he sees fellowship in the upper and downer experiences of life: "Rejoice with those who rejoice; mourn with those who mourn." The love others had for Paul brought him joy, just as his love for them brought them joy: "Your love has given me great joy and encouragement, because you, brother, have refreshed the hearts of the Lord's people" (Philemon 7).

Joy for the apostle Paul was not about his station in life or realizing his dreams or resting sure in his financial situation. Joy for him was about participating in the fellowship of differents because he was part of God's plan for the world. Joy, to put it directly, is a church-shaped disposition. Only folks in the church can experience what Paul means by joy.

I suspect we experience this kind of joy more often than we realize. One of the greatest writers of the twentieth century — in fact, *the* finest for some — was J. R. R. Tolkien. Tolkien struggled through discouragement with all his manuscripts and needed the encouragement of others to get the books off his desk. In Alister McGrath's wondrous biography of C. S. Lewis, he tells many stories about the friendship of Lewis and Tolkien, focusing on Lewis as the encouraging midwife to Tolkien's inestimable *The Hobbit.* But the story of how that book got published gets a summary in McGrath illustrating the shared joy and excitement of the pair:

Tolkien had lent the manuscript of *The Hobbit* to one of his students, Elaine Griffiths (1909 – 1996). Griffiths in turn drew the text to the attention of Susan Dagnall, a former Oxford student now working for the London publisher George Allen & Unwin for his evaluation. After securing a copy of the typescript, Dagnall passed it on to the publisher Stanley Unwin for his evalution. Unwin in turn asked his ten-year-old son, Rayner, to read it. Rayner gave it such an enthusiastic review that Unwin decided to publish it. The contract's deadline for submission gave Tolkien the motivation he so badly needed to complete the writing. On 3 October 1936, the work was complete....

Realising the potential of this new and unexpected market for hobbits, Allen & Unwin pressed Tolkien to write another "Hobbit-Book" — quickly. As Tolkien had no intention whatsoever of writing a sequel to his book, this demand proved to something of a challenge.[4]

Tolkien had too much to do to get on with another Hobbit book, and the whole project could easily have collapsed. But McGrath observes, "Only one other person seemed to be interested in the work: Lewis." After Lewis's death, Tolkien said this:

The unpayable debt that I owe to [Lewis] was not "influence" as it is ordinarily understood, but sheer encouragement.... Only from him did I ever get the idea that my "stuff" could be more than a private hobby. But for his interest and unceasing eagerness for more I should never have brought *The L. of the R.* to a conclusion.

A ten-year-old boy, an excited publisher, and an eager and joyous friend, C. S. Lewis, and we now have the grandeur of *The Lord of the Rings*. Joy passed from one to the other.

Recently I was thinking through the subject of encouragement because of an experience with a writer — Leslie Fields — who sent me her memoir because she knew I liked memoirs. This happened the same day my daughter shared her joy over her students' efforts to comfort the homeless by providing care packages, the same day Kris's sister wrote us about some new furniture arriving for her condominium in Florida, and the same day a student expressed appreciation in an email for something I had outlined in class that provided substance for a sermon he gave at church, which caused some joy in his listeners.

Joy is about sharing our lives, from the ordinary and routine to the sublime and special. Joy marks the gospel-shaped flourishing Christian. It surely marked the apostle Paul, the man who defies our happiness scales. I have tried, to quote Robert Louis Stevenson, "to find where joy resides, and give it a voice beyond singing."[5] Of this I'm quite confident, that gospel joy is found in Christ and in the fellowship of differents he has created.

APPENDIX

The Graces of Paul's Life

THE GRACE OF FINDING A VOICE

According to church tradition, Paul's family was from a Galilean village called Gischala,[1] approximately twelve miles northwest of Capernaum, where Jesus' ministry was based. When the Romans conquered the area, it is likely Paul's father became a Roman slave, was moved to Tarsus where he continued his observance of the Torah, and was later set free and acquired Roman citizenship. Paul was born somewhere around AD 1 in Tarsus, a premier city in the heart of Turkey (in Cilicia), where there was a flourishing, if snobbish, system of classical education. Tarsus was the Harvard of the Roman Empire.

Maybe because they recognized Paul's brilliance or because they feared the impact of Tarsus on their son, Paul's Torah-observant family either moved to Jerusalem when he was young or he was sent to Jerusalem when he was but a boy. Paul was educated there in Jerusalem, in the Torah, at the feet of the great Gamaliel, and eventually Paul became a leading Pharisee of the city. Paul was a blue blood when it came to those who cared most about the Torah and piety. He was also a blue blood because he was a Roman citizen. By God's grace, Paul found a voice, a Torah voice, a zealous obedience voice.

Here are some words that describe Paul before he became a follower of King Jesus, Messiah of Israel:

+ Roman citizen
+ trilingual: Greek, Hebrew, and its dialect, Aramaic
+ from Jerusalem
+ observant of the Torah
+ student of Rabbi Gamaliel
+ Pharisee
+ zealous for the Torah and for Pharisaism
+ competitive for the best form of Judaism
+ taught in Jerusalem Greek-speaking synagogues
+ persecuted the Hellenistic Jews who believed Jesus was Messiah and who were critical of the temple and perhaps some of the Torah

Of these terms, I would choose two as the most important: Torah and Pharisee. Paul's family was observant, Paul was observant, and Paul thought the Pharisees were the most observant of the many Jewish groups of his day. So observant was he that he opposed those who chose not to be observant.

Before his encounter with Jesus on the road to Damascus, then, Paul found his voice as a zealous, fierce observer of the Torah as the Pharisees interpreted it. Nothing mattered more to Paul than doing God's will.

THE GRACE OF A NEW LIFE AND MISSION

Paul's zeal to follow the Torah and protect the glory of God drove him to oppose an early group of Greek-speaking Jewish Christians, first supporting the martyrdom of Stephen, then chasing others from Jerusalem, and then acquiring permission from the high priest — Caiaphas, the one who tried Jesus — to hunt down the messianists all the way to Damascus. (Damascus was a two- or three-day journey from Capernaum, the north side of the Sea of Galilee.) Not far from Damascus, the Lord Jesus appeared to Saul, revealing to him that he was not simply opposing the messianists, but was actually opposing himself, Jesus. Here are Luke's words from Acts 9:1 – 6:

> Meanwhile, Saul was still breathing out murderous threats against the Lord's disciples. He went to the high priest and asked him for letters to the synagogues in Damascus, so that if he found any there who belonged to the Way, whether men or women, he might take them as prisoners to Jerusalem. As he neared Damascus on his journey, suddenly a light from heaven flashed around him. He fell to the ground and heard a voice say to him, "Saul, Saul, why do you persecute me?"
>
> "Who are you, Lord?" Saul asked.
>
> "I am Jesus, whom you are persecuting," he replied. "Now get up and go into the city, and you will be told what you must do."

Paul was never the same. He spilled his life to accomplish this calling: he would gospel Gentiles and he would fight fiercely to get messianic Jews and Gentile believers to fellowship and worship *together*. This new life and new vocation for Paul was because of God's forgiving, renewing, and empowering grace.

Paul did not *change religions* on the road to Damascus, but he was converted from being a Christ-opposing Pharisee to a Christ-honoring Pharisee. Paul will later tell a court that he was still a Pharisee (Acts 23:6). For Paul being a Pharisee did not mean one could not be a Christian, but it meant a special kind of Pharisee: a messianic Pharisee!

What is most notable about Paul's conversion outside Damascus was that he was graced with a new, special mission in life: *to gospel Gentiles in the Roman world*. Paul was uniquely ready for this mission, and one would have to say God had prepared him: he was a Roman citizen, he could speak Greek, he could preach, and he was fiercely courageous. These attributes kept him going for three decades.

THE GRACE OF FELLOWSHIP

In the flush and excitement of encountering the risen Lord and in the joy of his newly formed messianic faith, Paul may well have looked with dreamy eyes toward the mission Jesus gave to him: *to gospel Gentiles*. What he didn't know was how difficult the task would be at three levels: *the Bible, the people, and the body.*

Paul clearly spent hours and hours poring over what we call the Old Testament to see how Gentiles fit into the people of God. In his letters to the Galatians and to the Romans, Paul would pull out one verse after another supporting God's call on his life. What he would have to argue is that *he and his Pharisee-trained observant Jews did not see how important Gentiles were to God.* The major texts for Paul came to be Genesis 12:3: "All peoples on earth [Gentiles!] will be blessed through you [Abraham]," as well as Genesis 15:6: "Abram believed the LORD, and he credited it to him as righteousness."

Paul's theological and biblical argument was kosher, but getting other messianic Jews to agree was difficult — and getting them to live it out nearly impossible. After all, they surely wondered aloud, "Didn't God say circumcision was necessary? Didn't God say Gentile converts would have to embrace the God-given Torah? Didn't God give the Torah?" So we find major traces of this problem vexing Paul's ministries — the problem of gospeling Gentiles and welcoming them into the one people of God without having to become Jews and undergo the knife of circumcision. We see this in two of Paul's letters, Galatians and Romans, and this festering sore broke wide open leading to the Apostolic Council in Jerusalem in AD 49, where Peter, Barnabas, Paul, and then James offered public defenses for including Gentiles without demanding that they become Jewish converts.

Yes, this mission cost Paul physically. "I bear on my body the marks of Jesus," Paul wrote to the Galatians in 6:17, and this no doubt describes the physical remains of public beatings, stonings, and physical violence at the hands of both Gentiles who thought he was disloyal to the emperor and Jews who thought he, too, the student of Gamaliel, had apostasized from loyalty to the Torah. They treated him as he had treated those early messianic Jews in Jerusalem.

THE GRACE OF HOPE

We learn about the periods of Paul's life by the struggles of Christians in his churches. What we get from Paul is not an autobiographical reflection on how his mind developed, such as we get in Augustine's *Confessions*. What we get instead is a series of letters in which Paul responds to issues in churches.

Early in Paul's ministry, after he established the church in Thessalonica, the Christians there got too excited about Christian belief about God's future, that is, about eschatology and the return of Christ. So excited were they and so convinced that Jesus was about to return, they stopped working and started hanging out for him to return. One preacher I heard as a teenager was so amped up about the rapture and so convincing in his claims that I made an appointment with my pastor to ask him if I should even bother going to college! (He wisely said I should, just in case the preacher was wrong. He was right.) So what the Thessalonians experienced was just the first in a line of Christians whose enthusiasm about the return of Christ began to alter their way of life.

What did Paul teach them? First, that Jesus was coming again, that no one knows when, and that they can therefore have a life shaped wondrously by *hope*. Hope is living now in light of God's good hand of grace to come. Too many Christians today are "into" eschatology — things such as the rapture, the second coming, the tribulation, and world events — for all the wrong reasons. They are curious. Paul's teachings were about *hope* — hope for this world and for the kingdom and for life eternal. Paul didn't seek to satisfy curiosity. He sought to assure them that our gracious God would make all things right some day.

Second, Paul taught that Jesus would rescue them from oppression, sin, and death. When Jesus rescued them, they would be safe with God's good hand of grace forever and would enjoy life in God's kingdom. But that does not mean they won't suffer some before he comes. In fact, Paul tells them that the God-defying, seductive "man of lawlessness" will be unleashed before Jesus returns (2 Thessalonians 2:3).

Third, he taught that they were to be faithful in following Jesus until he comes. Paul told them to live a life "worthy of God, who calls you into his kingdom" (1 Thessalonian 2:12). He instructed them to "live a holy life" and a "quiet life" (4:7, 11). God's grace makes that kind of life possible now.

Finally, Paul taught that they were to go back to work (2 Thessalonians 3:11 – 13).

THE GRACE OF UNITY

Paul faced divisions in his rearview mirror. By the time he got to the next stop in his missionary work, someone seems to have informed him that things weren't going so well in the church he just left. He established a wonderful work of God in Galatia, but as soon as he moved on he heard the "Judaizers" had moved in and were convincing his grace-shaped Christians to get circumcised because it was necessary to become a Jew in order to become a full Christian. So in Galatia Paul was dealing with the pro-Judaizing Christians and the pro-Paul Christians.

When Paul looked back on the divisions in Corinth, he could see them battling about everything. They battled one another over wisdom and who was the most important leader in the church; they battled over how best to treat an incestuous man; they battled with one another in court; they battled over the goodness of marriage and the grounds for divorce; they battled over Paul's way of being an apostle; they battled over whether to eat foods that had been sacrificed to false gods; they battled over how sacred the Lord's Supper was; they battled over which spiritual gifts had the most glory; and they battled over questions (who? and when?) about the resurrection.

Romans does not start out looking like a letter addressing the same problems. In fact, for some, Romans seems to be a letter for systematic theologians. Not so. Paul's argument is that in Jesus Christ both Gentiles and Jews are admitted into the fellowship on the basis of what Jesus has done for them and through faith, faith alone, and not by doing the works of the Torah. In other words, we hear Galatians all over again: the Gentiles don't have to become Jews to be Jesus' people. In Romans this doesn't show up until chapter 14, but once you see it in blazing letters there, you need to start that letter all over again and see that Romans 1 – 8 establishes the ground rules for how Jewish believers and Gentiles believers are to dwell together in love, peace, and fellowship.

Some of you know how complicated Romans 9 – 11 is, and for some those three chapters seem to come from nowhere. But let me suggest that if you read Romans 14 – 16 first, you will see that Romans 1 – 8 set out the ground rules for what follows. Romans 9 – 11 is concerned, then, with showing that in accepting Gentiles into God's family without having to convert to Judaism, God was not abandoning his promises to Israel back in the Old Testament. The division between the "weak" (Jewish believers) and the "strong" (Gentile believers) was to give way to unity in the fellowship in Rome.

How did Paul deal with all these divisions? Paul had a strategy, not an easy one to accomplish, but it was gospel-centered: they were to die to self and to live unto others, and they were to do this by loving one another, by living a life of constrained freedom, and by living a holy life. This would lead to what happens when God's good hand of grace takes over — unity in the fellowship of the Spirit. This unity was embodied when the Gentile churches sacrificially and voluntarily gave funds for their mother church, the church of Jesus in Jerusalem.

THE GRACE OF THE CHURCH

Paul's letters do not enable us to map the theological life of the apostle. Instead, they give us episodes in his life. They give us fragments of a life. We are unwise if we think what we find in his later letters, say Philippians, is a new development because it doesn't appear until later in his life. If his letters were written as "my theology right now" briefs, then we would be able to trace his intellectual life. But they aren't that, so we can't do that. They are episodes, pastoral and theological episodes, in the life of a world-class traveling apostle.

Later in his life, then, in his letters to the churches in Colossae, Ephesus, and Philippi, and in his personal letter to Philemon, we see another theme in Paul's life: *the grace of God's good hand at work in the church in the world.* By this I mean we see Paul's grasp of what God is doing in the church in the scope of world and cosmic history — and we learn to see cosmic history by what God is doing in and through the church. If we read these letters and then read from Galatians right through Romans, we will gain the fullest perspective possible on Paul's thought. These letters reveal God's grace unleashed into the whole world.

Throughout these episodic letters of Paul, we learn the big picture about Christ as the preeminent ruling and saving one in all the cosmos, of the church as the body of Christ in this world, and of the plan of God for the unity of Jews and Gentiles in the one body of Christ because of the special mission of Paul, where God is at work now to include Gentiles in the one body of Christ. We learn of the cosmic battle now at work against the body of Christ, and how the church — as a church and as a family — is to live in the Roman world.

If I picked one passage in the prison letters of Paul about the grace of the church in this world, it would be Colossians 1:15 – 20:

> The Son is the image of the invisible God, the firstborn over all creation. For in him all things were created: things in heaven and on earth, visible and invisible, whether thrones or powers or rulers or authorities; all things have been created through him and for him. He is before all things, and in him all things hold together. And he is the head of the body, the church; he is the beginning and the firstborn from among the dead, so that in everything he might have the supremacy. For God was pleased to have all his fullness dwell in him, and through him to reconcile to himself all things, whether things on earth or things in heaven, by making peace through his blood, shed on the cross.

But it's hard not to pick Ephesians 2:14 – 18 as well:

> For he himself is our peace, who has made the two groups one and has destroyed the barrier, the dividing wall of hostility, by setting aside in

his flesh the law with its commands and regulations. His purpose was to create in himself one new humanity out of the two, thus making peace, and in one body to reconcile both of them to God through the cross, by which he put to death their hostility. He came and preached peace to you who were far away and peace to those who were near. For through him we both have access to the Father by one Spirit.

These two passages reveal the heart of Paul's entire gospel: Jesus is the center of it all, and in Jesus Christ, in the body of Christ, God's people are one: both Jews and Gentiles are one in Christ. This is how Paul says it in that beautiful set of lines in Ephesians 4:4 – 6:

There is one body and one Spirit, just as you were called to one hope when you were called; one Lord, one faith, one baptism; one God and Father of all, who is over all and through all and in all.

TIMELINE

Birth in Tarsus (approx. 10 BC to AD 1)
Relocation to Jerusalem (AD 15 – 20)
Death of Jesus (AD 30)
Conversion of Saul (AD 31 – 34)
Study, early ministry (AD 34 – 46)
Paul in Antioch (AD 40 – 47)
First missionary journey (AD 47 – 48)
Galatians (AD 49)
First Jerusalem Council (AD 49)
Second missionary journey (AD 49 – 52)
1 and 2 Thessalonians (AD 50 – 51)
Third missionary journey (AD 53 – 57)
In Ephesus (AD 52 – 55)
1 and 2 Corinthians (AD 55 – 56)
Romans (AD 57)
Return to Jerusalem and arrest (AD 57)

In prison in Caesarea (AD 57 – 59)
Trip to Rome (AD 59, fall)
Malta (AD 59 – 60, winter)
In Rome (Ad 60, early spring)
In prison in Rome (AD 60 – 62)
Colossians, Philemon, Ephesians, Philippians
Release and further ministry (AD 62 and later)
Reimprisonment and martyrdom (late AD 60s)
1 and 2 Timothy, Titus

Afterword

My friend Lynn Cohick read an earlier, much longer version of this book and offered encouragement and suggestions. Not long before this book was begun, I got in my hands the excellent book by Rodney Reeves called *Spirituality according to Paul*. My biggest fear was that Rodney, whose pastoral experience combined with a doctorate in New Testament studies made him a perfect candidate for the topic, would produce a book that would make mine unnecessary. But there was yet another way to talk about Paul, and I am grateful beyond words that Rodney read this book as a manuscript and offered suggestions. He has saved me from an error or two and made suggestions that found their way into this book.

My former colleague and friend, Joel Willitts, and I have had conversations about Paul for nearly a decade now, and I sense that he will hear himself at times in this book. He will also hear something no one else will hear — my responses to him. My brother-in-law, Ron Norman, read the manuscript and dashed off an encouraging note. But pride of place goes to my Paul classes at Northern Seminary, who not only read the book but gave feedback that has found its way at times into the book. Northern's commitment to make spiritual formation an element of all our classes gave me the momentum to keep at this book on Paul.

I am grateful, too, for my agent, Greg Daniel, and my editors at Zondervan: John Raymond, John Sloan, and Verlyn Verbrugge. A number of unnamed pastors and friends read various versions of chapter 12, and I will always be grateful for their wisdom and suggestions. Each of them made the chapter better.

Kris read through this book twice. She endured give and take on her suggestions, and we have discussed this book more than any book I have written. At times she found stories that ended up in the book. We dedicate this book to Jay and Susan Greener and to Amanda Holm and Erik Rosengren. Jay and Amanda are the pastors at Church of Redeemer, and they barely know how often my mind on Sundays wanders from what we are doing to what Paul was doing and back to what they are saying and doing. We are grateful to them for creating a fellowship of differents. Join us sometime and you'll see.

Ordinary Time
2014

Notes

Chapter 1: Growing Up in Church

1. Richard J. Foster, *Streams of Living Water: Celebrating the Great Traditions of Christian Faith* (San Francisco: HarperSanFrancisco, 1998).

Chapter 2: A Salad Bowl

1. Peter Oakes, *Reading Romans in Pompeii: Paul's Letter at Ground Level* (Minneapolis: Fortress, 2009), 96.
2. Ralph Ellison, *The Invisible Man* (New York: Random House, 1994), 15.
3. Ibid., 239.
4. Korie L. Edwards, *The Elusive Dream: The Power of Race in Interracial Churches* (New York: Oxford University Press, 2008).
5. www.christianitytoday.com/ct/2008/january/26.42.html.
6. Carolyn Custis James, *Half the Church: Recapturing God's Global Vision for Women* (Grand Rapids: Zondervan, 2011), 27.
7. http://oshetablogs.wordpress.com/2013/11/20/an-open-letter-to-my-sisters-in-the-suburbs/.
8. Joseph Epstein, *Once More around the Block: Familiar Essays* (New York: Norton, 1987), 155.
9. http://deeperstory.com/on-earth-as-it-is-in-heaven/.

Chapter 3: Space for Yes

1. Dorothy Sayers, *The Mind of the Maker* (San Francisco: HarperSanFrancisco, 1987), 12.
2. Christena Cleveland, *Disunity in Christ: Uncovering the Hidden Forces That Keep Us Apart* (Downers Grove, IL: InterVarsity Press, 2013), 12.

Chapter 4: Space for Grace

1. Please note that any italics added to Scripture quotations have been added in order to draw the reader's attention to certain parts of the text.
2. For the following list, see Galatians 2:4; Romans 2:4; 6:23; 1 Corinthians 1:2; 2 Corinthians 5:19; Ephesians 1:3; 2:6, 10; 4:32; Philippians 4:7, 19; 1 Timothy 1:14.
3. Frederick Buechner, *Beyond Words: Daily Readings in the ABC's of Faith* (San Francisco: HarperSanFrancisco, 2004), 139.
4. See www.christianity.com/theology/what-is-grace.html.

5. Anne Lamott, *Traveling Mercies: Some Thoughts on Faith* (New York: Random House, 1999), 143.

6. Kathleen Norris, *Amazing Grace: A Vocabulary of Faith* (New York: Riverhead, 1998), 151.

7. Sayers, *The Mind of the Maker*, 188.

8. Read Acts 26:9 – 11 for Paul's own summary of his past.

9. Many of the facts in this story of C. S. Lewis can be found in Alan Jacobs, *The Narnian: The Life and Imagination of C. S. Lewis* (San Francisco: HarperSanFrancisco, 2005). I borrow from pp. 4, 40, 41, 55, 56, 58, 62, 80, 89, 90, 96, 101, 131, 133, 148 – 49. Jacobs gets the name of the soldier next to Lewis wrong; the man's name was Harry Ayres. On this see Alister McGrath, *C. S. Lewis: A Life. Eccentric Genius. Reluctant Prophet* (Carol Stream, IL: Tyndale, 2013), 71. McGrath's chapter explaining Lewis' slow conversion is destined to be the classic explanation (pp. 131 – 59), even if some might be shocked at McGrath's temerity to suggest Lewis got the dates wrong when telling his story of conversion in *Surprised by Joy* (pp. 212 – 38). On the dates I follow McGrath. Other pages referred to are pp. 30, 42.

10. C. S. Lewis, *Mere Christianity* (New York: Macmillan, 1956), 94.

11. C. S. Lewis, *Spirits in Bondage* (San Diego: Harcourt, Brace Jovanovich, 1964), part 1, sec. 12.

12. C. S. Lewis, *Surprised by Joy: The Shape of My Early Life* (New York: Macmillan, 1956), 228 – 29. That chapter is called "Checkmate."

13. Lewis, *Surprised by Joy*, 221 – 22.

14. Ibid, 266.

15. C. S. Lewis, "Is Theology Poetry," in *Essay Collection and Other Short Pieces* (ed. L. Walmsley; New York: HarperCollins, 2000), 21.

Chapter 5: Love Is a Series of Prepositions

1. For a classical list of the 613 commandments, famous especially because of Maimonides, the great medieval rabbi, see http://en.wikipedia.org/wiki/613 _commandments.

2. I have for a long time paid attention to definitions of love. One good, accessible collection of definitions can be found at Maria Popova's blog (Brain Pickings): http://www.brainpickings.org/index/php/2013/01/01/what-is-love/

3. Stanley Hauerwas, "Sex and Politics: Bertrand Russell and 'Human Sexuality,'" *Christian Century* (April 19, 1978), 417 – 22.

4. See Leviticus 26:12; Jeremiah 7:23; 11:4; Ezekiel 14:11; Zechariah 8:8.

5. Leslie Leyland Fields, *Surviving the Island of Grace: A Memoir of Alaska* (New York: St. Martin's Press, 2002), 200, 215, 217, 326 – 27.

6. C. S. Lewis, *The Four Loves* (New York: Harcourt Brace Jovanovich, 1960), 91.

7. Humphrey Carpenter, *J. R. R. Tolkien: A Biography* (Boston: Houghton Mifflin, 2000), 152, 243.

8. Leslie Weatherhead, *The Transforming Friendship* (New York: Abingdon, 1929).

9. Dan Kimball, *Adventures in Churchland: Finding Jesus in the Mess of Organized Religion* (Grand Rapids: Zondervan, 2012), 73 – 82.

Chapter 6: Love Works

1. This is from the Babylonian Talmud, *Sanhedrin* 99b.
2. Lewis, *The Four Loves*, 169.
3. Jay Pathak and Dave Runyon, *The Art of Neighboring: Building Genuine Relationships Right Outside Your Door* (Grand Rapids: Baker, 2012), 35.
4. Acts 14:19-20; 16:1-3; 17:14-16; 18:5; 19:22; 20:4; 1 Thessalonians 1:1; 3:1-6; 2 Thessalonians 1:1; 1 Corinthians 4:17; 16:10-11; 2 Corinthians 1:1, 19; 11:9; Romans 16:21; Colossians 1:1; Philemon 1; Philippians 1:1; 2:19, 23; 1 Timothy 1:3, 18; 4:12, 14; 2 Timothy 1:5-6; 3:11, 15; 4:13, 21; Hebrews 13:23.

Chapter 7: Love Shares

1. I rely here on the research of Ronald F. Hock, *The Social Context of Paul's Ministry: Tentmaking and Apostleship* (Minneapolis: Fortress, 2007). See also Brian Rapske, *The Book of Acts and Paul in Roman Custody* (ed. Paul Winter; The Book of Acts in Its First Century Setting 3; Grand Rapids: Eerdmans, 1994), 106 – 8, who broadens Paul's craft to working with leather in general.
2. Mary-Ann Kirkby, *I Am Hutterite: The Fascinating True Story of a Young Woman's Journey to Reclaim Her Heritage* (Nashville: Nelson, 2010). The following story comes from pp. 141, 142, 179, 190, 202.
3. Christian Smith, Michael O. Emerson, and Patricia Snell, *Passing the Plate: Why American Christians Don't Give Away More Money* (New York: Oxford University Press, 2008), 175.
4. Kirkby, *I Am Hutterite*, 198.

Chapter 8: Tomatoes versus Maters

1. Martin Goodman, *The Roman World: 44 BC – AD 180* (2nd ed.; Routledge History of the Ancient World; London: Routledge, 2012), 17.
2. For an excellent selection of what slavery was like in the Roman world, see Jo-Ann Shelton, *As the Romans Did: A Sourcebook in Roman Social History* (2nd ed.; New York: Oxford University Press, 1998), 163 – 85.
3. Brady Boyd, *Let Her Lead: Creating a Better Future for Women in the Church* (Colorado Springs, CO: Bondfire Books, 2013), 14.
4. James D. G. Dunn, *The Acts of the Apostles* (Valley Forge, PA: Trinity Press International, 1996), 12.
5. Larry Martin, *The Life and Ministry of William J. Seymour, and a History of the Azusa Street Revival* (Pensacola, FL: Christian Life, 2006); Craig Borlase, *William Seymour: A Biography* (Lake Mary, FL: Charisma, 2006), esp. pp. 82, 125, 132, 133, 134, 147, 236.

Chapter 9: The Table of Connection

1. From http://ancienthistory.about.com/library/bl/bl_text_plinyltrs2.htm#VI.
2. From Justin Martyr, *First Apology* 67: www.earlychristianwritings.com/text/justinmartyr-firstapology.html. Here is what Justin Martyr said about the Eucharist itself in the previous chapter of this book: *First Apology* 66:

And this food is called among us Eukaristia [the Eucharist], of which no one is allowed to partake but the man who believes that the things which we teach are true, and who has been washed with the washing that is for the remission of sins, and unto regeneration, and who is so living as Christ has enjoined. For not as common bread and common drink do we receive these; but in like manner as Jesus Christ our Saviour, having been made flesh by the Word of God, had both flesh and blood for our salvation, so likewise have we been taught that the food which is blessed by the prayer of His word, and from which our blood and flesh by trans-mutation are nourished, is the flesh and blood of that Jesus who was made flesh. For the apostles, in the memoirs composed by them, which are called Gospels, have thus delivered unto us what was enjoined upon them; that Jesus took bread, and when He had given thanks, said, "This do ye in remembrance of Me, this is My body"; and that, after the same manner, having taken the cup and given thanks, He said, "This is My blood"; and gave it to them alone. Which the wicked devils have imitated in the mysteries of Mithras, commanding the same thing to be done. For, that bread and a cup of water are placed with certain incantations in the mystic rites of one who is being initiated, you either know or can learn.

Chapter 10: We Is Bigger than Me

1. See Edwin S. Gaustad, *Roger Williams* (New York: Oxford University Press, 2005), 4.
2. Dietrich Bonhoeffer, *Life Together and Prayerbook of the Bible* (ed. Eberhard Bethge; trans. G. L. Müller; Dietrich Bonhoeffer Works 5; Minneapolis: Fortress, 1996), 36.
3. Lewis, *The Four Loves*, 60.
4. Henry David Thoreau, *Walden, or, Life in the Woods* (Everyman's Library; New York: Knopf, 1992), 288; Robert D. Richardson Jr., *Henry Thoreau: A Life of the Mind* (Berkeley, CA: University of California Press, 1986), 188, 191, 215, 240, 299.

Chapter 11: Holiness as Devotion to God

1. Flannery O'Connor, *Flannery O'Connor: Collected Words* (Library of America 39; New York: Library of America, 1988), 1061.
2. Lyle W. Dorsett, *A Passion for God: The Spiritual Journey of A.W. Tozer* (Chicago: Moody Press, 2008). I refer in what follows to pp. 64, 66, 121, 122, 132, 135, 138, 160.

Chapter 12: Sexual Bodies in a Church

1. Everything about this topic seems to create heated debates, including the terms we use. For instance, in Matthew Vines's recent book the terms "affirming" and "non-affirming" are used. But one must ask if the traditional view is not more accurately labeled with a positive term instead of a negative term; thus, "affirming of hetero-sexual marriage and relations." See Matthew Vines, *God and the Gay Christian: The Biblical Case in Support of Same-Sex Relationships* (New York: Random House/Convergent, 2014). I will use "same-sex" with terms like "relations" (for sexual acts) and "attraction" (instead of "orientation" or "desire"). The word "orientation" has

come under fire with the thoroughly preposterous claim being made that sexual "orientation" was not known until the modern world. Not so. Aristotle, *Nicomachean Ethics* 7.5.3 – 5, speculates on the causes of same-sex "orientation." And Aristotle was not alone in discussing the origins of same-sex attraction.

The literature continues to grow, but for our purposes I mention two books, one more scholarly and one more popular, for those who believe same-sex relations or marriage are supported in the Bible or Christian thinking, and two for those who think the Bible and Christian tradition affirm heterosexual marriage and not same-sex relations/marriage. For the first, James V. Brownson, *Bible, Gender, Sexuality: Reframing the Church's Debate on Same-Sex Relationships* (Grand Rapids: Eerdmans, 2013); Matthew Vines, *God and the Gay Christian*. For the second, William J. Webb, *Slaves, Women and Homosexuals: Exploring the Hermeneutics of Cultural Analysis* (Downers Grove, IL: InterVarsity Press, 2001); John R. W. Stott, *Same-Sex Partnerships? A Christian Perspective* (Grand Rapids: Revell, 1998). I simply cannot engage here each and every counterpoint or supporting argument to what I discuss.

2. For a dense but solid description, see Roy E. Ciampa, "'Flee Sexual Immorality': Sex and the City of Corinth," in *The Wisdom of the Cross: Exploring 1 Corinthians* (ed. Brian S. Rosner; Nottingham, UK: Apollos/Inter-Varsity Press, 2011), 100 – 133. See also Nigel Spivey and Michael Squire, *Panorama of the Classical World* (Los Angeles: J. Paul Getty Museum, 2004), 48 – 61.

3. The famous poet Virgil preferred boys, and the later study of him by Aelius Donatus, which many think comes from Suetonius, *Life of Virgil*, reads: "His sexual desire was more inclined to boys, among whom he especially loved Cebes and Alexander" (9). Ovid, another Greek poet, in his *The Art of Love*, said this: "I hate sex that doesn't gratify both partners, and that is why I'm less enthralled with boys" (2.683 – 684).

4. At the very time Paul's ministry was flourishing, a contemporary philosophical movement, called Stoicism, was resisting the sexuality of the Roman world.

5. Cicero, *Speech in Defense of Caelius* 20.48.

6. For a full collection of texts from the Greco-Roman world, see Thomas K. Hubbard, ed., *Homosexuality in Greece and Rome: A Sourcebook of Basic Documents* (Berkeley, CA: University of California Press, 2003); for the first century, see pp. 383 – 442.

7. That Greek and Roman males knew of long-term or marital same-sex relations is found in the ancient evidence, but the pervasiveness of the evidence is disputed. For instance, in Plato's famous *Symposium*, Aristophanes, a Greek poet, speaks of a same-sex relationship in these terms: "who continue with one another throughout life … desiring to join together and to be fused into a single entity with his beloved and to become one person from two" (192E). And a number of Stoic philosophers criticized Roman same-sex practices, including Suetonius, a contemporary of Paul and the Roman emperor Nero, who mocked and lambasted Nero's perverse marriage to Sporus, who had been "castrated and [the doctors] tried to transform him into an actual woman" (*Nero* 28). These two examples, one from the world of what we might call "faithful and monogamous" and the other from the perverse,

reflect the spectrum of the Roman world. The best recent discussion is by Thomas K. Hubbard, "Peer Sexuality," in Thomas K. Hubbard, ed., *A Companion to Greek and Roman Sexualities* (London: Blackwell, 2014), 128–49.

8. Lucian, *Dialogues of the Courtesans* 5.

9. Each of these texts is disputed, but those debates cannot be engaged in this context. See footnote 1 above.

10. The expression "out of order" comes from Donald J. Wold, *Out of Order: Homosexuality in the Bible and the Ancient Near East* (Grand Rapids: Baker, 1998).

11. Jesus never mentions same-sex relations unless they are to be seen in Luke 7:25, where a man "dressed in fine [soft] clothes" *could* be referring to typical Roman same-sex relations.

12. I agree with many who contend we are not to elevate homosexuality above the others in this list, but this chapter's focus requires a concentration on that subject.

13. Here is another one, this one from the list of regulations for Gentile converts in Acts 15:19–20: "It is my judgment, therefore, that we should not make it difficult for the Gentiles who are turning to God. Instead we should write to them, telling them to abstain from food polluted by idols, from sexual immorality, from the meat of strangled animals and from blood." For James Gentiles are known for "sexual immorality."

14. Some have suggested that Paul does not mean absolute, total, and unchanging nonassociation. So perhaps he means, "Do not associate indiscriminately with...." It is clear Paul wants such folks to be restored to fellowship.

15. It is common for the word "natural" to be adjusted to the word "conventional" or "customary" since in 1 Corinthians 11:14 Paul uses the same term for males having short hair and women having long hair, and in that context the term may mean "conventional." Thus, for this viewpoint, if "natural" in Romans 1 means "conventional," Paul's argument for same-sex relations is less forceful. However, the word "natural" covers a range of senses, from the conventional to the God-created way of nature, which is what he means in Romans 1. At Paul's time the Stoic Seneca the Younger (*Moral Epistles* 122.7) argued against same-sex relations on the basis of "nature."

16. www.desiringgod.org/blog/posts/an-alternative-script-for-same-sex-attraction.

17. The debate about same-sex legal marriages (and civil unions) complicates the matter. First, it is about law and what is legal; second, what the Supreme Court or state courts decide to be law does not govern what the church believes. So, same-sex marriage might be law that does not make it, for the traditionalist, "right." The church should not confuse its own ethical beliefs and practices with what the state has decided.

18. Wesley Hill, *Washed and Waiting: Reflections on Christian Faithfulness and Homosexuality* (Grand Rapids: Zondervan, 2010).

19. Ibid., 13.

20. An important book detailing numbers, even if the discussion has moved well beyond these conclusions, is Stanton L. Jones and Mark A. Yarhouse, *Ex-Gays? A Longitudinal Study of Religiously Mediated Change in Sexual Orientation* (Downers Grove, IL: IVP Academic, 2007).

21. Hill, *Washed and Waiting*, 145, 150.
22. http://spiritualfriendship.org/2012/09/20/an-unformed-pauline-thought-on
-living-and-dying-with-christ/.

Chapter 13: Salvation as Process

1. Found in Exodus 12, but with resonances throughout the Bible. The most notable
resonance is Isaiah 40, but a close second is the opening to Mark's gospel (1:1 – 3).
But there are others, including Deuteronomy 26:5 – 9; Psalms 78, 105, and 106.
2. I rely here on the exceptional research of Augustine Thompson, *Francis of Assisi: A
New Biography* (Ithaca, NY: Cornell University Press, 2012), 3 – 17.
3. From Ronald J. Sider, Philip N. Olson, and Heidi Rolland Unruh, eds., *Churches
That Make a Difference: Reaching Your Community with Good News and Good
Works* (Grand Rapids: Baker, 2002), 182.

Chapter 14: A New Freedom

1. Greg A. Boyd, *Benefit of the Doubt: Breaking the Idol of Certainty* (Grand Rapids:
Baker, 2013), 97 – 111.
2. Wayne Gordon, *Who Is My Neighbor? Lessons from a Man Left for Dead* (Ventura,
CA: Gospel Light, 2010). This paragraph expresses the chapter titles in Wayne's
book.

Chapter 15: A New Faithfulness

1. The best study of Sheldon is by Timothy Miller, *Following in His Steps: A Biography of Charles M. Sheldon* (Knoxville: University of Tennessee Press, 1987). I refer
to pp. 15, 65, 99, 183.
2. The story can be found at Randy Harris, *Living Jesus: Doing What Jesus Says in the
Sermon on the Mount* (Abilene, TX: Leafwood, 2012).
3. Derwin Gray, *Limitless Life: You Are More Than Your Past When God Holds Your
Future* (Nashville: Nelson, 2013).
4. Eugene Peterson, *A Long Obedience in the Same Direction: Discipleship in an Instant
Society* (Downers Grove, IL: InterVarsity Press, 2000).

Chapter 16: A New Guidance

1. David E. Fitch and Geoff Holsclaw, *Prodigal Christianity: 10 Signposts into the Missional Frontier* (Leadership Network; San Francisco: Jossey-Bass, 2013), 81.
2. Dallas Willard, *Hearing God: Developing a Conversational Relationship with God*
(Downers Grove, IL: InterVarsity Press, 1999).
3. This story comes from an astounding collection of dreams and visions of Jesus
among Muslims in the Middle East in Tom Doyle and Greg Webster, *Dreams and
Visions: Is Jesus Awakening the Muslim World?* (Nashville: Nelson, 2012), 17 – 22
(also quoting 58 – 59).
4. Tass Saada, *Once an Arafat Man: The True Story of How a PLO Sniper Found a
New Life* (Carol Stream, IL: Tyndale, 2008). Pages referred to: 24 – 25, 33 – 34,
108, 118, 157 – 70, 192.

Chapter 17: A New Politics

1. H. L. Mencken, *A Mencken Chrestomathy* (New York: Knopf, 1949), 624. He also said a Christian was one "who is willing to serve three Gods, but draws the line at one wife."
2. F. J. Bremer, *John Winthrop: America's Forgotten Founding Father* (Oxford/New York: Oxford University Press, 2003). I refer to pages 76, 94, 97, 110, 156, 177.
3. Eberhard Busch, *Karl Barth: His Life from Letters and Autobiographical Texts* (trans. John Bowden; London: SCM, 1976), 255, 257, 259.
4. S. R. Llewelyn and J. R. Harrison, eds., *New Documents Illustrating Early Christianity* (New Documents 10; Grand Rapids: Eerdmans, 2012), 64–75.
5. See my book, *Kingdom Conspiracy: Returning to the Radical Mission of the Local Church* (Grand Rapids: Brazos, 2014).

Chapter 18: We Have Landed, but We Want the Land

1. Dunn, *Acts of the Apostles*, 12.
2. Gerald F. Hawthorne, *The Presence and the Power: The Significance of the Holy Spirit in the Life and Ministry of Jesus* (Dallas: Word, 1991), 35.

Chapter 19: The Exposure Challenge

1. Dietrich Bonhoeffer, *Discipleship* (Dietrich Bonhoeffer Works 4; Minneapolis: Fortress, 2001), 87 [German, p. 81]. Footnote 11 on p. 87 is mistaken; it has the German word *fährt* instead of the German word *führt*. The former word means "drives" while the latter means "leads."
2. John R. W. Stott, *The Contemporary Christian: Applying God's Word to Today's World* (Downers Grove, IL: InterVarsity Press, 1992), 146 (see all of pp. 146–57).
3. Ibid., 157.
4. I owe this observation about neediness to Rodney Reeves.
5. The others are found at Romans 12:3–8; Ephesians 4:11; and 1 Peter 4:10–11.
6. Nikki A. Toyama and Tracey Gee, *More Than Serving Tea: Asian American Women on Expectations, Relationships, Leadership and Faith* (Downers Grove, IL: InterVarsity Press, 2006), 156–73.
7. Timothy Keller, *Center Church: Doing Balanced, Gospel-Centered Ministry in Your City* (Grand Rapids: Zondervan, 2012), 178.

Chapter 20: Pete the Mechanic

1. As noted in chapter 7, Paul likely worked with leather to make a variety of products.
2. Two texts for this can be found in *Mishnah 'Abot* 2:2 and 4:57. : "Rabban Gamaliel, son of R. Judah the Patriarch, says, 'Fitting is learning in Torah along with a craft, for the labor put into the two of them makes one forget sin. And all learning of Torah which is not joined with labor is destined to be null and cause sin. And all who work with the community-let them work with them for the sake of Heaven.'" "R. Sadoq... 'Thus have you learned: Whoever derives worldly benefit from teachings of Torah takes his life out of this world.'"

3. For a good study of this theme, see Bruce W. Longenecker, *Remember the Poor: Paul, Poverty, and the Greco-Roman World* (Grand Rapids: Eerdmans, 2010).
4. Hock, *The Social Context of Paul's Ministry*, 36.
5. A really good book on this topic is Adam McHugh, *Introverts in the Church* (Downers Grove, IL: InterVarsity Press, 2009).
6. J. R. R. Tolkien, *Tree and Leaf* (Boston: Houghton Mifflin, 1989), 75 – 95. My friend Katie Prudek pointed out to me the autobiographical element in this story. An edited version of my piece is located at The High Calling: www.thehighcalling. org/culture/less-valuable-and-more-serious- - -work-and-life-sketch#.UZJpmZX-vz7c. Tolkien's story expresses a theology of work, and I recommend the following: Miroslav Volf, *Work in the Spirit: Toward a Theology of Work* (Eugene, OR: Wipf & Stock, 2001); Darrell Cosden, *The Heavenly Good of Earthly Work* (Peabody, MA: Hendrickson, 2006).

Chapter 21: Teacher with the Big Fancy Hat

1. Rodney Reeves, *Spirituality according to Paul: Imitating the Apostle of Christ* (Downers Grove, IL: InterVarsity Press, 2011), 47.
2. Ibid., 50 – 51.
3. Dwight N. Peterson, "Choosing Weakness," *Covenant Companion* (February 2012), 6 – 9.
4. George Macdonald, *Unspoken Sermons* (Whitethorn, CA: Johannesen, 1999), 27. I have adjusted slightly to facilitate inclusive language.
5. Marcus Brotherton, *"Teacher": The Henrietta Mears Story* (Ventura, CA: Regal, 2006), pp. 42, 81.

Chapter 22: On a Walk with Kris

1. Scot McKnight, "Happiness: Given, Lost, Regained," *Books & Culture*, 14, no. 6 (November/December 2008): 44 – 46. I borrow from this article in what follows; all quotations are from that article.
2. Jennifer Michael Hecht, *The Happiness Myth: Why What We Think is Right Is Wrong – A History of What Really Makes Us Happy* (San Francisco: HarperSan-Francisco, 2007), 9.
3. Lynn H. Cohick, *Philippians* (Story of God Bible Commentary New Testament 11; Grand Rapids: Zondervan, 2013), 185.
4. A. McGrath, *C. S. Lewis: A Life*, 198. A complementary account can be found in Carpenter, *J. R. R. Tolkien: A Biography*, 179 – 86.
5. From his essay, "The Lantern-Bearers," in *The Art of the Personal Essay: An Anthology from the Classical Era to the Present* (ed. Phillip Lopate; New York: Anchor Doubleday, 1994), 220.

Appendix: The Graces in Paul's Life

1. God prepared Paul to be the great integrator, though it took an eye-twittering experience with Jesus himself to accept the challenge. There is an early Christian tradition, from the fourth-century church father Jerome, informing us that Paul's family was originally from Gischala in Galilee. As a result of a war in Galilee with

Rome the family later moved to Tarsus (perhaps as slaves, though they were later set free). Paul spent a decade or more in Tarsus but as a young man moved to Jerusalem to study Torah. Here is what Jerome wrote:

Paul, formerly called Saul, an apostle outside the number of the twelve apostles, was of the tribe of Benjamin and the town of Giscalis [Gischala] in Judea [Galilee]. When this [town] was taken by the Romans he removed with his parents to Tarsus in Cilicia. Sent by them to Jerusalem to study law he was educated by Gamaliel a most learned man whom Luke mentions.... As Sergius Paulus Proconsul of Cyprus was the first to believe on his preaching, he [Paul] took his name from him because he had subdued him to faith in Christ....

(From Jerome, *Lives of Illustrious Men* 5; http://biblehub.com/library/various /jerome_and_gennadius_lives_of_illustrious_men_/chapter_v_paul.htm).

Scripture Index

Subject and Name Index